Indian Gaming Law
and Policy

INDIAN GAMING LAW AND POLICY

SECOND EDITION

Kathryn R.L. Rand
DEAN
FLOYD B. SPERRY PROFESSOR
SCHOOL OF LAW
UNIVERSITY OF NORTH DAKOTA

Steven Andrew Light
ASSOCIATE VICE PRESIDENT FOR ACADEMIC AFFAIRS
PROFESSOR OF POLITICAL SCIENCE AND PUBLIC ADMINISTRATION
UNIVERSITY OF NORTH DAKOTA

CO-DIRECTORS
INSTITUTE FOR THE STUDY OF TRIBAL GAMING LAW AND POLICY
UNIVERSITY OF NORTH DAKOTA

CAROLINA ACADEMIC PRESS
Durham, North Carolina

Library of Congress Cataloging-in-Publication Data

Rand, Kathryn R. L., 1968- author.
 Indian gaming law and policy / Kathryn R.L. Rand, Steven Andrew
Light. -- Second edition.
     pages cm
 Includes bibliographical references and index.
 ISBN 978-1-59460-956-5 (alk. paper)
 1. Gambling on Indian reservations--Law and legislation--United
States. I. Light, Steven Andrew, author. II. Title.
 KF8210.G35R36 2014
 344.73'099--dc23
                        2014017119

CAROLINA ACADEMIC PRESS
700 Kent Street
Durham, North Carolina 27701
Telephone (919) 489-7486
Fax (919) 493-5668
www.cap-press.com

Printed in the United States of America

This book is dedicated to
Dorothy Light,
Tom and Alice Jean Rand,
Doug Rand,
and our entire families for their unconditional support.

CONTENTS

Preface and Acknowledgments

We are fortunate to have the chance to publish this second edition of a book whose subject, the world of casinos owned and operated by American Indian tribes, is incredibly dynamic, despite its foundation in a federal law whose text has remained the same since we last visited it eight years ago. In that time, so-called "Indian gaming"—as an economic development tool, an industry, and a cultural phenomenon—has continued to grow and change.

In 2006, we observed that legalized gambling had become prevalent in popular culture, noting that one could hardly flip the television dial without seeing a show glamorizing Las Vegas, featuring a high-stakes poker tournament, or depicting tribal casinos. The same observation could be made today, except more so, what with the ubiquity of Powerball, the legalization of online gaming in three states (so far), the potential spread of commercial casinos to states like New York or Massachusetts, and the expansion of political contestation over tribes' "off-reservation" casinos. As it has become increasingly normalized, the novelty of legalized gambling's spread has, to some degree, worn off, but Indian gaming still seems to be in the news all the time, whether the story is about a state seeking a cut of a tribe's casino profits, or a tribe's attempts to acquire new trust land to open a casino.

Today there is much more and, we think, much better journalism about Indian gaming, and a greater number of scholars in diverse fields have taken up the challenge to develop broader, deeper, and more contextualized accounts of tribal gaming. Gaming law is taught at a number of law schools, universities, and tribal colleges, using books like this one, and there are many more attorneys who have developed a successful gaming practice or become gaming commissioners. The ranks have swelled dramatically in the number of American Indian lawyers and judges, policymakers, and human resource managers—not to mention tribal regulators—who have both training and experience in gaming law and policy.

Yet the body of knowledge about Indian gaming remains incomplete and, at times, ill-informed, both "in the field" and in the educational or day-to-day journalistic arenas. As such, we believe the second edition of this book will continue to fill an important gap by providing an accurate and complete account of *Indian gaming now*—how it came about, what it is, how it is regulated, and why it is so highly politicized.

The law and policy of tribal gaming are the most complicated and politically fraught of any area of tribal-state-federal relations today. These two domains— law and policy—are inextricably linked in the field of Indian gaming, and indeed, due largely to the complex history of the federal government's relationship to tribes, in any area related to American Indians. And so, we ask: Can a legal practitioner negotiate the parameters of the law of Indian gaming without delving into the politics that create the law and shape its application? Can a lawmaker effectively and fairly weigh policy options without comprehending the complex legal and regulatory environment of tribal gaming? And can anyone fully understand Indian gaming without being aware of the significance of tribal sovereignty as it relates to the law, politics, and policy of Indian gaming? We think the answers to these questions are a resounding "No," again providing a compelling rationale for the existence of this book and related accounts of tribal gaming.

The first edition of this book grew out of our own search for materials that straightforwardly and fully explained the law and policy of Indian gaming. By assembling such information in a single text, we hoped to provide a readily accessible resource for practitioners and policymakers, students and scholars, and anyone else interested in Indian gaming.

Succeeding well enough in that endeavor leads us to the second edition of this book, along with our excitement over the fact that the Indian gaming industry has grown, changed, and matured in ways that have been advantaged by what we set out to accomplish: to provide accurate and complete information that people want and need. In this second edition, we include updates addressing the U.S. Supreme Court's landmark 2009 *Carcieri* decision, recent state and federal efforts toward legalization of online gaming and the accompanying opportunities and pitfalls for tribes, the maturation of the tribal gaming industry, impacts of the recent national economic recession and the law (or lack thereof) governing tribal casino bankruptcy, the continuing politicized nature of tribal-state compact negotiations including recent federal court decisions on revenue sharing and the legality of administrative compacts, unionization at tribal casinos, and the ongoing integration of Indian gaming into tribal, national, and state economies, laws, and politics.

Our own collaboration to develop and promote greater understanding of Indian gaming issues began nearly two decades ago, when the industry was in its relative infancy compared to today. We have found that our respective disciplines—law, and political science and public administration—perhaps uniquely position us to take an interdisciplinary approach to researching what inherently is a field that crosses disciplines. At the University of North Dakota, we founded the Institute for the Study of Tribal Gaming Law and Policy more than a decade ago to facilitate quality research and informed public discourse on Indian gaming.[1] Our fundamental belief is that to serve the public good, accurate and complete information, along with a foundational respect for tribal sovereignty, should drive the law and policy of Indian gaming.

* * *

Thanks to our colleagues at the University of North Dakota School of Law and the Department of Political Science and Public Administration in the University of North Dakota College of Business and Public Administration, as well as in the Office of the Provost and Vice President for Academic Affairs, for their ongoing support. As we each have advanced our professional careers in ways we could not have foreseen eight years ago, including the move into university administration, we continue to be thankful for the opportunity to maintain our footing in teaching, research, and service related to Indian gaming.

The first edition of this book benefited from the research assistance of Melissa Burkland and John Hoff and the administrative assistance of Kelly Jordet and Karen Bowles. The second edition has benefited from the research assistance of Christopher J. Ironroad and the students in Kathryn's 2010 and 2012 Indian Gaming Law classes, as well as Steve's 2010 Indian Gaming and American Politics course. At Carolina Academic Press, thanks to Keith Sipe for his enthusiasm for this project, to Bob Conrow for guiding us through the publication process, and to everyone else at the Press, including Paul McFarland and Tim Colton, for their help along the way. For this second edition, our thanks extend to Charlsey Rutan, who helped us determine the need for a new edition and, with Chris Harrow, Jae Aoh, and Jessica Newman, guided us through the publication process. Thanks also to Meg Daniel, who expertly prepared the index for both editions. Any errors in this book are, of course, our own. We welcome comments and suggestions from interested readers.

Kathryn R.L. Rand
Steven Andrew Light

Grand Forks, North Dakota
May 2014

---

1. The Institute is a component of the University of North Dakota School of Law's Northern Plains Indian Law Center. See Institute for the Study of Tribal Gaming Law and Policy, http://www.law.und.nodak.edu/npilc/gaming/index.php (last visited Mar. 23, 2014).

Indian Gaming Law
and Policy

CHAPTER 1

INTRODUCTION

The casino is not a statement of who we are, but only a means to get us to where we want to be. We had tried poverty for 200 years, so we decided to try something else.

—Ray Halbritter, Nation Representative,
Oneida Indian Nation of New York[1]

Ray Halbritter was referring to his own tribe, the Oneida Indian Nation of New York, and its highly successful Turning Stone Resort and Casino, but the sentiment might have applied to each of the more than 240 tribes that have opened gaming establishments as a means of tribal economic development. In just over three decades, so-called "Indian gaming," or the industry of tribally owned and operated casinos, has become big business in the United States.[2] Generating $26.9 billion in revenue in 2012, tribal gaming accounts for more than a quarter of the gambling industry's gross nationwide. Despite the dampening effects of the recent national economic recession, Indian gaming continues to grow.[3]

The growth of tribal gaming is only part of the ever-expanding legalized gambling industry. Gambling, with roots in games of chance played by ancient Egyptians, Greeks, Romans, and Chinese as well as indigenous popula-

---

1. As quoted in Ray Halbritter and Steven Paul McSloy, "Empowerment or Dependence? The Practical Value and Meaning of Native American Sovereignty," *New York University Journal of International Law and Policy* 26 (1994): 568.

2. "Indian gaming" is a legal term that is firmly embedded in mainstream and popular discourse. Throughout this book, we refer interchangeably to Indian gaming and tribal gaming, as well as to American Indians, Native Americans, Native people, and tribal members. We also refer to "federal Indian law," another legal term of art. We recognize that to some, each of these terms carries the baggage of history and potentially problematic connotations.

3. See National Indian Gaming Commission (NIGC), "Gaming Tribe Report," Feb. 11, 2014, http://www.nigc.gov/Reading_Room/List_and_Location_of_Tribal_Gaming_Operations.aspx (last visited Mar. 26, 2014); NIGC, "Gaming Revenue Reports," http://www.nigc.gov/Gaming_Revenue_Reports.aspx (last visited Mar. 26, 2014).

tions in North America, is a popular pastime, once widely seen as a sin or vice, and now seemingly as American as apple pie.[4] During the twentieth century, in what sometimes is called the "third wave" of gambling in the United States, legalized gambling emerged and, nurtured by gangster-visionaries like Bugsy Segal, became generally accepted, in a number of forms. Most notable perhaps were the large-scale casinos in Las Vegas, Reno, and Atlantic City, replete with card games, craps tables, roulette wheels, and slot machines, along with restaurants, hotels, nightclub-style entertainment, and showgirls. The casinos, epitomized by those in Las Vegas, became places "where reality is suspended"—by the 1990s, exotic destinations at which volcanoes erupt, pirate battles are waged, and drinks are free. Today, paradoxically, Las Vegas maintains its reputation as "Sin City"—what happens in Vegas stays in Vegas, not only in movies like *The Hangover*, but for bachelors and bachelorettes, fraternity and sorority members, middle-aged thrill-seekers, and retirees alike— while rivaling Disneyland as a family-friendly destination for some 40 million visitors a year.[5]

Far more readily accessible across the United States than full-scale casinos, legalized gambling in the mid- and late twentieth century also included pari-mutuel betting at horse and dog tracks, charitable games, and state-operated gambling. When New Hampshire instituted a state lottery in 1964, states began to look to gambling as a means of raising direct government revenue. Charitable organizations used gambling as fundraising events; beyond bingo, charities offered blackjack and other casino-style games—all for a good cause, of course.[6] As the congressionally sanctioned National Gambling Impact Study Commission concluded in 1999, "the United States has been transformed from a nation in which legalized gambling was a limited and a relatively rare phenomenon into one in which such activity is common and growing."[7]

---

4. See generally, for example, Gerda Reith, *The Age of Chance: Gambling and Western Culture* (New York: Routledge, 1999); John M. Findlay, *People of Chance: Gambling in American Society from Jamestown to Las Vegas* (New York: Oxford University Press, 1986); see also Mike Roberts, "The National Gambling Debate: Two Defining Issues," *Whittier Law Review* 18 (1997): 581–89 (providing a short account of gambling's long and storied history).

5. Las Vegas Convention and Visitors Authority, "Las Vegas Stats & Facts," http:// www.lvcva.com/stats-and-facts/ (last visited Mar. 26, 2014). For an entertaining account of the rise of Las Vegas's casino resorts, see David G. Schwartz, *Suburban Xanadu: The Casino Resort on the Las Vegas Strip and Beyond* (New York: Routledge, 2003).

6. See, for example, Roberts, "National Gambling Debate," 586–87.

7. National Gambling Impact Study Commission, *Final Report* (1999), 1-1, http://gov info.library.unt.edu/ngisc/index.html (last visited Apr. 6, 2005). Despite its age, the Study

Today, as Table 1.1 indicates, Americans can place bets on dog and horse races in 40 states, buy lottery tickets in 44 states, gamble for charity in 48 states, and play at commercial casinos or racinos in 23 states. All but two states, Utah and Hawaii, permit some form of gaming. Altogether, an estimated 70% of Americans wager some $900 billion, making legalized gambling in 48 states and the District of Columbia an $88.6 billion industry in 2010.[8]

Table 1.1 Legalized Gambling by Type and State

Type of Gaming	Number of States
Commercial casinos (includes stand-alone and racetrack casinos)	23
Lotteries	44 (and D.C.)
Indian casinos	29
Pari-mutuel wagering	40
Charitable gambling	48 (and D.C.)
All forms	**48 (and D.C.)**

Sources: Adapted from American Gaming Association, "Types of Gaming By State," http://www.americangaming.org/industry-resources/research/fact-sheets/states-gaming (last visited Mar. 26, 2014).

Indian gaming's growth has far outpaced that of other venues and, in many ways, has driven the overall expansion of legalized gambling. Across the United States, 29 states are home to more than 450 tribal gaming operations.[9] Table 1.2 demonstrates the wide variation in Indian gaming venues from state to state. Thirteen states are home to five or fewer tribal gaming facilities. By contrast, 65 tribes in California run 70 casinos, and 30 tribes in Oklahoma operate a total of 117 gaming facilities. This diversity complicates the administration

---

Commission's final report remains the most recent federal study of legalized gambling and, in many ways, its findings remain relevant.

8. See Richard K. Miller & Associates, *Casinos, Gaming, & Wagering* (2011); American Gaming Association, "Types of Gaming By State," http://www.americangaming.org/industry-resources/research/fact-sheets/states-gaming (last visited July 20, 2012).

9. As the landscape for the Indian gaming industry changes frequently, and tribes are subject to federal and sometimes state reporting requirements that are more limited than those for privately held or publicly traded commercial entities, exact numbers can be difficult to pin down. The NIGC put the total number of tribal gaming facilities at 474 in 2014. NIGC, "Gaming Tribe Report," Feb. 11, 2014, http://www.nigc.gov/Reading_Room/List_and_Location_of_Tribal_Gaming_Operations.aspx (last visited Apr. 6, 2014).

Table 1.2 Indian Gaming Venues by State

State	Total Number of Indian Gaming Venues	Total Number of Tribes Operating Gaming Facilities
Alabama	3	1
Alaska	2	2
Arizona	26	15
California	70	65
Colorado	2	2
Connecticut	2	2
Florida	8	2
Idaho	9	4
Iowa	1	1
Kansas	4	4
Louisiana	4	4
Michigan	23	12
Minnesota	39	11
Mississippi	3	1
Missouri	3	1
Montana	15	7
Nebraska	6	3
Nevada	3	2
New Mexico	21	13
New York	8	4
North Carolina	2	1
North Dakota	11	5
Oklahoma	117	30
Oregon	9	8
South Dakota	14	8
Texas	1	1
Washington	34	23
Wisconsin	30	11
Wyoming	4	2
Total: 29	474	245

Sources: Adapted from NIGC, "Gaming Tribe Report," Feb. 11, 2014, http://www.nigc.gov/ Reading_Room/List_and_Location_of_Tribal_Gaming_Operations.aspx (last visited Apr. 6, 2014); Alan P. Meister, *Indian Gaming Industry Report, 2014 Ed.* (Newton, MA: Casino City Press, 2014).

and regulation of tribal gaming. As states, tribes, and the federal government struggle with regulating a booming industry within the complicated context of tribes' distinctive and federally acknowledged political status as sovereign nations, Indian gaming raises substantial questions of law and public policy that do not have easy answers.

Given the size, scope, and prominence of the tribal gaming industry across the United States, it is imperative that legal practitioners, public policymakers, industry officials, and the general public have accurate and complete information about the laws and policies that shape Indian gaming today. The breadth and complexity of the legal, regulatory, and policy environments in which Indian gaming occurs on a tribe-by-tribe and state-by-state basis, against the background of the complicated history of federal Indian law and policy and tribal-state and tribal-federal relations, can be both perplexing and daunting. Yet mastery of these areas is just what is—or should be—expected of practicing attorneys, tribal, state, or federal regulators, lawmakers, and industry insiders of all stripes. Current students who will enter the field and shape its future, as well as the journalists who cover it now, also require sound understanding of the foundation upon which tribal gaming is constantly evolving.

In the second edition of this book, we provide a comprehensive description of the law and policy surrounding tribal gaming, as well as synopses of key current issues in the field. From the history of tribal gaming, to landmark U.S. Supreme Court decisions, to regulatory schemes established by federal law, to the political realities of tribal-state-local interactions and controversies, this book contains a full yet accessible account of Indian gaming law and policy.

The Interactive Roles of Law and Politics

Stated simply, Indian gaming is gaming conducted on tribal lands by federally acknowledged tribal governments. When federal Indian policy shifted in the latter twentieth century from attempts to undercut tribal sovereignty or even "terminate" tribes to encouraging tribal self-determination and economic self-sufficiency, a few tribes experimented with high-stakes bingo halls as a means of raising revenue. As the fledgling Indian gaming industry grew, tribes and states vied for regulatory authority over reservation casinos. The federal Indian Gaming Regulatory Act of 1988 (IGRA) grew out of a political compromise between state and non-Indian gaming interests in controlling the spread of gambling on the one hand, and tribal and federal interests in effectuating reservation economic development on the other.[10]

Tribal gaming differs from commercial gambling in Atlantic City or Las Vegas in that it is conducted by tribal governments, making it more akin to state lotteries than to commercial casinos or charitable gambling. Not all tribes game, of course, and not all tribal casinos are wildly successful financial ventures. Indian gaming encompasses a wide range of reservation casinos, from modest and marginally profitable rural bingo halls to hugely profitable Las Vegas-style destination casino-resort complexes near major metropolitan areas. For every tribal gaming facility that earns over $250 million annually, there are 10 facilities that generate less than a tenth of that amount. Nearly one in five tribal gaming facilities earns less than $3 million annually, often just enough to keep the casino open and to fund a handful of essential public services for tribal members.[11] Table 1.3 highlights the wide disparity in revenue generated by tribal gaming operations.

Table 1.3 Indian Gaming Operations by Revenue

2011 Revenue of …	Number of Tribal Gaming Facilities	Total Revenue (in millions)
$250 million and over	23	$10,422
$100 million to $250 million	55	$9,066
$50 million to $100 million	52	$3,640
$25 million to $50 million	55	$1,903
$10 million to $25 million	98	$1,630
$3 million to $10 million	70	$413
Under $3 million	68	$81
Total	421	$27,154

Source: NIGC, "Gaming Revenues 2007–2011," June 20, 2012, http://www.nigc.gov/Gaming_Revenue_Reports.aspx (last visited Mar. 26, 2014).

---

10. 25 U.S.C. §§ 2701–21 (2001). For a full treatment of IGRA's legal and political compromise, see Steven Andrew Light and Kathryn R.L. Rand, *Indian Gaming and Tribal Sovereignty: The Casino Compromise* (Lawrence, KS: University Press of Kansas, 2005).

11. In 2011, 23 tribal gaming facilities earned $250 million or more, while 236 earned $25 million or less. Sixty-eight facilities earned less than $3 million in 2011. NIGC, "Gaming Revenues 2007–2011," June 20, 2012, http://www.nigc.gov/Gaming_Revenue_Reports.aspx (last visited Mar. 26, 2014). As we note above, the NIGC's total count of tribal gaming facilities varies from other reports, and from the figures we cite in Table 1.2.

Indian gaming is subject to a unique and complex federal regulatory scheme, involving layers of federal, state, and tribal regulation. Through IGRA, Congress established a federal independent regulatory agency with specific authority over tribal gaming (the National Indian Gaming Commission or NIGC), delegated regulatory power to the states, and set the terms for tribal regulation of gaming. In the 26 years since Congress enacted IGRA, states and tribes alike have challenged the statute's constitutionality and litigated its murkier provisions. The NIGC and the federal Secretary of the Interior have promulgated extensive and detailed regulations. Accordingly, the law of Indian gaming has grown only more complex since IGRA's passage.

Practitioners in the field must navigate federal laws and regulations, both civil and criminal, concerning tribal recognition and tribal lands, the types of gaming allowed on reservations, use of gaming revenue, negotiation of tribal-state agreements governing casino-style gaming, management contracts, minimum internal control standards, financial reporting requirements, and excise taxes, to name just a few. Tribal laws and regulations, specific to the tribal government operating the gaming facility, cover many of the same topics, as well as a number of additional subjects, including employee and vendor licensing, minimum age requirements, liquor laws, environmental standards, employment benefits, hiring preferences, and background checks. State law, too, is relevant, ranging from a governor's authority under a state constitution to negotiate tribal-state compacts required by IGRA, to the scope of gambling permitted by public policy, to food safety standards and worker compensation schemes. In short, an incredibly wide range of law applies to Indian gaming.

With regulatory authority stemming from the federal government, 29 states, and some 245 tribes, it may be impossible to gather all applicable law between the covers of a single volume.[12] Instead, we discuss the major parameters of Indian gaming law—landmark U.S. Supreme Court cases, current federal, state, and tribal statutes and regulations, and case law from federal and state courts—as well as provide guidance in conducting legal research in the area.

Law is not the only force at play, as Indian gaming has been shaped as much by politics.[13] IGRA also necessitates and governs tribal, state, federal, and even

---

12. Yet we try to do just that in our comprehensive casebook designed for the next level of detailed instruction or training, especially for law school or graduate education. See Kathryn R.L. Rand and Steven Andrew Light, *Indian Gaming Law: Cases and Materials* (Durham, NC: Carolina Academic Press, 2008).

13. See Kathryn R.L. Rand, "At Odds? Perspectives on the Law and Politics of Indian Gaming," *Gaming Law Review* 5 (2001): 297.

local intergovernmental relations. As a practical matter, therefore, IGRA created the terms under which the politics of Indian gaming have played out over the last 26 years. Indeed, following the Supreme Court's 1996 invalidation of one of the IGRA's enforcement mechanisms, Indian gaming policy has evolved through political compromise as much as through litigation and law reform.[14] More recently, policymakers' concerns appear to have shifted from whether tribal gaming enterprises comply with applicable law to whether tribal gaming itself—legal or not—is a desirable political outcome.

Throughout the United States, states and tribes have struggled to balance their respective interests in Indian gaming, sometimes working as partners pursuing shared policy goals, other times locking horns in political and legal battles. As IGRA's policy implications have played out, tribal-state negotiations have expanded to include such topics as relinquishment of tribal treaty rights and revenue-sharing requirements. Whether such provisions are fair to include under IGRA's compacting framework often is overshadowed by the necessity of political compromise to get things done. States have been successful in demanding concessions from tribes and, in some cases, thwarting tribes' efforts to start or expand gaming enterprises. Tribes, for their part, have wielded increasing political clout through lobbying, state or local referenda and voter initiatives, and negotiation with local governments based largely on the economic benefits of Indian gaming to non-Native communities.

Today a myriad of political actors create, implement, and enforce the law and policy governing tribal gaming. After 26 years of federal regulation, one conclusion is clear: Indian gaming, perhaps more so than any other legal or political issue facing tribes in the last half-century, is a subject of ever-increasing popular awareness and public policy debate.

A Note on Tribal Sovereignty

Indian gaming is fundamentally different than most forms of gambling, from church bingo nights to the slots at Las Vegas's MGM Grand, Caesars Palace, or Wynn Casino and Resort, because it is conducted by tribal governments as an exercise of their sovereign rights. Tribal sovereignty—a historically rooted doctrine recognizing tribes' inherent rights as independent nations, preexisting the United States and its Constitution—is the primary legal and political foundation of federal Indian law and policy and thus, Indian gaming. Yet the legal doctrine of tribal sovereignty is perhaps the most misunderstood as-

---

14. Seminole Tribe v. Florida, 517 U.S. 44 (1996).

pect of tribal gaming. This in large part is due to the convoluted body of federal Indian law and resultant public policy that has shaped the doctrine over the course of more than 200 years.[15]

Prior to the arrival of Western colonizers, Native American tribes were sovereign nations in the territory that became the United States. Although recognizing the sovereign status of the tribes, the colonizers believed that tribal sovereignty rightly was limited both by settlers' "manifest destiny" and the perceived primitive nature of indigenous societies. The foundations of the modern legal doctrine of tribal sovereignty, which governs the relationship among the tribes, the federal government, and the states, reflects these early colonial conceptions. The doctrine was established by Chief Justice John Marshall in the U.S. Supreme Court's infamous "Marshall Trilogy," handed down in the early 1800s. In the Trilogy, the Court held that all tribes were incorporated into the United States through a "doctrine of discovery," through which "civilized" Western colonizers had rights that trumped those of the "savage" tribes in the United States and its territories. Tribes thus were "domestic dependent nations," possessing only limited sovereignty subject to Congress's asserted plenary power over tribes under the U.S. Constitution's Indian Commerce Clause.[16]

The Marshall Trilogy came during the first post-Constitution stage of federal Indian policy, the hallmarks of which were forced relocation and land ces-

---

15. In this section, we draw upon Kathryn R.L. Rand and Steven A. Light, "Virtue or Vice? How IGRA Shapes the Politics of Native American Gaming, Sovereignty, and Identity," *Virginia Journal of Social Policy and Law* 4 (1997): 385–96. For a highly readable summary of the relationship of the United States Constitution to Native American nations and tribes, see David E. Wilkins and Heidi Kiiwetinepinesiik Stark, *American Indian Politics and the American Political System*, 3rd ed. (Lanham, MD: Rowman and Littlefield, 2010), Chapter 2. For a thorough treatment of the legal doctrine of tribal sovereignty, see David E. Wilkins, *American Indian Sovereignty and the U.S. Supreme Court: The Masking of Justice* (Austin: University of Texas Press, 1997). For an argument that tribes' inherent right of self-determination, rather than the federal legal doctrine of tribal sovereignty, should guide Indian gaming law and policy, see Light and Rand, *Indian Gaming and Tribal Sovereignty*. For a tribe-specific account of changing conceptions of sovereignty, see Jessica R. Cattelino, *High Stakes: Florida Seminole Gaming and Sovereignty* (Durham, NC: Duke University Press, 2008).

16. See generally *Worcester v. Georgia*, 31 U.S. (6 Pet.) 515 (1832); *Cherokee Nation v. Georgia*, 20 U.S. (5 Pet.) 1 (1831); *Johnson v. M'Intosh*, 21 U.S. (8 Wheat.) 543 (1823); see also U.S. Const., art. I, §8, cl. 3 ("The Congress shall have Power ... to regulate commerce ... with the Indian tribes...."). For a critical analysis of the Marshall Trilogy and Congress's so-called plenary power, see Walter R. Echo-Hawk, *In the Courts of the Conqueror: The 10 Worst Indian Law Cases Ever Decided* (Golden, CO: Fulcrum Publishing, 2010); David E. Wilkins and K. Tsianina Lomawaima, *Uneven Ground: American Indian Sovereignty and Federal Law* (Norman: University of Oklahoma Press, 2001).

sions. After halting treaty making with the tribes in 1871, the United States adopted a policy of forced assimilation designed to eradicate Native traditions and culture. During the 1920s and 1930s and throughout the middle of the twentieth century, federal Indian policy reflected the termination and allotment era, in which tribal lands were sold to non-Natives and American Indians were provided incentives to move off-reservation. After the Civil Rights Movement, the federal government developed and promulgated a new policy of tribal self-determination in part designed to reduce perceived tribal reliance on the federal government. By the 1970s and 1980s, this policy drove cuts in federal assistance to tribes while encouraging tribal economic self-sufficiency. Leveraging limited reservation resources to promote economic growth and development proved extremely difficult, however, and many tribes faced the continuing realities of crushing poverty and other economic and social ills. As we discuss in Chapter 2, some tribes soon hit upon bingo and other forms of gaming as a viable economic development strategy that at first glance was not subject to state interference.

American Indian tribes now have a special status outside as well as within the American federal system that is, under federal law, defined and circumscribed by the historical development of the legal and political doctrine of tribal sovereignty. In essence, the modern legal doctrine means that the United States recognizes tribes as independent sovereign nations whose location within the boundaries of a state does not subject them to the application of state law, yet nevertheless are subject to Congress's asserted plenary power and bound by the trust relationship between the federal government and tribes.[17] Tribes therefore have a unique and paradoxical semi-sovereign status under federal law, and accordingly may be regulated by Congress.[18]

As they establish and delimit the law and policy of Indian gaming, the peculiarities of this situation are relatively obvious, but seldom noted. Tribal governments' right to conduct gaming on reservations stems from their status as preconstitutional sovereign nations. IGRA, however, creates a set of limitations on that sovereign right. In particular, under IGRA, tribes that choose to

---

17. Rand and Light, "Virtue or Vice?", 382; see also Wilkins and Stark, *American Indian Politics*, Chapter 2.

18. Although beyond the scope of this book, it is important to understand that the federal legal doctrine is not the only, and certainly not the best, definition of tribal sovereignty. A broader and more accurate definition, rooted in tribal rather than U.S. legal and political conceptions, is that tribal sovereignty is tribes' inherent right of self-determination, with legal, political, cultural, and spiritual dimensions. For a thorough treatment of Indian gaming centered on indigenous perspectives on tribal sovereignty, see Light and Rand, *Indian Gaming and Tribal Sovereignty*.

game must submit to federal and, for casino-style gaming, state regulation. Thus, Congress has mandated that those tribes that choose to open casinos must compromise their inherent sovereignty in order to pursue gaming as a strategy for reservation economic development. But far beyond Congress's intentions as represented by IGRA, subsequent legal developments have dramatically increased the political power that states wield over tribal gaming.[19]

A Note on Gambling Law

Legalized gambling is different than most industries in the United States. Gambling was regarded both as a religious sin and a moral vice in the past and accordingly was prohibited in nearly all 50 states. More recently, legalized gambling has expanded rapidly, giving rise to state lotteries, riverboat casinos, sports wagering, pari-mutuel betting, charitable gaming, and, of course, tribal gaming, in 48 states and the District of Columbia.[20] The gambling market has depended almost exclusively upon government decisions regarding prohibition versus regulation to foster its growth: market expansion was made possible only by the repeal or modification of anti-gambling laws.[21]

The legalization of gambling in most jurisdictions has not diminished the intense government scrutiny of the industry. Government at federal, state, and local levels retains an extensive regulatory role over legalized gambling, deciding what forms of gambling are allowed, where and when games may be conducted and under what conditions, who may work for or own a gambling establishment, and who may gamble. Although complex and varied, gambling regulations historically share two key social-control functions: ensuring the integrity of the games and preventing the infiltration of organized and common crime.[22] Regulatory schemes also are intended to facilitate common economic development goals related to gambling enterprises, such as revitalization of local and regional economies, job creation, and generation of tax revenue.[23]

---

19. We initially developed this argument in Steven Andrew Light and Kathryn R.L. Rand, "Resolving the Paradox: Three Frameworks for Developing Indian Gaming Law and Policy," *Nevada Law Journal* 4 (2004): 262–84.

20. NGISC, *Final Report*, 1-1. For a multidisciplinary examination of the morality and politics of gambling in the United States, see Alan Wolfe and Erik C. Owens, eds., *Gambling: Mapping the American Moral Landscape* (Waco, TX: Baylor University Press, 2009).

21. NGISC, *Final Report*, 1-4.

22. Id. at 3-1; Cory Aronovitz, "The Regulation of Commercial Gaming," *Chapman Law Review* 5 (2002): 181.

23. Aronovitz, "The Regulation of Commercial Gaming," 182–86.

At the federal level, Congress has enacted a number of far-reaching statutes concerning gambling, including the Johnson Act, which prohibits the illegal possession or interstate transportation of "gambling devices,"[24] the Wire Act, which prohibits the use of wire communications to transmit bets,[25] the Racketeering Influenced and Corrupt Organizations Act, which combats the infiltration of organized crime in interstate commerce, including gambling,[26] and, of course, IGRA, which regulates tribal gaming.

States and localities, with the broadest authority to regulate gambling within their borders, have extensive laws and regulations governing gambling. Nevada's and New Jersey's regulatory schemes serve as somewhat divergent prototypical models for state regulation based on different policy goals.[27] The Nevada model "seeks to maximize economic benefits of gaming, and allows the industry to meet market demands with little regulatory involvement," while the New Jersey model "focuses on the potential negative impacts of gaming, and establishes a comprehensive regulatory framework that strictly governs virtually every aspect of the business."[28] Variants of these models govern the proliferation of riverboat and commercial casinos, sports books, and state lotteries across the United States.

Perhaps the most important development in gambling law is online and mobile gambling, the next wave of legalized gambling in the United States. The defining characteristics of Internet and mobile services include their unparalleled ability to cross virtual and physical borders, the difficulty of and public wariness regarding government regulation of personal privacy and behavior, and the pervasive integration of online and mobile services into all aspects of modern life. Accompanying the proliferation of offshore and allegedly wager-free poker sites such as Full Tilt Poker and PokerStars, Congress indirectly banned online gaming through the federal Unlawful Internet Gambling Enforcement Act of 2006 (UIGEA).[29] The UIGEA prohibits banks, credit card companies, or other financial institutions from collecting on debts incurred on an Internet gaming web site.[30] Yet the online gaming market is too large, too

---

24. 15 U.S.C. §§ 1171–78 (2001).

25. 18 U.S.C. § 1084 (2001).

26. Id. § 1961 et seq. (2001).

27. NGISC, *Final Report*, 3-5; Aronovitz, "The Regulation of Commercial Gaming," 190.

28. Aronovitz, "The Regulation of Commercial Gaming," 190.

29. 31 U.S.C. §§ 5361–5367.

30. Id. The law "prohibits gambling businesses from knowingly accepting payments in connection with the participation of another person in a bet or wager that involves the use of the Internet and that is unlawful under any federal or state law." Id. It excludes most fantasy sports and legal intrastate and intertribal gaming.

fluid, and too under-regulated for the federal, state, or tribal governments to ignore.

Lending urgency to otherwise burgeoning pressure for federal legislation was the fall 2011 legal opinion by the U.S. Department of Justice that the federal Wire Act did not ban states from conducting online lottery sales within their borders.[31] The opinion found that the Wire Act does not reach online lotteries that do not involve wagering on "sporting events or contests."[32] Because of that conclusion, the opinion signaled that online lotteries also do not conflict with the UIGEA. The Justice Department's opinion opened the door to state legalization and regulation of online gaming. Many states were seeking new sources of revenue to overcome the effects of the recent economic recession, so it was no surprise that California, Delaware, Florida, Nevada, New Jersey, and a dozen more states have considered or enacted legislation to legalize online poker or casino-style gaming.[33] Delaware was first out of the gates, with Nevada and New Jersey close behind. Some assumed that Congress would preempt the field with federal legislation, especially as bills to legalize online poker had been under consideration for several years. Yet these efforts did not find serious traction in Congress until 2012, when Senator Harry Reid (D-NV) led attempts to legalize Internet poker and also to recognize a tribal role through the separate Tribal Online Gaming Act (TOGA).[34]

The TOGA in bill form assigned primary oversight and regulatory authority of tribal online gaming to the U.S. Secretary of Commerce via an Office of Tribal Online Gaming. Had the bill passed, this in practice would have created a federal regulatory framework separate from that under IGRA and the authority of the National Indian Gaming Commission, a complicating and even

---

31. "Whether Proposals by Illinois and New York to Use the Internet and Out-of-State Transaction Processors to Sell Lottery Tickets to In-State Adults Violate the Wire Act," Memorandum Opinion for the Assistant Attorney General, Criminal Division, U.S. Department of Justice, Sept. 20, 2011, http://www.justice.gov/olc/2011/state-lotteries-opinion.pdf (last visited July 27, 2012).

32. Id. at 1.

33. Michael Cooper, "As States Weigh Online Gambling, Profit May Be Small," *New York Times*, Jan. 17, 2012, http://www.nytimes.com/2012/01/18/us/more-states-look-to-legalize-online-gambling.html (last visited July 27, 2012).

34. Tribal Online Gaming Act of 2012, S. ___, Discussion Draft, 112th Cong. 2d. Sess. (2012), available at http://www.indian.senate.gov/sites/default/files/upload/files/TOGA-Sec-by-Sec-final.pdf (last visited Mar. 26, 2014). For a discussion of possible policy issues related to tribal online gaming, see Kathryn R.L. Rand and Steven Andrew Light, "Indian Gaming on the Internet: How the Indian Gaming Ethic Should Guide Tribes' Assessment of the Online Gaming Market," *Gaming Law Review & Economics* 15 (2011): 681–91.

troubling development to some.[35] However, in the face of political and limited but significant commercial opposition, neither the TOGA nor other federal online gaming legislation has moved forward, despite building pressure from the states and recently converted proponents from the commercial industry, including the American Gaming Association.[36] As other states, including Illinois, Iowa, Massachusetts, and Texas, consider legalization and states like Nevada and New Jersey ponder interstate compacting to leverage market strength, how, whether, and when online or mobile gaming will include tribal gaming is yet to be determined. Yet by spring 2014, tribes such as the Alturas Indian Rancheria Tribe in rural California, seeking to launch the first tribal online gaming effort, the Cheyenne & Arapaho Tribes in Oklahoma, developing a site catering to gamblers outside the U.S., and the Lac du Flambeau Band of Lake Superior Chippewa in Wisconsin, working on "fun-play" online gaming and seeking partners through the Tribal Internet Gaming Alliance, all were pushing the envelope on online gaming.[37]

To a large extent, state and local gambling laws simply do not apply to Indian gaming. Tribal sovereignty and Congress's constitutional authority place regulatory power over Indian gaming primarily with the tribes and federal government. But state interests are not absent from Indian gaming—far from it. As we discuss in detail throughout this book, states play a key part in determining the size and scope of tribal gaming. The states' growing role is a product of congressional delegation through IGRA, judicial interpretation, and the variable and highly politicized nature of tribal-state relations governed by the complex law and policy of Indian gaming.

35. See, e.g., Kathryn R.L. Rand and Steven Andrew Light, Statement for the Record Before the U.S. Senate Committee on Indian Affairs (July 26, 2012), http://www.gpo.gov/fdsys/pkg/CHRG-112shrg78446/html/CHRG-112shrg78446.htm (last visited Mar. 26, 2014).

36. See Karoun Demirjian, "American Gaming Association Backing Effort to Legalize Online Poker," *The Policy Racket* (*Las Vegas Sun*), Dec. 10, 2010, http://www.lasvegassun.com/blogs/policy-racket/2010/dec/10/american-gaming-association-backing-effort-legaliz/ (last visited Mar. 26, 2014); Frank J. Fahrenkopf, Jr., "Federal Online Gambling Legislation Needed Now More Than Ever," *Global Gaming Business*, Feb. 1, 2012, available at http://www.indian.senate.gov/sites/default/files/upload/files/TOGA-Sec-by-Sec-final.pdf (last visited Mar. 26, 2014).

37. Pamela M. Prah, "Tribes, States Eye Multibillion-dollar Online Gaming," *USA Today*, Dec. 11, 2013, http://www.usatoday.com/story/news/nation/2013/12/11/indian-tribes-states-eye-online-gambling/3986473/ (last visited Mar. 26, 2014).

Plan of Book

In Chapter 2, we describe the history of Indian gaming, examining both traditional tribal games and tribes' early for-profit gambling enterprises. By the late 1970s, tribes began to turn gaming into a strategy for self-determination and economic development to combat the challenges of reservation socioeconomic conditions. The U.S. Supreme Court, in a landmark case, *California v. Cabazon Band of Mission Indians*, recognized tribes' sovereign right to open and operate gaming establishments. This set the stage for Congress's enactment of the Indian Gaming Regulatory Act of 1988.

In Chapter 3, we set forth and discuss in detail IGRA's key provisions regulating Indian gaming at the tribal, state, and federal levels. In particular, we address what constitutes an Indian tribe and Indian lands, including newly acquired lands. The U.S. Supreme Court's shocking 2009 decision in *Carcieri v. Salazar* and Congress's even more surprising failure to pass a legislative "fix" in the wake of the case have complicated the question of Indian lands for tribes recognized after 1934, as cases following *Carcieri* show. We further examine the National Indian Gaming Commission's structure and authority, definitions of and requirements for Class I, Class II, and Class III gaming, the tribal-state compact requirement for casino-style gaming, restrictions on gaming revenue, and criminal prohibitions and penalties.

Chapter 4 turns to the subsequent and formative legal developments that have shaped Indian gaming. Federal and state case law, along with federal regulations, have elaborated on IGRA's requirements. There is a long-standing split in the federal circuit courts of appeal as to the proper interpretation of state public policy as it relates to IGRA; we discuss the differing approaches to the issue. IGRA's statutory distinctions among gaming classes have been further defined by the courts, with important regulatory implications. In 1996, the Supreme Court examined IGRA in the context of state sovereign immunity, resulting in a significant loss for tribes. We lay out the Court's decision in *Seminole Tribe v. Florida* and the federal regulations promulgated to recover some of IGRA's intent. Finally, we discuss other constitutional challenges to IGRA.

In Chapter 5, we outline the role of politics and policymaking in further shaping Indian gaming. Beginning with regulatory agencies at the federal, tribal, and state levels, we identify the key political players in compacting and other policy governing tribal gaming, which have come to include diverse non-governmental as well as governmental actors. After *Seminole Tribe* removed tribes' ability to force states to negotiate the terms for casino-style gaming within their borders, the states began to wield newfound political authority over tribes. Against that background, IGRA's requirement that tribes negotiate compacts with states has created an increasingly rugged landscape for government-to-government relations on Indian gaming. We close with a discussion of increased tribal political clout, as tribes to an unprecedented degree have used gaming revenue to develop, fund, and execute strategies to exercise political influence over state-level elections and policymaking.

Chapter 6 turns to a discussion of policy outcomes. Although public officials routinely engage in cost-benefit analyses of tribal gaming's socioeconomic impacts, there unfortunately remains a lack of accurate and complete information to guide informed discussion and policymaking. We summarize much of the research, noting particular areas of convergence as well as disagreement or inconclusive results. We then examine how politics and policymaking play out in four issues at the forefront of public debate: tribal-state revenue sharing, tribal treaty rights, federal recognition of tribes, and gaming on newly acquired lands, usually labeled "off-reservation" casinos.

In Chapter 7, we conclude by examining briefly what the future holds for tribal gaming, raising evolving law and policy in the areas of online gaming, tribes as debtors with commercial creditors, and unionization of tribal casinos. We note the trends that will shape the environment for legalized gambling, tribal economic development, and tribal-state relations, as well as the likelihood of law reform.

As a rapidly developing, complicated area of law and public policy, Indian gaming presents significant research opportunities—and challenges—for policymakers, practitioners, students, and scholars alike. In the Appendices, we discuss how to research Indian gaming and provide the necessary resource guideposts to navigate and chart the future trajectories of this complex field.

CHAPTER 2

Indian Gaming before 1988

Although the rapid and widespread expansion of tribal gaming facilities is a recent phenomenon, roughly dating from the passage of the federal Indian Gaming Regulatory Act (IGRA) in 1988, tribal gaming is rooted in a tradition of social games and wagering common to many tribes. "Indian gaming," as the term is used today, however, refers to gaming as a means of American Indian tribal self-governance, self-sufficiency, and economic development, a trend that began with a few reservation bingo halls and card rooms in the 1970s and early 1980s. Controversy over the regulation of tribal gaming spread almost as rapidly as Indian gaming itself, culminating in two legal landmarks: the U.S. Supreme Court's 1987 decision in *California v. Cabazon Band of Mission Indians* and Congress's passage of IGRA.

Traditional Tribal Games

The tribes of North America share a rich history of traditional tribal gaming. Many tribal games have their roots in cultural creation stories and myths. Often, the rules of the game were determined by the elements of the story and the characters portrayed. The mythical foundation also provided the sacred circumstances of the game and frequently taught a moral lesson.[1] Traditional tribal games reflect a profound relationship between the game, the community, and spirituality. Contestants prepared mentally, physically, and spiritually for the game with the participation and help of the community. This spiritual as-

---

1. Stewart Culin, *Games of the North American Indians* (New York: Dover Publications, Inc., 1975 (republication of Accompanying Paper, "Games of the North American Indians," in W.H. Holmes, *Twenty-Fourth Annual Report of the Bureau of American Ethnology to the Smithsonian Institution, 1902–1903* (Washington, DC: Government Printing Office, 1907))), 31–32; Kathryn Gabriel, *Gambler Way: Indian Gaming in Mythology, History and Archaeology in North America* (Boulder, CO: Johnson Books, 1996), 19.

pect highlighted the importance of the contestants' personal conduct during the game, including responsibility to team members and fairness to the opposition. In that respect, tribal games resembled ceremonies more than sporting events.[2]

Although each tribe is unique—and often a game is unique to a particular tribe—universal tribal games or categories of games exist in Native American history and culture.[3] Two broad categories of traditional games are games of dexterity and games of chance, both of which often involved gambling or wagering.[4]

Games of dexterity historically were defined by physical skill, such as speed and agility in foot races and lacrosse, and strength and coordination in hoop-and-pole and archery games. Besides the athletes themselves, community members participated in dexterity contests by placing bets on the games. Wagering was part of the social activity surrounding the games; the more significant the game was to the community, the higher the stakes.[5] Betting on games of dexterity was common, especially in foot racing; additionally, there were specific games of chance in which wagering played an integral part for the players and the community.[6]

Games of chance included dice games and various forms of guessing games, such as stick games and the moccasin game, and traditionally involved wagering as part of the play.[7] Dice games were universally popular among American Indian tribes.[8] The game consisted of players throwing dice, sometimes made of stones, buttons, seeds, or similar objects, against a blanket or a hide. Each player's score was determined by how the dice landed on the ground.[9] Stick games, a type of guessing game, involved an uneven number of sticks grouped together. One player divided the group of sticks into two groups, and the opposing player guessed which group contained an even or uneven number of sticks, or which group of sticks contained a special stick.[10] The moccasin game was another guessing game, widely known today as the shell game. An object was placed under one of a number of moccasins and the player

---

2. Joseph B. Oxendine, *American Indian Sports Heritage* (Champaign, IL: Human Kinetics Publishers, 1988), 3–5, 15–17.

3. Id. at xix.

4. Id. at 141; Culin, *Games of the North American Indians*, 31.

5. Oxendine, *American Indian Sports Heritage*, 81–82.

6. Id. at 81–82, 142.

7. Id. at 142.

8. Culin, *Games of the North American Indians*, 44–45.

9. Oxendine, *American Indian Sports Heritage*, 144, 149.

10. Id. at 149–50.

guessed which moccasin hid the object.[11]

Although one common Western view, at least at different times throughout history, is that gambling is evil or immoral, tribal communities generally did not share that perspective.[12] For many tribes, wagering was viewed as an act of generosity that helped as a matter of course to redistribute wealth within the community.[13] Traditional indigenous gambling myths place a "sacred significance" on wagering and express a "divine origin, power, and symbolism of the games." They often depict "good" gamblers, who play according to the rules and in appropriate context and moderation, and "bad" gamblers, who cheat or wager excessively. In Native mythology, the good gambler prevails over the bad gambler and restores the balance in nature.[14]

The stakes, and thus the rewards for winning, were as varied as the types of games. Depending on the prestige of the game, players would wager money, clothing, jewelry, guns, horses, saddles, and lodges. Besides the cautionary tales of gambling myths, tribal communities commonly addressed potential negative effects of gambling through various social norms and practices. Bets could only be placed in the amount of goods or cash the gambler had available at the time, creating wagering limits. Community members looked unfavorably on those who gambled excessively, and gamblers were not allowed to incur debt. Because gambling was a means of redistributing wealth, the community took steps to ensure gambling did not impoverish individuals.[15]

As an integral component of traditional tribal games, tribal communities viewed gambling as part of their social and cultural heritage.[16] Traditional tribal games, like other American Indian customs and practices, were impacted by increasing contact with Europeans and the pressures of colonization and westward expansion. The influence of colonial religious teachings and the laws and policies of the United States actively discouraged gambling by tribal members. At the same time, white settlement had negative effects on the wealth of tribal communities, so that there simply was less leisure time to play and fewer goods to wager.[17] Nevertheless, many tribes have retained traditions of games of chance and wagering, and continue to play these games in modern times, often in conjunction with social or religious ceremonies and events.

11. Id. at 151.
12. Gabriel, *Gambler Way*, 22–23.
13. Oxendine, *American Indian Sports Heritage*, 143.
14. Gabriel, *Gambler Way*, 17.
15. Oxendine, *American Indian Sports Heritage*, 144, 156.
16. Id. at 142, 156.
17. Id. at 141–44.

MODERN INDIAN GAMING

Reservation Economic Development

The colonization of the New World and subsequent history of federal-tribal relations in the United States more widely resulted in what has been termed the "Indian problem."[18] Through the early twentieth century, the so-called problem involved western settlement of tribal lands, "solved" through armed conflict, treaties, and forced relocation of tribal members onto reservations.[19] In more recent years, the Indian problem has referred to the widespread, extraordinary poverty and accompanying socioeconomic difficulties on many reservations. By the late twentieth century, over a third of reservation Indians lived in poverty and unemployment rates topped 50% in many tribal communities.[20] Native Americans living on reservations had lower life expectancy and higher infant mortality rates than the general U.S. population, along with higher incidences of violent crime, suicide, substance abuse, mental health problems, and mortality from illnesses such as diabetes, tuberculosis, and alcoholism.[21]

At the same time, the federal government adopted a policy of "self-determination" toward tribes, including encouragement of tribal economic development. However, high barriers to tribal enterprise on reservations contributed to extreme levels of poverty and unemployment on reservations. Typ-

---

18. See, for example, Murray L. Wax and Robert W. Buchanan, eds., *Solving "The Indian Problem": The White Man's Burdensome Business* (New York: New York Times, 1975).

19. See generally, for example, Stephen Cornell, *Return of the Native: American Indian Political Resurgence* (New York: Oxford University Press, 1988), 33–50; Angie Debo, *A History of the Indians of the United States* (Norman: University of Oklahoma Press, 1970).

20. See Frank Pommersheim, *Braid of Feathers: American Indian Law and Contemporary Tribal Life* (Berkeley, CA: University of California Press, 1995), 7. In 1990, the U.S. Census found that 31% of Native Americans, living both on and off the reservation, earned incomes below the poverty line, the largest percentage of the five identified racial groups in the United States. U.S. Census Bureau, *Social and Economic Characteristics, American Indian and Native Alaska Areas* (Washington, DC, 1990) (hereinafter cited as 1990 U.S. Census, *American Indians*). High poverty rates have persisted into the twenty-first century, despite avenues for economic uplift that include the spread of Indian gaming. Twenty-nine percent of American Indians and Alaska Natives fell below the poverty line in 2012, the highest rate of any racial or ethnic group, and nearly double the nation's average poverty rate of 15.9%. U.S. Census Bureau, "Facts for Features: American Indian and Native Alaskan Heritage Month: November 2013," https://www.census.gov/newsroom/releases/archives/facts_for_features_special_editions/cb13-ff26.html (last visited Mar. 31, 2014).

21. See, for example, U.S. Commission on Civil Rights, *A Quiet Crisis: Federal Funding and Unmet Needs in Indian Country* (Washington, DC, July 2003), 34–35.

ically, reservations afforded few opportunities for successful commercial business ventures or efforts to market on-reservation goods and services to non-Native populations.[22] Nevertheless, and against the odds, many tribes pursued some form of economic development in the face of depressed reservation economies and the Reagan Administration's policy of encouraging tribal self-sufficiency and economic development while cutting funding to Indian programs.[23]

In the late 1970s and early 1980s, a few tribes, notably in California and Florida, opened high-stakes bingo palaces as a means of raising revenue. As one of the few viable strategies for reservation economic development, bingo presented an attractive option to tribal governments: start-up costs were relatively low, the facilities had a minimal impact on the environment, and the game had potential for high returns on the tribes' investment.[24]

Bingo was legal in both California and Florida, as it was in many states at the time, but state law stringently regulated bingo enterprises through both civil and criminal penalties. Based on federal Indian law's general prohibition against state regulation of tribes, the tribes offered games in their bingo halls that did not comply with state gambling regulations. The states, however, argued that state regulation had been authorized by Congress and attempted to fine or shut down the tribal bingo and card games for violations of state law.[25]

The Seminole Tribe contracted with a private company to build and operate a high-stakes bingo hall on the tribe's reservation in southern Florida, within driving distance of Fort Lauderdale and Miami. Although Florida law permitted charitable bingo, it set several restrictions on the games, including a $100 ceiling on jackpots, and violations were punished through criminal penalties. Learning of the Seminoles' plans for a high-stakes bingo palace, the Broward County sheriff announced that he would enforce the state bingo laws on the tribe's reservation. The tribe sued in federal court to enjoin application of state law within the bounds of its reservation.

---

22. See, for example, Kathryn R.L. Rand and Steven A. Light, "Raising the Stakes: Tribal Sovereignty and Indian Gaming in North Dakota," *Gaming Law Review* 5 (2001): 334.

23. For an overview of federal Indian policy during the Reagan era, see Samuel R. Cook, "Ronald Reagan's Indian Policy in Retrospect: Economic Crisis and Political Irony," *Policy Studies Journal* 24 (1996): 11–27.

24. See generally Eduardo E. Cordeiro, "The Economics of Bingo: Factors Influencing the Success of Bingo Operations on American Indian Reservations," in Stephen Cornell and Joseph P. Kalt, eds., *What Can Tribes Do? Strategies and Institutions in American Indian Economic Development* (Los Angeles: UCLA American Indian Studies Center, 1992).

25. Florida's and California's position on the issue had some support from the limited federal grant of authority in Public Law 280, which we discuss in more detail below.

Florida's defense centered on the congressional grant of legal authority over tribes in Public Law 280. Enacted by Congress in 1953, Public Law 280 gave certain states a broad grant of criminal jurisdiction and a limited grant of civil jurisdiction over tribes within their borders.[26] Based on federal law, Florida had assumed criminal jurisdiction over tribes located in the state.[27] Assessing Congress's authorization of state jurisdiction under Public Law 280, the Court of Appeals for the Fifth Circuit reasoned in *Seminole Tribe v. Butterworth* that the state only had authority to enforce criminal prohibitions on tribal land. It could not enforce its civil regulatory laws against the tribe.[28] The court concluded that Florida's bingo laws, although enforced through criminal penalties, were not a criminal prohibition against bingo generally. The laws instead comprised a civil regulatory scheme and thus were unenforceable: "Where the state regulates the operation of bingo halls to prevent the game of bingo from becoming a money-making business, the Seminole Indian tribe is not subject to that regulation and cannot be prosecuted for

---

26. Act of Aug. 15, 1953, ch. 505, 67 Stat. 588–590 (codified as amended at 18 U.S.C. 1162, 28 U.S.C. 1360 and other scattered sections in 18 and 28 U.S.C. (2001)). In Public Law 280, Congress expressly granted to six states (California, Minnesota, Nebraska, Oregon, Wisconsin, and Alaska, sometimes referred to as "mandatory" states) jurisdiction over specified Indian reservations located within those states, and provided a process for the assumption of jurisdiction by other states (sometimes referred to as "voluntary" states) over reservations within their borders. The statute's grant of criminal jurisdiction stated:

> Each of the States [listed] ... shall have jurisdiction over offenses committed by or against Indians in the areas of Indian country listed ... to the same extent that such State ... has jurisdiction over offenses committed elsewhere within the State ... and the criminal laws of such State ... shall have the same force and effect within such Indian country as they have elsewhere within the State....

18 U.S.C. § 1162(a). The statute's grant of civil jurisdiction was more limited:

> Each of the States [listed] ... shall have jurisdiction over civil causes of action between Indians or to which Indians are parties which arise in the areas of Indian country listed ... to the same extent that such State has jurisdiction over other civil causes of action, and those civil laws of such State that are of general application to private persons or private property shall have the same force and effect within such Indian country as they have elsewhere within the State....

28 U.S.C. § 1360(a).

27. As explained by the Fifth Circuit, a provision of Public Law 280, later repealed by Congress, allowed states to unilaterally assert jurisdiction over "criminal offenses [and] civil causes of action" on reservation lands by duly passing state legislation. Florida passed Fla. Stat. § 285.16, which assumed criminal jurisdiction over reservation Indians. See Seminole Tribe of Florida v. Butterworth, 658 F.2d 310, 313 (5th Cir. 1981) (quoting 67 Stat. 590 (1953) (repealed by Pub. L. 90-284, Title IV, § 403, 82 Stat. 79 (1968))).

28. Seminole Tribe, 658 F.2d at 313.

violating the limitations imposed."[29] Because Florida generally allowed bingo, subject to restrictions, the game did not violate the state's public policy and thus did not fall within Public Law 280's ambit of allowable state jurisdiction.

In California, the Barona Group of the Capitan Grande Band of Mission Indians had followed the Seminoles' lead and contracted with a private management company to open a bingo palace on the tribe's reservation in San Diego County. Both the state of California and the county allowed charitable bingo games, subject to the restrictions of state law. Local law enforcement, asserting that the state restrictions applied on the tribe's reservation, threatened to shut down the bingo operation and arrest its patrons. Although California's bingo law was similar to the Florida law examined in *Seminole Tribe v. Butterworth*, California's position was strengthened by the fact that Congress had expressly granted it both criminal and some civil jurisdiction through Public Law 280. In *Barona Group v. Duffy*, the Court of Appeals for the Ninth Circuit nevertheless adopted the reasoning of *Seminole Tribe* and held that because California generally allowed bingo games, bingo did not violate state public policy, and thus the state lacked authority to enforce its bingo regulations against the tribe.[30]

The holdings in *Barona Group* and *Seminole Tribe* led a number of tribes to explore gaming as a means of reservation economic development.[31] Indian gaming facilities at the time, operated by more than 80 tribes across the country, primarily consisted of bingo and a few card rooms offering poker and blackjack. Even without slot machines or other lucrative casino-style games, the tribal gaming industry grew rapidly in the 1980s, grossing over $110 million in 1988.[32]

---

29. Id. at 314–15.

30. Barona Group of the Capitan Grande Band of Mission Indians v. Duffy, 694 F.2d 1185 (9th Cir. 1982). The court noted that the tribe's bingo operation shared a similar policy goal with the state's bingo laws:

> [T]he stated purpose of the tribal bingo ordinance is to collect money "for the support of programs to promote the health, education and general welfare" of the Barona Tribe. This intent to better the Indian community is as worthy as the other charitable purposes to which bingo proceeds are lawfully authorized under the California statute. Although the Barona bingo operation does not fully comply with the letter of the [state] statutory scheme, it does at least fall within the general tenor of its permissive intent.

Id. at 1190.

31. In Wisconsin, for example, a federal district court reached a nearly identical result in Oneida Tribe of Indians v. Wisconsin, 518 F. Supp. 712 (W.D. Wis. 1981), holding that the state's bingo laws were regulatory rather than prohibitory and thus inapplicable on the Oneida reservation.

32. I. Nelson Rose, Commentary, "The Indian Gaming Act and the Political Process," in William R. Eadington, ed., *Indian Gaming and the Law*, 2d ed. (Reno: Institute for the

Despite federal court rulings limiting state power over tribal gaming, some states continued to enforce their gambling regulations on reservations.

California v. Cabazon Band of Mission Indians

Two tribes in California, the Cabazon and Morongo Bands of Mission Indians, operated bingo halls and a card club on their reservations in Riverside County, near Palm Springs and within driving distance of Los Angeles. The tribes' games were open to the public and catered to non-Indians coming onto the reservations to play. California law permitted charitable bingo games, but restricted the amount of jackpots to $250 per game and the use of gaming profits to charitable purposes. Violations of the state regulations were punishable as criminal misdemeanors. Riverside County ordinances similarly regulated bingo games, and also prohibited poker and other card games. The tribes challenged both the state's and the county's enforcement of their regulations in federal court, and the case culminated in the U.S. Supreme Court's landmark 1987 decision in *California v. Cabazon Band of Mission Indians*.[33]

As it did in *Barona Group*, California argued that Public Law 280's grant of state jurisdiction over tribes in California constituted congressional abrogation of tribal sovereignty and thus authorized the application of state and local law on the tribes' reservations. In *Bryan v. Itasca County*, the U.S. Supreme Court had ruled that Public Law 280's grant of civil jurisdiction was not a blanket authority for the states to regulate the tribes generally; instead, it applied only to private civil litigation in state court.[34] The Court's interpretation of Public Law 280 was based on its reading of congressional intent not to grant states broad civil regulatory authority over tribes, as that "would result in the destruction of tribal institutions and values."[35] Accordingly, if California's gambling laws were civil regulatory laws, then the state would not have authority to enforce them against the tribes under the federal statute. On the other hand, Public Law 280's grant of state criminal jurisdiction was more extensive: if California's gambling laws were criminal prohibitions against gambling, then the state would have authority to enforce them against the tribes under the statute.

Study of Commercial Gambling and Gaming, 1998), 4; Sioux Harvey, "Winning the Sovereignty Jackpot: The Indian Gaming Regulatory Act and the Struggle for Sovereignty," in Angela Mullis and David Kamper, eds., *Indian Gaming: Who Wins?* (Los Angeles: UCLA American Indian Studies Center, 2000), 16–17.

33. 480 U.S. 202 (1987).

34. 426 U.S. 373 (1976).

35. Cabazon, 480 U.S. at 208. The Ninth Circuit had followed this line of reasoning in *Barona Group*. See Barona Group, 694 F.2d at 1187–88.

In deciding whether California's gambling statutes were criminal prohibitions or civil regulations, the determinative question was not simply whether the state law carried a criminal penalty. Instead, the Supreme Court adopted the policy-based approach of the Ninth Circuit Court of Appeals in *Barona Group v. Duffy*:

> [A court should draw] a distinction between state "criminal/prohibitory" laws and state "civil/regulatory" laws: if the intent of a state law is generally to prohibit certain conduct, it falls within Pub. L. 280's grant of criminal jurisdiction, but if the state law generally permits the conduct at issue, subject to regulation, it must be classified as civil/regulatory and Pub. L. 280 does not authorize its enforcement on an Indian reservation. The shorthand test is whether the conduct at issue violates the State's public policy.[36]

The Court then examined California's public policy concerning gambling, noting that it operated a state lottery and permitted bingo, card games, and parimutuel betting on horse races:

> California does not prohibit all forms of gambling. California itself operates a state lottery and daily encourages its citizens to participate in this state-run gambling. California also permits parimutuel horse-race betting. Although certain enumerated gambling games are prohibited under [California's penal code], games not enumerated, including the games played in the Cabazon card club, are permissible. The Tribes assert that more than 400 card rooms similar to the Cabazon card club flourish in California, and the State does not dispute this fact. Also, ... bingo is legally sponsored by many different organizations and is widely played in California.

Based on this overview of California's gambling policy, the Court determined that "[i]n light of the fact that California permits a substantial amount of gambling activity, including bingo, and actually promotes gambling through its state lottery, we must conclude that California regulates rather than prohibits gambling in general and bingo in particular."[37]

---

36. Cabazon, 480 U.S. at 209.

37. Id. at 210–11. The Court noted that there appeared to be little, if any, authority supporting the application of Riverside County's gambling ordinances on the tribes' reservations, as Public Law 280 authorized the application of state, rather than local, law. The Court reasoned, however, that even if the county ordinances could apply on reservations under Public Law 280, they too were regulatory rather than prohibitory. Id. at 212 n.11.

California argued that although bingo, as played within the constraints of state law, did not violate state public policy, the high-stakes bingo played on the tribes' reservations did, as reflected in the state's criminal prohibition against such games. But the Court cautioned that the distinction between criminal/prohibitory and civil/regulatory state laws was not a bright line and the fact that "an otherwise regulatory law is enforceable by criminal as well as civil means does not necessarily convert it into a criminal law within the meaning of Pub. L. 280."[38] Instead, said the Court, "[t]he applicable state laws governing an activity must be examined in detail before they can be characterized as regulatory or prohibitory."[39]

California also argued that Congress had authorized application of state law through the federal Organized Crime Control Act of 1970, which made certain violations of state gambling laws violations of federal law as well.[40] The Supreme Court disagreed, reasoning that the Act was a federal statute, and thus the federal government rather than the states had jurisdiction to enforce it. Federal jurisdiction over tribes was within Congress's constitutionally granted plenary power, as construed by the Supreme Court, and did not raise the same tribal sovereignty issues as did state jurisdiction.[41] The Court concluded that nothing in the Act gave jurisdiction to the states to enforce federal law generally or against tribes in particular.[42]

Finally, the *Cabazon* Court considered whether any exceptional circumstances might allow state regulation of the tribes even in the absence of express congressional authorization. Such circumstances, the Court explained, are rare and depend on the doctrine of federal preemption: "state jurisdiction is pre-empted if it interferes or is incompatible with federal and tribal interests reflected in federal law, unless the state interests at stake are sufficient to justify the assertion of state authority."[43] The Court noted that the relevant federal interests at stake were "traditional notions of Indian sovereignty and the congressional goal of Indian self-government, including its 'overriding goal' of encouraging tribal self-sufficiency and economic development."[44] These "important federal interests" were reflected in federal statutes, statements of executive

---

38. Id. at 211.

39. Id. at 211 n.10.

40. 18 U.S.C. § 1955 (2001). A similar argument was raised, with similar results, in United States v. Farris, 624 F.2d 890, 894–95 (9th Cir. 1980).

41. We discuss this distinction in Chapter 1.

42. Cabazon, 480 U.S. at 213–14.

43. Id. at 216 (quoting New Mexico v. Mescalero Apache Tribe, 462 U.S. 324, 333–34 (1983)) (alterations omitted).

44. Id.

policy, and actions of the U.S. Secretary of the Interior that encouraged Indian gaming as a means of tribal economic development. As the Court explained, the tribes' interests paralleled those of the federal government:

> These [federal] policies and actions, which demonstrate the Government's approval and active promotion of tribal bingo enterprises, are of particular relevance in this case. The Cabazon and Morongo Reservations contain no natural resources which can be exploited. The tribal games at present provide the sole source of revenues for the operation of the tribal governments and the provision of tribal services. They are also the major sources of employment on the reservations. Self-determination and economic development are not within reach if the Tribes cannot raise revenues and provide employment for their members.[45]

California contended that while the tribes' interests in economic development might be strong, their interests in conducting gaming enterprises that relied in large part on a non-Indian customer base were not. The state further argued that its regulation of gaming on the tribes' reservations should be allowed under a prior case allowing state taxation of cigarettes sold to non-Indians in tribal smokeshops. There, the U.S. Supreme Court had held that the state's interest in collecting taxes from cigarette sales to non-Indians was sufficient to warrant application of state law in the absence of express congressional authorization because there was not a "significant" tribal interest at stake: the tribes were simply marketing "an exemption from state taxation to persons who would normally do their business elsewhere."[46] Here, however, the Cabazon and Morongo Bands were not "merely marketing an exemption from state gambling laws," reasoned the Court, thus distinguishing the tribes' gaming enterprises from tribal smokeshops:

> [T]he Tribes are not merely importing a product onto the reservations for immediate resale to non-Indians. They have built modern facilities which provide recreational opportunities and ancillary services to their patrons, who do not simply drive on to the reservations, make purchases and depart, but spend extended periods of time there enjoying the services the Tribes provide. The Tribes have a strong incentive to provide comfortable, clean, and attractive facilities and well-

---

45. Id. at 218–19.
46. Washington v. Confederated Tribes of Colville Indian Reservation, 447 U.S. 134, 155 (1980).

run games in order to increase attendance at the games.... [The tribes] are generating value on the reservations through activities in which they have a substantial interest.[47]

California also argued that its interest in controlling crime was sufficient to warrant state regulation, insisting that enforcement of state gambling laws on the reservations was necessary to prevent the infiltration of organized crime in tribal gaming operations. The state reasoned that the tribes' high-stakes bingo halls and card games were more susceptible to criminal elements than were the state's stringently regulated charitable bingo operations. After noting that there was no indication that the tribes' bingo halls and card club had been infiltrated by organized crime, the Court decided that on balance, the "compelling" federal and tribal interests at hand outweighed California's interest and thus preempted state regulation.[48]

Justice Stevens, joined by Justices O'Connor and Scalia, dissented: "Unless and until Congress exempts Indian-managed gambling from state law and subjects it to federal supervision, I believe that a State may enforce its laws prohibiting high-stakes gambling on Indian reservations within its borders."[49] Stevens argued that the Court should interpret Public Law 280 as permitting general state civil regulation of tribes, particularly with regard to commercial transactions between Indians and non-Indians on the reservation, and took special issue with the Court's construction of California's public policy regarding gambling:

> The Court reasons ... that the operation of high-stakes bingo games does not run afoul of California's public policy because the State permits some forms of gambling and, specifically, some forms of bingo. I find this approach to "public policy" curious, to say the least. The State's policy concerning gambling is to authorize certain specific gambling activities that comply with carefully defined regulation and that provide revenues either for the State itself or for certain charitable purposes, and to prohibit all unregulated commercial lotteries that are operated for private profit. To argue that the tribal bingo games comply with the public policy of California because the State permits some other gambling is tantamount to arguing that driving over 60 miles an

---

47. Cabazon, 480 U.S. at 219–20.
48. Id. at 221.
49. Id. at 222 (Stevens, J., dissenting).

hour is consistent with public policy because the State allows driving at speeds of up to 55 miles an hour.[50]

Even in the absence of express congressional authorization, Justice Stevens would have found that California's "economic and protective" interests warranted state regulation of Indian gaming, relying on the reasoning of the Court's smokeshop case: "Whatever revenues the tribes receive from their unregulated bingo games drain funds from the state-approved recipients of lottery revenues — just as the tax-free cigarette sales [in tribal smokeshops] diminished the receipts that the tax collector otherwise would have received."[51] It was "painfully obvious" to Stevens that only the tribes' "exemption" from state regulation made the bingo halls attractive to customers "who would normally do their gambling elsewhere," and all but guaranteed the tribes' financial success. Stevens reasoned that the tribal gaming establishments were really no different from smokeshops, in that the tribes had "no tradition or special expertise in the operation of large bingo parlors."[52] Further, Stevens found the state's interest in controlling organized crime more persuasive than did the Court. "Comprehensive regulation of the commercial gambling ventures that a state elects to license," Stevens wrote, "is obviously justified as a prophylactic measure even if there is presently no criminal activity associated with casino gambling in the state."[53]

Stevens' concluding remarks seemed prescient. The tribes and the federal government "may well be correct, in the abstract, that gambling facilities are a sensible way to generate revenues that are badly needed by reservation Indians," he wrote. "But the decision to adopt, or reject, or to define the precise contours of such a course of action, and thereby to set aside the substantial public policy concerns of a sovereign State, should be made by the Congress of the United States."[54]

Political Responses to Cabazon

The Supreme Court's consideration of the *Cabazon* case fueled lobbying efforts of both states and tribes for federal legislation governing Indian gaming.[55] Congress was aware of the controversy over tribal gaming: the growth in

---

50. Id. at 224–25 (Stevens, J., dissenting) (citation and footnote omitted).
51. Id. at 226 (Stevens, J., dissenting).
52. Cabazon, 480 U.S. at 225–26 (Stevens, J., dissenting).
53. Id. at 227 (Stevens, J., dissenting).
54. Id.
55. See Joseph M. Kelly, "Indian Gaming Law," *Drake Law Review* 43 (1995): 504–5.

Indian gaming during the 1980s and the accompanying tensions between state power and tribal sovereignty attracted Congress's attention as early as 1983, when Representative Morris Udall (D-Ariz.) introduced a bill allowing for federal regulation of gambling on reservation lands.[56] The Udall bill did not pass, and such was the fate of a number of similar Indian gaming bills.[57] By 1985, in congressional hearings on Indian gaming, the Department of the Interior estimated that about 80 tribes were conducting gaming on their reservations, some grossing nearly $1 million each month. The operation of Indian gaming was far from uniform: although many tribes owned and operated their gaming establishments, others had contracted with outside management companies and a few were owned and operated by individual tribal members.[58]

The states urged Congress to authorize state regulation of tribal gaming operations, emphasizing the danger of organized crime and the appropriate role of the states in regulating gambling generally. As Arizona's Attorney General put it, "[T]he prime responsibility for establishing and enforcing public policy on matters with such a particularly localized impact as those relating to gambling are uniquely within the province of the States and not the Federal Government."[59] Nevada professed a particular concern that any incidence of organized crime at a tribal casino would trigger a federal crackdown on state-licensed gaming as well.[60] The states also asserted economic interests in regulating Indian gaming, asking Congress to abolish the tribal "exemption" from state regulation to place tribes on a level playing field with private and charitable gaming operations and to allow state taxation of Indian gaming enterprises.

Many tribes opposed state regulation of Indian gaming, and lobbied Congress to codify exclusive tribal regulation, both to preserve tribal sovereignty generally and to protect Indian gaming as an economic development strategy for tribal governments. The success of some tribal bingo operations demonstrated gaming's potential as one of the very few viable avenues for reservation economic development and job creation. In Florida, for example, the Seminole Tribe's bingo hall had helped to slash reservation unemployment

---

56. See H.R. 4566, 98th Cong., 1st Sess. (1983).

57. See Roland J. Santoni, "The Indian Gaming Regulatory Act: How Did We Get Here? Where Are We Going?," *Creighton Law Review* 26 (1992–93): 395–99 (discussing several Indian gaming bills).

58. Harvey, "Winning the Sovereignty Jackpot," 18.

59. Gambling on Indian Reservations and Lands: Hearings on S. 902 Before the Senate Select Comm. on Indian Affairs, 99th Cong., 1st Sess. 107 (1985) (statement of Arizona Attorney General Robert Corbin).

60. Rose, Commentary, 4–5.

from 60% to less than 20%, while in California, the Morongo Band's bingo operation created 35 new jobs and grossed over $300,000 in its first year.[61] Anticipating that Congress would insist on some form of regulation of Indian gaming, however, the tribes supported federal regulation over state regulation. As one tribal leader put it, "Any proposed legislation must be consistent with the general rule that State laws ordinarily do not extend to an Indian reservation."[62]

Initially, proposed federal legislation concerning Indian gaming was motivated by an anticipated decision against the tribes in *Cabazon*, and thus focused on preserving tribal gaming as a means of reservation economic development by preempting state regulation.[63] The Supreme Court's decision in *Cabazon*, however, "threw the ball into Congress's lap to do something, fast," catalyzing proponents of both state and federal regulation.[64] According to U.S. Senator Harry Reid (D-Nev.), a supporter of state regulation of Indian gaming,[65] after the Court decided *Cabazon*, "there was little choice except for Congress to enact laws regulating gaming on Indian lands. The alternative would have been for the rapid and uncontrolled expansion of unregulated casino-type gambling on Indian lands."[66] Yet Reid also saw a need for a compromise between the state and tribal positions, as well as the necessity of ensuring that gaming remained a viable strategy for tribal governments to generate much-needed revenue in accordance with federal interests in tribal self-sufficiency and economic development.

Reid, alongside Udall and Senator Daniel Inouye (D-Haw.), chairs of the House Interior Committee and the Senate Indian Affairs Committee respectively, as well as Senators Daniel Evans (R-Wash.), Thomas Daschle (D-S.D.), and

---

61. Harvey, "Winning the Sovereignty Jackpot," 17; Cordeiro, "The Economics of Bingo."

62. Gambling on Indian Reservations and Lands: Hearings on S. 902 (statement of Donald Antone, Sr., Governor of the Gila River Indian Community). See generally Santoni, "The Indian Gaming Regulatory Act," 399–403 (discussing lobbying efforts and congressional debates).

63. Alexander Tallchief Skibine, "*Cabazon* and Its Implications for Indian Gaming," in Mullis and Kamper, eds., *Indian Gaming: Who Wins?*, 68. For a detailed discussion of Indian gaming bills introduced in Congress, see Santoni, "The Indian Gaming Regulatory Act," 395–403.

64. Rose, Commentary, 3; Skibine, "*Cabazon* and Its Implications," 68.

65. See Gaming Activities on Indian Reservations and Lands: Hearings on S. 555 and S. 1303 Before the Senate Select Comm. on Indian Affairs, 100th Cong., 1st Sess. 82 (1987) (statement of Sen. Harry Reid).

66. Harry Reid, Commentary, "The Indian Gaming Act and the Political Process," in Eadington, ed., *Indian Gaming and the Law*, 17.

John McCain (R-Ariz.), introduced various bills to regulate Indian gaming. One key innovation was to categorize types of gambling and to assign regulatory authority accordingly. Traditional tribal games of chance, associated with tribal ceremonies and carrying little risk of corruption, were left to exclusive tribal jurisdiction. With almost a decade of tribal experience and relatively few problems, tribal governments would continue to regulate bingo and similar games, with some federal oversight.

Congress saw casino-style gambling, however, as carrying greater risks and raising different issues than bingo. As Reid explained, "[t]here was no intention of diminishing the significance of the *Cabazon* decision," but the Supreme Court's reasoning, in the eyes of the bill's drafters, was tied to the bingo and poker games at issue in the case, rather than casino gambling.[67] As a "cash business," many believed that casino gaming necessarily attracted corruption and crime, whether organized or unorganized. As one commentator noted, "The problem was not that it was Indian gambling, but that it was gambling, period."[68] The states' interests in preventing the infiltration of organized crime and controlling gambling generally appeared most persuasive in the context of casino-style gaming. In one bill, introduced just six days before *Cabazon* was decided, a tribe would have been required to submit to state regulation of casino-style gaming;[69] in another bill, introduced after *Cabazon*, a new National Indian Gaming Commission would have been authorized to promulgate regulations governing casino-style gaming.[70] Subsequent legislative efforts focused on finding a compromise between the two approaches to regulating casino gambling on reservations—state regulation or some combination of tribal and federal regulation—while protecting tribal and federal interests in Indian gaming.[71]

In mid-1988, the Senate Select Committee on Indian Affairs reported favorably on a version of the bill mandating state regulation of tribal casino-style gaming, as introduced by Senators Inouye, Evans, and Daschle in 1987.[72] The Senate Committee version incorporated a middle ground, requiring "tribal-state compacts," in which a state and tribe would negotiate the regulatory structure for casino-style gaming on the tribe's reservation. According to the Committee report,

---

67. Id. at 18.
68. Rose, Commentary, 5.
69. See S. 555, 100th Cong., 1st Sess. (1987).
70. See H.R. 2507, 100th Cong., 1st Sess. (1987); S. 1303, 100th Cong., 1st Sess. (1987).
71. See Santoni, "The Indian Gaming Regulatory Act," 403–4.
72. S. Rep. 100-446, 100th Cong., 2d Sess., 1988 U.S.C.C.A.N. 3071.

Consistent with these principles [of tribal sovereignty and the exclusivity of federal law over tribes], the Committee has developed a framework for the regulation of gaming activities on Indian lands which provides that in the exercise of its sovereign rights, unless a tribe affirmatively elects to have State laws and State jurisdiction extend to tribal lands, the Congress will not unilaterally impose or allow State jurisdiction on Indian lands for the regulation of Indian gaming activities. The mechanism for facilitating the unusual relationship in which a tribe might affirmatively seek the extension of State jurisdiction and the application of State laws to activities conducted on Indian land is a tribal-State compact.... [The bill] does not contemplate and does not provide for the conduct of [casino-style] gaming activities on Indian lands in the absence of a tribal-State compact. In adopting this position, the Committee has carefully considered the law enforcement concerns of tribal and State governments, as well as those of the Federal Government, and the need to fashion a means by which differing public policies of these respective governmental entities can be accommodated and reconciled. This legislation is intended to provide a means by which tribal and State governments can realize their unique and individual government objectives, while at the same time, work together to develop a regulatory and jurisdictional pattern that will foster a consistency and uniformity in the manner in which laws regulating the conduct of gaming activities are applied.[73]

The compact provision, according to the report, was "the best mechanism to assure that the interests of both sovereign entities are met with respect to the regulation of complex gaming enterprises."[74] Senator Reid credited the compact requirement with breaking the "logjam" of competing interests holding up the federal legislation, as "[the bill] provided protection to the states without violating either the *Cabazon* decision or the concept of Indian sovereignty."[75]

* * *

The Senate as well as the House quickly passed the revised bill as the Indian Gaming Regulatory Act—what universally would be referred to as "IGRA"—on October 17, 1988.[76] A vastly different era of tribal gaming had begun.

---

73. Id. at 3075–76.

74. Id. at 3083.

75. Reid, Commentary, 19. We describe the tribal-state compact requirement in detail in Chapter 3.

76. Pub. L. 100-497 (codified at 25 U.S.C. §§ 2701–21 (2001)).

CHAPTER 3

THE INDIAN GAMING REGULATORY ACT OF 1988

Congress's formal findings and its declaration of policy in the Indian Gaming Regulatory Act of 1988 (IGRA) reflect both the varied interests involved in tribal gaming and Congress's intent to create a comprehensive regulatory framework that balanced tribal sovereignty and reservation economic development with state interests in controlling crime and regulating gambling generally.

Following extensive hearings, Congress enacted IGRA on the basis of a number of formal findings, including these:

- a number of tribes had opened gaming establishments as means of generating tribal government revenue;
- several tribes had entered into outside management contracts, but federal standards governing such contracts were not clear;
- federal law did not provide clear guidance on appropriate regulation of Indian gaming generally;
- a principal goal of federal Indian policy was to promote tribal economic development, tribal self-sufficiency, and strong tribal government; and
- tribes have exclusive regulatory jurisdiction over tribal gaming that is not prohibited by either federal law or state public policy.[1]

Thus, the congressional purposes served by IGRA were to codify tribes' sovereign right to conduct gaming on Indian lands as a means of promoting tribal economic development, self-sufficiency, and strong tribal governments, while providing sufficient regulation to ensure legality and to protect the financial interests of gaming tribes. Additionally, Congress enacted IGRA to establish an independent federal regulatory authority in the form of the National Indian Gaming Commission (NIGC).[2]

---

1. 25 U.S.C. §2701.
2. Id. §2702.

In this chapter, we detail IGRA's provisions and describe the roles of tribes, states, and the federal government in regulating Indian gaming. We focus in particular on the provision that has had the greatest impact on tribes as well as the industry, and garnered the most legal and political controversy: the tribal-state compacting requirement for casino-style gaming.

Indian Tribes and Indian Lands

IGRA provides that "Indian gaming" is gaming conducted by an "Indian tribe" on "Indian lands." An Indian tribe is defined as a tribe or other organized group that is eligible for federal Indian programs and services and has been federally acknowledged as possessing powers of self-government.[3] Indian lands are defined as reservation lands as well as trust and restricted lands over which a tribe exercises governmental authority.[4]

In recent years, the U.S. Department of the Interior's tribal acknowledgment process has come under escalating political scrutiny, largely because of the continuing controversy over Indian gaming and the perception that federal recognition is a "license" for tribes to open casinos. In 2002, the Department announced that it was undertaking a "strategic plan" for revamping the recognition process; however, such efforts stalled out in both the Bush and Obama administrations. In 2013, Assistant Secretary for Indian Affairs Kevin Washburn again announced the Interior Department's intent to revise the administrative recognition process.[5] Similarly, proposed transfers of off-reservation land into trust for the benefit of a tribe became politically charged throughout the 2000s, as an increasing number of tribes, many of which recently were granted federal acknowledgment, sought to acquire land for casinos near major metropolitan areas.[6] We revisit these and similar issues in Chapters 5 and 6.

---

3. Id. § 2703(5).

4. Id. § 2703(4); see also 25 C.F.R. § 502.12.

5. Office of the Assistant Secretary-Indian Affairs, "Washburn Announces Consideration of Revisions to Federal Acknowledgement Regulations," Press Release, June 21, 2013, http://www.bia.gov/News/index.htm (last visited July 24, 2013).

6. See, for example, Alex Tallchief Skibine, "The Indian Gaming Regulatory Act at 25: Successes, Shortcomings, and Dilemmas," *Federal Lawyer* 60 (2013): 35; Steven Andrew Light and Kathryn R.L. Rand, "The Hand That's Been Dealt: The Indian Gaming Regulatory Act at 20, *Drake Law Review* 57 (2009): 413, 437–41.

Indian Tribes

To be eligible for federal Indian programs and services, particularly those ad-ministered by the Interior Department, a tribe ordinarily must be acknowledged, or "recognized," by the federal government. A tribe may be federally recognized through treaty, statute, executive or administrative order, or long-standing prac-tice of the federal government treating the tribe as a political entity.[7] Many fed-erally acknowledged tribes have long histories of federal recognition, marked by legal and political interactions with the United States in the eighteenth and nineteenth centuries. Others have sought recognition in recent years, often through federal statute or the Interior Department's acknowledgment process.[8]

In 1978, the Department adopted mandatory recognition criteria to assess the eligibility of Native American groups that had not been federally recog-nized. In essence, the group must show that it has maintained a "substantially continuous" tribal existence and has functioned as an autonomous govern-ment entity "from historical times until the present." This status includes con-tinuous identification as an "American Indian entity" since 1900 through interactions, as a tribe, with federal, state, local, or tribal governments, historical records, and anthropological scholarly opinion; existence as a "distinct com-munity" from the first sustained contact with colonizers to the present, in-cluding evidence of political leadership and authority over members and appropriate governing documents; and a membership consisting of descen-dants of a tribe that existed in historical times and who are neither members of other tribes nor have been subject to termination of tribal status by Congress.[9]

---

7. William Canby, Jr., *American Indian Law in a Nutshell*, 3d ed. (St. Paul, MN: West Group, 1998), 4–7.

8. In 2003, the Interior Department's Branch of Acknowledgment and Research (BAR) was realigned and renamed the Office of Federal Acknowledgement (OFA). Information about the OFA's procedures and decisions is available through the Interior Department's website. See Office of Federal Acknowledgement, http://www.bia.gov/WhoWeAre/AS-IA/OFA/ (last visited Aug. 30, 2013).

9. 25 C.F.R. §§ 83.1, 83.7. The Federally Recognized Indian Tribe List Act of 1994, Pub. L. 103-454, 108 Stat. 4791, requires the annual publication in the Federal Register of a list of all federally recognized tribes. For detailed discussions of federal tribal recognition, see Sara-Larus Tolley, *Quest for Tribal Acknowledgment: California's Honey Lake Maidus* (Nor-man, OK: University of Oklahoma Press, 2006); Mark D. Myers, "Federal Recognition of Indian Tribes in the United States," *Stanford Law and Policy Review* 12 (2001): 271–86. For a critical account of Indian gaming's influence on tribal acknowledgement, see Renee Ann Cramer, *Cash, Color, and Colonialism: The Politics of Tribal Acknowledgement* (Norman, OK: University of Oklahoma Press, 2005).

Indian Lands

During the second half of the nineteenth century, the federal government established reservations for tribes to accommodate westward expansion. Many reservations originally were established by treaty and later diminished by federal statute or executive order. The lands within the bounds of current reservations qualify as Indian lands under IGRA. Additionally, IGRA's definition of Indian lands includes what typically are called "trust" lands, or lands held in trust by the United States for the benefit of a tribe, and "restricted" lands, or lands protected from alienation (absolute conveyance of real property) but not held in trust by the federal government, so long as the tribe exercises governmental authority over the land.[10] Indian lands do not include fee land allotments. Thus, in order to qualify as Indian lands under IGRA, non-reservation land must meet three requirements: the tribe must exercise jurisdiction over the land, fee title to the land must be restricted or not freely alienable, and the tribe must exercise governmental power over the land.[11]

For most tribes with reservations, the question of whether a location qualifies as Indian lands is straightforward. For some tribes with less clearly defined reservations, and for other tribes pursuing casinos nearer non-tribal metropolitan areas, however, the question may depend on a complex history of tribal-federal interactions. In a case concerning a tract of non-reservation

---

10. IGRA defines "Indian lands" as "all lands within the limits of any Indian reservation" and "any lands title to which is either held in trust by the United States for the benefit of any Indian tribe or individual or held by any Indian tribe or individual subject to restriction by the United States against alienation and over which an Indian tribe exercises governmental power." 25 U.S.C. § 2703(4); see also 25 C.F.R. § 502.12. Until the introduction of the term "Indian lands" in IGRA, most federal laws used the term "Indian country," with a similar, but not identical, definition. See 18 U.S.C. § 1151 (defining "Indian country").

11. Kansas v. United States, 249 F.3d 1213, 1228 (10th Cir. 2001); see also United Keetoowah Band of Cherokee Indians v. U.S., 567 F.3d 1235, 1250 (10th Cir. 2009). In Match-E-Be-Nash-She-Wish Band of Pottawatomi Indians v. Engler, 304 F.3d 616 (6th Cir. 2002), the Court of Appeals for the Sixth Circuit held that a state was not obliged to enter into tribal-state compact negotiations for Class III gaming unless and until the tribe possessed "Indian lands" under IGRA. The Ninth Circuit reached a similar conclusion in Guidiville Band of Pomo Indians v. NGV Gaming, Ltd., 531 F.3d 767 (9th Cir. 2008), and in Big Lagoon Rancheria v. California, Nos. 10-17803 & 10-17878, ___ F.3d ___ (9th Cir. Jan. 21, 2014), the court clarified that the "Indian lands" must be the proposed location for the tribe's casino, stating that "a tribe's right to request negotiations—and to sue if the state does not negotiate in good faith—depends on its having jurisdiction over Indian lands on which it proposes to conduct class III gaming."

land owned by the Miami Tribe of Oklahoma, for example, the federal district court relied on an 1867 treaty, 1873 and 1882 congressional enactments, an 1891 claim settlement with the federal government, a 1960 action to collect interest on the settlement, and other historical events to conclude that the tribe did not have jurisdiction over the tract of land.[12]

A few courts have examined the meaning of IGRA's requirement that a tribe "exercise governmental power" over the lands. The U.S. Court of Appeals for the First Circuit, in *Rhode Island v. Narragansett Indian Tribe*, held that the exercise of governmental power, though dependent on tribal jurisdiction, required "the presence of concrete manifestations of that authority."[13] In deciding that the Narragansett tribe exercised authority over the lands in question, the court took into account the tribe's establishment of a housing authority, its status as the functional equivalent of a state under federal environmental laws, and its administration of government programs such as health care, job training, social services, and public safety.[14] In *Cheyenne River Sioux Tribe v. South Dakota*, the district court listed the following factors as relevant in determining whether a tribe exercised governmental power over lands: whether the lands were developed, whether tribal members resided on the lands, and whether the tribe provided any governmental services, including law enforcement, on the lands.[15]

Carcieri v. Salazar

The Supreme Court's 2009 decision in *Carcieri v. Salazar* abruptly threw into doubt the Interior Secretary's seemingly well-settled ability to take land into trust for tribes recognized after 1934. The case concerned the Narragansett Tribe, which achieved federal acknowledgement in 1983. When the Secretary approved the tribe's application to take into trust 31 acres of land owned by the tribe in Charleston, Rhode Island, the state sued. Both a federal district court and the First Circuit found in favor of the tribe, but the Supreme Court reversed.[16]

---

12. See Miami Tribe of Oklahoma v. United States, 927 F. Supp. 1419 (D. Kan. 1996) (*Miami Tribe I*); Miami Tribe of Oklahoma v. United States, 5 F. Supp. 2d 1213 (D. Kan. 1998) (*Miami Tribe II*).

13. 19 F.3d 685, 703 (1st Cir. 1994). Conversely, in Kansas ex rel. Graves v. United States, 86 F. Supp. 2d 1094 (D. Kan. 2000), the district court held that evidence of the tribe's exercise of governmental power, without evidence that the tribe had jurisdiction to exercise that power, should not satisfy IGRA's definition of Indian lands.

14. Narragansett Indian Tribe, 19 F.3d at 703.

15. 830 F. Supp. 523, 528 (D.S.D. 1993), *aff'd*, 3 F.3d 273 (8th Cir. 1993).

16. Carcieri v. Kempthorne, 497 F.3d 15 (1st Cir. 2007), *rev'd sub nom.* Carcieri v. Salazar, 555 U.S. 379 (2009).

The Court's analysis largely turned on its reading of the 1934 federal Indian Reorganization Act's (IRA) statutory language, and the related application of basic principles of administrative law. The IRA authorizes the Secretary to take land into trust for the benefit of a "recognized Indian Tribe now under Federal jurisdiction."[17] In the decades since the IRA's passage, the Interior Department has held land in trust for tribes federally acknowledged after 1934, whether by Congress or through the Interior Department's administrative acknowledgement process. The question of whether "now" in the IRA means in 1934, or at the time the Secretary acts to take land into trust, had been held by the lower courts to be ambiguous enough to merit deference under principles of administrative law to the Secretary's interpretation.[18]

The Supreme Court in *Carcieri*, however, deemed the phrase unambiguous. Writing for the majority, Justice Clarence Thomas found the meaning of "now" to be unambiguously understood to be tantamount to its dictionary definition: at "the present time; at this moment; at the time of speaking." The Court therefore concluded that "the term 'now under Federal jurisdiction'... unambiguously refers to those tribes that were under the federal jurisdiction of the United States when the IRA was enacted in 1934."[19] Under this interpretation, Congress "spoke" in 1934, and in so doing, did not grant authority to the Interior Secretary to act in future instances of "now." Accordingly, the Secretary did not have authority to take land into trust for any tribe that came under federal jurisdiction after 1934. Further, the Court subsequently decided that trust acquisitions could be challenged even when the land already is held in trust.[20]

---

17. Section 5 of the IRA authorizes the Secretary of the Interior to acquire interests in land for the purpose of providing land for "Indians," defined in section 19 as "persons of Indian descent who are members of any recognized Indian tribe now under Federal jurisdiction." Wheeler-Howard (Indian Reorganization) Act, Pub. L. No. 73-383, 48 Stat. 984 (1934) (codified as amended at 25 U.S.C. §§ 461–479 (2006)).

18. See Chevron U.S.A. Inc. v. Natural Resources Defense Council, Inc., 467 U.S. 837, 843 (1984).

19. Carcieri v. Salazar, 555 U.S. at 395.

20. In Match-E-Be-Nash-She-Wish Band of Pottawatomi Indians v. Patchak, 132 S. Ct. 2199 (2012), the Court allowed a *Carcieri* challenge to a proposed tribal casino to proceed despite the fact that the suit was filed three years after the Interior Secretary took the land into trust. The Bureau of Indian Affairs then promulgated a "*Patchak* patch" intended to clarify how administrative land-into-trust decisions may be appealed. See Land Acquisitions: Appeals of Land Acquisition Decisions, Final Rule by Bureau of Indian Affairs, 78 Fed. Reg. 67928 (Nov. 13, 2013).

Called by one commentator "[p]erhaps the most disruptive recent case" by the Supreme Court,[21] the controversial decision was followed by calls for Congress to adopt a statutory "fix." Linguistically, a fix would be quite simple: Congress simply would authorize the Interior Secretary to take land into trust for any federally acknowledged tribe, regardless of when it had been recognized. Politically, however, the issue was divisive, as land into trust and gaming, particularly on newly acquired lands, had come to be seen as synonymous. At the time of this writing a legislative response remained elusive.[22]

Litigation (or the threat of the same) pursuant to *Carcieri* continues to increase uncertainty and complicate the ability of many tribes to pursue what had seemed to be a matter clearly under the Interior Secretary's authority. In *Big Lagoon Rancheria*, California and the Big Lagoon Rancheria had engaged in protracted compact negotiations (and litigation) for years. In 2009, the tribe sued the state for failure to negotiate in good faith. The Ninth Circuit relied on *Carcieri* to conclude that the state had no obligation to negotiate with the tribe, as the proposed casino location did not constitute Indian lands under IGRA. The court reasoned that because the tribe was not under federal jurisdiction in 1934, the Secretary's past decision to take the land into trust was invalid under *Carcieri*, and as a result the land could not qualify as Indian lands.[23]

Big Lagoon Rancheria demonstrated what pitfalls were likely to continue in the absence of a *Carcieri* fix. In November 2013, Assistant Secretary for Indian Affairs Kevin Washburn testified,

> In the wake of the *Carcieri* decision, both the Department and many tribes have been forced to spend an inordinate amount of time analyzing whether the tribes were under Federal jurisdiction in 1934 and thus entitled to have land taken into trust. We testified before [the Senate Indian Affairs] Committee, just over a year ago, on the burdens, costs and uncertainty on the fee to trust process that resulted from the *Carcieri* decision. We stated then, and it continues to remain true, that once this analysis is completed, if the Department decides to take land into trust and provides notice of its intent, the *Carcieri* decision

---

21. "The decision may place the future land acquisitions of perhaps as many as 100 tribes at risk." Matthew Fletcher, "The Tenth Justice Lost in Indian Country," *Federal Lawyer* 58 (2011): 36.

22. See, e.g., Rob Capriccio, "Another Shot at a Clean *Carcieri* Fix in the House," *Indian Country Today*, Feb. 14, 2013, http://indiancountrytodaymedianetwork.com/2013/02/14/another-shot-clean-carcieri-fix-house-147674 (last visited Apr. 1, 2014).

23. See Big Lagoon Rancheria v. California, Nos. 10-17803 & 10-17878, ___ F.3d ___ (9th Cir. Jan. 21, 2014).

makes it likely that we will face costly and complex litigation over whether applicant tribes were under federal jurisdiction in 1934.[24]

Newly Acquired Lands

IGRA generally prohibits Class II and Class III gaming on Indian lands placed in trust after October 17, 1988, IGRA's date of passage.[25] Such lands are commonly referred to as "newly acquired" or "after acquired" lands. There are, however, a number of general and state- and tribe-specific exceptions.

First, a tribe may conduct gaming on newly acquired lands that are located within the tribe's existing reservation or that are contiguous to the reservation's boundaries.[26] Second, for tribes without reservations as of October 17, 1988, gaming is not prohibited on newly acquired lands if the lands are within the tribe's last recognized reservation and within the state in which the tribe currently resides.[27]

Third, an exception is made when gaming on newly acquired lands is "in the best interest of the tribe and its members, and would not be detrimental to the surrounding community." Specifically, the Secretary of the Interior must make such a determination after consulting with the tribe, the state, local officials, and officials of nearby tribes. Further, the state's governor must concur in the Secretary's determination.[28] The consultation and governor's concurrence requirements create potential political obstacles to the likelihood that a tribe may conduct gaming on newly acquired lands under the "best interests" exception.[29]

---

24. Kevin K. Washburn, Statement Before the U.S. Senate Committee on Indian Affairs (Nov. 20, 2013).

25. 25 U.S.C. §2719(a). Congress has authorized the Interior Secretary to acquire lands and place them in trust for the benefit of a tribe. 25 U.S.C. §465; see also 25 C.F.R. pt. 151. Congress also may exercise its own power to place land into trust.

26. 25 U.S.C. §2719(a)(1).

27. Id. §2719(a)(2)(B). A special exception applies to tribes without reservations that have acquired trust lands in Oklahoma. Gaming is allowed on newly acquired lands in Oklahoma if the lands are within the tribe's former reservation or if the lands are contiguous to the tribe's current trust or restricted lands. Id. §2719(a)(2)(A).

28. Id. §2719(b)(1)(A).

29. For most of IGRA's history, only three tribes operated gaming on newly acquired lands under this exception: the Keweenaw Bay Indian Community of the Lake Superior Bands of Chippewa Indians operates a casino in Choclay Township, outside of Marquette, Michigan; the Forest County Potawatomi have a casino in Milwaukee, Wisconsin; and the Kalispell Tribe conducts gaming in Airway Heights, Washington. In the early 2000s, growing political controversy over what some called "reservation shopping" seemed to result in a de facto moratorium on federal and/or gubernatorial approval. See Heidi McNeil Staudenmaier,

The constitutionality of the governor's concurrence requirement was challenged in *Confederated Tribes of Siletz Indians v. United States*.[30] There, the Interior Secretary had disallowed a tribal casino on newly acquired lands near Salem, Oregon, because Democratic Governor Barbara Roberts refused to agree that gaming on the lands was in the best interest of the tribe and not detrimental to the surrounding community. The tribe contended that the concurrence requirement violated both the Appointments Clause of the U.S. Constitution,[31] because the governor was exercising authority without being duly appointed to a federal post, and separation of powers principles, because the concurrence requirement reassigned authority from the Interior Secretary to state governors. The Court of Appeals for the Ninth Circuit rejected both arguments, holding that IGRA does not give state governors "primary authority" to determine applicability of the exception and that Congress appropriately conditioned the Secretary's delegated power to take land into trust on state concurrence.[32] The Seventh Circuit reached a similar conclusion in *Lac Courte Oreilles Band v. United States*.[33]

"Off-Reservation Native American Gaming: An Examination of the Legal and Political Hurdles," *Nevada Law Journal* 4 (2004): 311–12. More recently, however, the Obama administration's Interior Secretary has issued a handful of approvals under the "best interests" exception, including for the Keweenaw Bay Indian Community, the Enterprise Rancheria of Maidu Indians, the North Fork Rancheria of Mono Indians (all in 2011), and the Menominee Indian Tribe of Wisconsin (in 2013). We discuss the issue of gaming on newly acquired lands further in Chapters 5 and 6.

  30. 110 F.3d 688 (9th Cir. 1997).

  31. U.S. Const., art. II, §2, cl. 2 ("[The President] shall appoint ... all other Officers of the United States....").

  32. 110 F.3d at 696, 698.

  33. 367 F.3d 650 (7th Cir. 2004). There, the Interior Secretary had determined that an off-reservation casino near Hudson, Wisconsin, would be in the best interests of the tribes and would not be detrimental to the surrounding community. Republican Governor Scott McCallum refused to concur in the Secretary's determination, defeating the tribes' proposal. The tribes challenged the governor's authority under 25 U.S.C. §2719(b)(1)(A) on a number of grounds, including the separation of powers doctrine, nondelegation doctrine, Appointments Clause, state sovereignty, and the federal government's trust obligation to the tribes. None of these arguments persuaded the Seventh Circuit that the provision was unconstitutional. Id.

  At the time of this writing, a state lawsuit was pending in California, challenging the governor's authority under state law to concur in the Secretary's "best interests" determination. By contrast, this suit was filed not by tribes but by a prominent non-Indian citizens' group that continually opposes the expansion of Indian gaming in that state. See Stand Up for California! v. Brown (Case No. MCV062850, Cal. Sup., filed Mar. 27, 2013).

  One commentator has suggested amending IGRA to remove the governor's concurrence

Fourth, gaming is allowed on newly acquired lands when the lands are placed in trust as a settlement of a land claim, or as the initial reservation of a federally recognized tribe, or as the restoration of lands for a tribe whose federal recognition is restored.[34] Finally, IGRA includes specific exceptions for the St. Croix Chippewa Indians in Wisconsin and the Miccosukee Tribe of Indians in Florida.[35]

The National Indian Gaming Commission

Composition

As the apex of its regulatory structure, IGRA established the NIGC, an independent federal regulatory agency within the Interior Department. The Commission consists of three members who each serve three-year terms: a chair, appointed by the president with the advice and consent of the Senate, and two associate members, appointed by the Secretary of the Interior. At least two commissioners must be enrolled members of a tribe, and no more than two commissioners may be members of the same political party. By majority vote, the Commission selects one of the two associate members to serve as Vice Chair.[36]

---

requirement, so that tribal gaming on newly acquired lands simply would be a point of tribal-state negotiation during the compacting process required for Class III gaming. See Brian P. McClatchey, Note, "A Whole New Game: Recognizing the Changing Complexion of Indian Gaming by Removing the 'Governor's Veto' for Gaming on 'After-Acquired Lands,'" *University of Michigan Journal of Law Reform* 37 (2004): 1227–74.

34. 25 U.S.C. §2719(b)(1)(B). In *City of Rossville v. Norton*, for example, the district court held that the federal government's placement into trust of a 50-acre parcel of land pursuant to the Auburn Indian Restoration Act was a "restoration of lands." 219 F. Supp. 2d 130 (D.D.C. 2002).

35. These tribe-specific exceptions also reference particular lands. 25 U.S.C. §2719(b)(2). In 2005, the Interior Department's Office of Indian Gaming Management (now known as the Office of Indian Gaming) produced a "checklist" for gaming-related land acquisitions based on the requirements of 25 U.S.C. §2719, 25 C.F.R. pt. 151, and federal environmental laws. The checklist details the submission process for an acquisition request, including explanations of the supporting documentation required for each of the exceptions under 25 U.S.C. §2719. See Office of Indian Gaming Management, "Checklist for Gaming Acquisitions, Gaming-Related Acquisitions, and IGRA Section 20 Determinations" (Mar. 2005).

36. 25 U.S.C. §2704. The NIGC's current members are Acting Chair Jonodey Osceola Chaudhuri and Associate Commissioner Daniel Little. Chaudhuri, appointed to a three-year term by the Interior Secretary in September 2013, is a member of the Muscogee Creek Nation and is a former Senior Counselor to the Department of the Interior's Assistant Secretary for Indian Affairs. Little, a former manager of National Governmental Affairs for the

The NIGC is staffed by an Office of General Counsel and an Office of the Chief of Staff. The Commission's Chief of Staff heads Divisions of Compliance, Public Affairs, and Finance. The Division of Compliance includes regional directors in six offices, located in Portland, Sacramento, Phoenix, Tulsa, St. Paul, and Washington, D.C.[37] The Commission is funded by fees assessed against tribal gaming operations, but also may request appropriations from Congress.[38] In 2013, the Commission issued a strategic plan for 2014–2018 that included goals of continuing an "assistance, compliance, and enforcement" initiative, enhancing technical assistance and training, improving and updating regulations, improving consultation and communication with tribal regulatory authorities as well as federal and state agencies, and increasing efficiency, transparency, and accountability.[39]

Regulatory Authority

The Commission "shall promulgate such regulations and guidelines as it deems appropriate to implement the provisions of" IGRA.[40] The NIGC has issued a number of federal regulations, scattered throughout Title 25 of the Code of Federal Regulations, and located roughly in Parts 501 to 580.[41] Perhaps most notably, in 1999, the NIGC promulgated "minimum internal control standards," or MICS, for tribal gaming operations. Tribes must at a minimum adopt these highly detailed standards, which cover aspects of gaming ranging from requiring that a bingo ball be displayed to patrons before it is called to requiring two employees to initial a corrected error on a slot machine count. The MICS regulate the operation of specific games offered at tribal casinos, as

---

Mashantucket Pequot Tribe and Foxwoods Resort Casino in Connecticut, as well as a Policy Analyst for the Connecticut legislature, was appointed to a three-year term by the Interior Secretary in April 2010. The Vice Chair seat remained unfilled as of this writing. Of recent note, former Chair Tracie Stevens, a member of the Tulalip Tribes of Washington, was the first Native American woman to chair the Commission. See NIGC, "Commissioners," http:// www.nigc.gov/About_Us/Commissioners.aspx (last visited Apr. 6, 2014).

37. See NIGC, "Organizational Chart," http://www.nigc.gov/Portals/0/NIGC%20Uploads/aboutus/Organizational%20Chart.pdf (last visited Apr. 1, 2014).

38. 25 U.S.C. §2717; 25 C.F.R. pt. 514.

39. NIGC, Strategic Plan for Fiscal Years 2014-2018 (2013), http://www.nigc.gov/LinkClick.aspx?fileticket=gV9TuiUoWuk%3D&tabid=917 (last visited Apr. 1, 2014).

40. 25 U.S.C. §2706(b)(10).

41. An easily accessible source for the Commission's regulations is NIGC, "Commission Regulations," http://www.nigc.gov/Laws_Regulations/Commission_Regulations.aspx (last visited Apr. 1, 2014).

well as cage and credit, internal audits, surveillance, electronic data processing, and complimentary services and items.[42]

Investigative and Enforcement Powers

The Commission has authority, through the power to close Indian gaming operations and to impose civil fines, to enforce IGRA's provisions, federal regulations promulgated by the Commission, and the tribes' own gaming regulations, ordinances, and resolutions. Before exercising its enforcement powers, the NIGC must issue a written complaint alleging the violation in "common and concise language."[43] The Commission also has authority to conduct inspections of tribal gaming operations and to "demand access to ... all papers, books, and records respecting ... any ... matter necessary to carry out the duties of the Commission under" IGRA, as well as the power to subpoena witnesses, hold hearings, and receive testimony and evidence.[44] Commission regulations further detail the execution of its investigative and enforcement powers.[45]

The Commission Chair has the authority to temporarily close a tribal gaming operation for "substantial violation" of IGRA, federal regulation, or tribal law. Commission regulations set forth 13 specific substantial violations that may trigger the Chair's temporary closure.[46]

The Chair also has authority to levy and collect civil fines against the operator of a tribal gaming establishment for violations of IGRA, federal regulation, or tribal law, not to exceed $25,000 per violation. The Chair reviews each vi-

---

42. 25 C.F.R. pts. 542, 543. The MICS were last revised in 2012.
43. 25 U.S.C. § 2713(a)(3).
44. Id. §§ 2706(b)(4), (8), 2715.
45. 25 C.F.R. pts. 571, 573.
46. Substantial violations include (1) failure to correct a violation within a reasonable time, (2) failure to pay the Commission's annual fee, (3) operation of a gaming establishment without a duly approved tribal ordinance, (4) operation of a gaming establishment without a tribal license, (5) operation of a gaming establishment without completing the required background investigations, (6) defrauding the tribe, (7) operation of a gaming establishment by a management company without a duly approved management contract, (8) submitting false or misleading information to the Commission or the tribe, (9) refusing to allow inspection of a gaming operation, (10) failure to suspend a gaming license in accordance with the Commission's direction, (11) operation of Class III games without a valid tribal-state compact, (12) posing a threat to the environment or to public health or safety through the operation of a gaming establishment, and (13) operation of gaming on Indian lands not eligible for gaming. Id. § 573.4(a).

olation and assesses a fine according to the economic benefit of noncompliance, the seriousness of the violation and the extent to which it threatens the integrity of Indian gaming generally, whether the operator has a history of violations, whether the violation is negligent or willful, and whether the operator made a good-faith effort to correct the violation after notification. The operator is entitled to provide relevant information to the Chair and to request a reduction or waiver of the fine. The Chair and the operator also may enter into a settlement agreement.[47] The NIGC's final decision on a civil fine levied by the Chair is reviewable in federal district court.[48] Commission regulations detail the collection of civil fines and other debts.[49]

Approval and Oversight Powers: Tribal Ordinances, Management Contracts, and Tribal Regulation

The Commission's other key powers relate to approving tribal gaming ordinances and management contracts, and its oversight role in regulating tribal bingo operations and some limited card game operations. The Commission's determinations, including those regarding approval of tribal ordinances, management contracts, and petitions for "self-regulation," are final agency decisions and accordingly may be appealed in federal district court.[50]

The Chair's approval of tribal ordinances or resolutions relating to bingo and casino-style gaming is a prerequisite for tribal operation of the games, and Commission regulations detail the submission process. Under IGRA, the Chair "shall" approve an ordinance if it comports with IGRA's requirements for the type of gaming involved, including limits on use of net revenue, audits of gaming and contracts, and background and licensing requirements. If the Chair disapproves an ordinance, the tribe or other interested party may appeal the Chair's decision to the Commission.[51]

Similarly, the Chair has the power to approve management contracts for the operation and management of bingo and casino-style gaming establishments. Although Indian gaming casinos generally must be owned and operated by a tribe, a tribe may enter into limited management contracts for the

---

47. 25 C.F.R. §§ 575.4–.6.
48. 25 U.S.C. §§ 2705(a)(2), 2713(a), 2714; 25 C.F.R. pt. 575.
49. 25 C.F.R. pt. 513.
50. 25 U.S.C. § 2714 ("Decisions made by the Commission pursuant to sections 2710, 2711, 2712, and 2713 of this title shall be final agency decisions for purposes of appeal to the appropriate Federal district court pursuant to chapter 7 of Title 5.").
51. 25 U.S.C. §§ 2705(3), 2710; 25 C.F.R. pts. 522, 523, 524.

operation of its casino.[52] Prior to approval of a proposed management contract, the Chair is required to obtain background information, including a "complete financial statement," on "each person or entity (including individuals comprising such entity) having a direct financial interest in, or management responsibility for" the proposed management contract.[53] The Chair has the power to question any person identified as having a direct financial interest or management responsibility.[54] To be approved, the contract must provide monthly accounting procedures and financial reports, allow tribal officials access to the gaming operations and the ability to verify daily revenues, guarantee a minimum payment to the tribe, cap the repayment of development and construction costs, and provide grounds for termination. Additionally, the contract must not exceed five years (or, upon the request of the tribe and authorization of the Chair, seven years if necessary based on capital investment and income projections).[55] Commission regulations further detail the required content of management contracts and procedures for submitting proposed management contracts to the Chair.[56]

Generally speaking, IGRA requires the Chair to exercise the "skill and diligence" of a trustee in approving proposed management contracts, and to disapprove a proposed management contract for a number of reasons.[57] A person identified as having a direct financial interest or management responsibility may not be an elected member of the tribe's governing body, convicted of a felony or a gaming offense, or a person whose background "pose[s] a threat to the public interest or to the effective regulation and control of gaming or create[s] … dangers of unsuitable, unfair, or illegal practices, methods, and activities in the conduct [or business] of gaming."[58] Any of these circumstances will trigger mandatory disapproval. Additionally, misrepresentations or refusal to respond to the Chair's questions by a person with a direct financial interest

---

52. 25 U.S.C. §§ 2711, 2710(d)(a). Management contracts are defined by 25 C.F.R. § 502.15.

53. 25 U.S.C. § 2711(a)(1); 25 C.F.R. pt. 537. The proposed management contract responsibility is defined by federal regulation. 25 C.F.R. §§ 502.17, 502.18.

54. 25 U.S.C. § 2711(a)(2).

55. Id. § 2711(b).

56. 25 C.F.R. pts. 531, 533. For two highly useful discussions of the practical "ins and outs" of the NIGC's management contract approval process, see Kevin K. Washburn, "The Mechanics of Indian Gaming Management Contract Approval," *Gaming Law Review* 8 (2004): 333–46, and Heidi McNeil Staudenmaier, "Negotiating Enforceable Tribal Gaming Management Agreements," *Gaming Law Review* 7 (2003): 31–36.

57. 25 U.S.C. § 2711(e); 25 C.F.R. § 533.6(b).

58. 25 U.S.C. § 2711(e)(1)(D).

or management responsibility similarly requires the Chair to disapprove the contract. The management contractor's attempt to unduly influence the tribal government or its failure to comply with the terms of the proposed contract or the tribe's gaming ordinances also will prove fatal for the contract.[59]

Finally, the Commission has oversight powers over tribal regulation of gaming operations, including the power to approve tribal regulatory ordinances and to oversee tribal licensing of key employees and management officials.[60] Commission regulations detail the content of background investigations for tribal licensing as well as the procedures for submitting proposed licenses to the Commission.[61] The tribe must notify the NIGC of the results of the background investigation before it issues a license to an individual employee, and again when it issues the license. The Commission has 30 days to object to the tribe's issuance of a license, and may direct the tribe to suspend or revoke a tribal license based on "reliable evidence" that the employee's background disqualifies her from casino employment.[62] Commission regulations also detail the NIGC's investigatory and oversight powers.[63] The Commission's oversight of tribal bingo operations includes the power to issue a "certificate of self-regulation" to a tribe.[64]

Classes of Gaming

One of IGRA's key innovations was its categorization of tribal gaming for regulatory purposes. Stated simply, IGRA allocates jurisdictional responsibility for regulating Indian gaming according to the type of gaming involved. In

---

59. Id. §2711(e).

60. Id. §2710(b)(2), (c), (d)(1)(A).

61. 25 C.F.R. pts. 556, 558.

62. The background investigation must be designed to uncover an individual's criminal record, activities, reputation, habits, and associations that may undermine effective regulation of the gaming or add to the danger of illegality or unfairness in the conduct of the gaming. Any person with such a background is ineligible for employment in the casino. 25 U.S.C. §§2710(b)(2)(F), 2710(c)(1), (2).

63. 25 C.F.R. pts. 571, 573.

64. In 2013, the NIGC finalized revisions to its self-regulation rules, found in 25 C.F.R. pt. 518. The revisions streamlined the process for review and approval of a tribe's petition for a self-regulation certificate and also reduced the annual reporting requirements for self-regulating tribes. Self-Regulation of Class II Gaming, Final Rule by National Indian Gaming Commission, 78 Fed. Reg. 20236 (Apr. 4, 2013).

so doing, IGRA establishes three classes of gaming, as shown in Table 3.1: Class I, or social or traditional tribal games; Class II, or bingo and similar games as well as nonbanked card games; and Class III, or casino-style games.[65]

Table 3.1 Classes of Gaming under IGRA

Class I	Class II	Class III
• Traditional tribal games, as defined by § 2703(6) – social games for low-value prizes – tribal ceremonial games • Falls under exclusive tribal regulatory jurisdiction • Not subject to IGRA • See § 2710(a)(1)	• "Bingo," as defined by § 2703(7) – bingo and other similar games, such as pull-tabs, if played at same location – nonbanked card games, if conducted in compliance with state law – includes such games played with technologic aids • Allowed in states that permit such gaming • Falls under tribal regulatory jurisdiction • Subject to IGRA – limits on revenue use – annual outside audits – contract audits – background checks • NIGC oversight, including – monitoring Class II games – inspection of Class II operations • NIGC may grant "certificate of self-regulation" to tribe after three years • See §§ 2710(a), (b), (c); 2705; 2706	• "Casino-style gaming," as defined by § 2703(8) – all forms of gaming not included in Class I or Class II – typically slot machines, banked card games, electronic facsimiles of games, and other casino games • Allowed in states that permit such gaming • To conduct Class III games, tribe must negotiate a tribal-state compact with state • Falls under tribal/state jurisdiction according to compact • Compact must be approved by Secretary of Interior • Subject to IGRA – limits on revenue use – annual outside audits – contract audits – background checks • NIGC oversight • See §§ 2710(d); 2705; 2706

Source: Indian Gaming Regulatory Act, 25 U.S.C. §§ 2701–21 (2001).

---

65. As we discuss in Chapter 4, Commission regulations further detail which games fall within Class II or Class III.

Class I — Traditional Tribal Games

As defined by IGRA, Class I gaming includes social games played for low-value prizes and traditional forms of tribal gaming associated with Native American ceremonies. Class I gaming is regulated exclusively by the tribe and is not subject to IGRA's provisions.[66]

Many tribes historically have played and continue to play various games and contests involving gambling as part of their traditional ceremonies and celebrations. There has been little, if any, litigation or controversy over Class I gaming.

Class II — Bingo and Nonbanked Card Games

Class II games are often referred to in shorthand as "bingo," although they encompass a wider range of games, including nonbanked card games. Under IGRA, Class II games include bingo (traditional bingo as well as some qualifying video or computer versions) and other games similar to bingo, such as pull-tabs, lotto, and punch boards, if played in the same location as bingo.[67]

In the familiar game of bingo, players purchase cards with numbers printed on a grid. The player wins (or loses) according to how many numbers on a card match the numbers called, and what patterns are formed on the card by the matching numbers (usually a straight or diagonal line). The first player to form a line on his card wins by shouting or otherwise announcing "Bingo!" Lotto is a game similar to bingo, played by covering numbers on a card as they are called and won by covering a straight line.[68] Pull-tabs, or "break opens,"

---

66. 25 U.S.C. §§2703(6), 2710(a)(1).

67. Id. §2703(7); 25 C.F.R. §§502.3, 502.9. IGRA provides a legal definition of bingo:
[T]he game of chance commonly known as bingo (whether or not electronic, computer, or other technologic aids are used in connection therewith) —
(I) which is played for prizes, including monetary prizes, with cards bearing numbers or other designations,
(II) in which the holder of the card covers such numbers or designations when objects, similarly numbered or designated, are drawn or electronically determined, and
(III) in which the game is won by the first person covering a previously designated arrangement of numbers or designations on such cards....
25 U.S.C. §2703(7)(A)(i). NIGC regulations similarly define bingo (and lotto), albeit in simpler language. See 25 C.F.R. §502.3.

68. "Lotto" also is used to refer to lotteries. In this version, lotto is played by selecting a small set of numbers (usually six) from a larger set (usually 49). Prizes are awarded according to how many numbers selected by the player match a set of randomly drawn numbers. "Powerball" is a popular variant of lotto. The "lottery" version of lotto, however, is classified

are instant-win tickets. A player buys a paper ticket from a deck of tickets and pulls the perforated tab to reveal a symbol indicating whether the player has won. Punch boards are similar to pull-tabs: a player purchases a slot on the board and punches it out to reveal a symbol indicating whether the player has won. Tip jars also are similar to pull-tabs. A player purchases a ticket dealt from a large jar; symbols or numbers on the ticket indicate whether the player has won. Instant bingo essentially is a pull-tab or scratch-off game modeled after a bingo card: if the purchased ticket reveals numbers forming a winning bingo configuration, the player wins.

Nonbanked card games also are categorized as Class II games, so long as the card games are conducted in compliance with state law regarding hours of operation and wager and pot limits. In a nonbanked card game, such as poker, players play against each other, rather than the "house" or a "bank."[69] Class II gaming specifically excludes banked card games, such as baccarat, chemin de fer (a player-banked version of baccarat, sometimes called French or "European-style" baccarat), and blackjack, as well as slot machines and other electronic facsimiles of games of chance.[70]

Permissible video or computer versions of Class II games are games played with "electronic, computer, or other technologic aids," but not games that are "electronic or electromechanical facsimiles of any game of chance."[71] A technologic aid is not a game in itself, but "merely assists" in the playing of a game and is "readily distinguishable" from a slot-machine-like facsimile of a game. Technologic aids include computers, telephones, cables, televisions, satellites, bingo blowers, and similar devices that are operated in accordance with federal communications law.[72] Electronic facsimiles, on the other hand, are games "played in an electronic or electromechanical format that replicates a game of chance by incorporating all of the characteristics of the game."[73] Electronic

---

as a Class III game under IGRA. See Oneida Tribe of Indians v. Wisconsin, 951 F.2d 757, 760–63 (7th Cir. 1991); Spokane Indian Tribe v. United States, 972 F.2d 1090, 1093–95 (9th Cir. 1992). The NIGC subsequently included lotteries in its definition of Class III gaming. See 25 C.F.R. § 502.4(d).

69. Some card games offered at tribal casinos in specific states (Michigan, North Dakota, South Dakota, and Washington) that would otherwise be classified as Class III games were "grandfathered" as Class II games under IGRA. 25 U.S.C. § 2701(7)(c).

70. Id. § 2703(7). Slot machines and similar electronic games are sometimes referred to as "stand-alone electronic gambling devices" or EGDs. See, for example, National Gambling Impact Study Commission (NGISC), *Final Report* (1999), 1-2, http://govinfo.library.unt.edu/ngisc/index.html (last visited Mar. 27, 2005).

71. 25 U.S.C. § 2703(7)(a)(i), (B)(ii).

72. 25 C.F.R. § 502.7.

73. Id. § 502.8.

facsimiles generally qualify as gambling devices as defined by the federal Johnson Act, which prohibits the possession and operation of any "gambling device" on Indian land unless authorized by IGRA.[74] Electronic facsimiles of games are thus illegal unless operated in compliance with IGRA's requirements for Class III gaming. The distinction between Class II "technologic aids" and Class III "electronic facsimiles" is controversial and constantly is tested by new machines. We discuss issues related to classification of games in more detail in Chapter 4.

Echoing the Supreme Court's conception of state public policy in *California v. Cabazon Band of Mission Indians*, IGRA allows a tribe to operate Class II gaming on tribal lands in states that permit such gaming for any purpose by any person. If the state in which the tribe is located prohibits bingo and other Class II games, then IGRA does not authorize the tribe to conduct such games, even on the tribe's reservation. Similarly, Class II gaming is limited to "such gaming [that] is not otherwise specifically prohibited on Indian lands by Federal law."[75]

Before opening a Class II casino, a tribe must adopt a regulatory ordinance, approved by the NIGC Chair, and must issue a gaming license for each establishment conducting Class II games.[76] The tribal ordinance must incorporate several specific provisions:

- The tribe must have sole proprietary interest in and responsibility for the gaming operation.[77]
- The tribe must use net gaming revenues for only five specified purposes: (1) to fund tribal government operations or programs, (2) to provide

---

74. See 15 U.S.C. §1175(a); 25 U.S.C. §2710(d)(6). The Johnson Act defines "gambling device" as a slot machine or "any other machine or mechanical device" used primarily for gambling that delivers money through an element of chance, such as a roulette wheel. Gambling devices also include "any subassembly or essential part" used in connection with a gambling device. 15 U.S.C. §1171(a).

75. 25 U.S.C. §2710(b)(1)(A).

76. Id. §2710(b)(1).

77. Id. §2710(b)(2)(A), (b)(4). As an exception to this requirement, IGRA allows tribes to license and regulate Class II casinos owned by private entities only if the private entity meets the requirements for state licensure as well. IGRA also contains a "grandfather" clause for privately owned establishments that were in operation in 1986, so long as the tribe receives at least 60% of the net revenue (subject to the revenue restrictions described below), the private owner pays the required assessment to fund the NIGC, and the gaming operation does not change in "nature and scope." Id.

for the general welfare of the tribe and its members, (3) to promote economic development, (4) to make charitable donations, and (5) to fund local, non-tribal government agencies. Tribes also may authorize per capita payments to their members.[78]

• The tribe must provide annual outside audits of the gaming operation to the Commission.[79]

• The tribe must provide independent audits of all contracts for supplies, services (other than legal or accounting services), or concessions that exceed $25,000 annually.[80]

• The tribe must ensure that the construction, maintenance, and operation of the gaming establishment adequately protect the environment and public health and safety.[81]

• The tribe must provide an adequate system to conduct background investigations and ongoing oversight of the casino's primary management officials and key employees.[82]

Class II gaming is regulated by the tribes with NIGC oversight, including monitoring the games, inspecting gaming facilities, and conducting background investigations. The Commission also may inspect and audit a Class II casino's records of gross revenues.[83]

After satisfactory operation and regulation of a Class II casino for at least three years, a tribe may request "self-regulation" status. NIGC regulations detail procedures for submission of a petition for self-regulation.[84] Under IGRA, the Commission must determine whether the tribe meets three requirements before issuing a certificate of self-regulation. First, the tribe must have conducted its games honestly and fairly. This includes effective and honest ac-

---

78. Id. § 2710(b)(2)(B), (b)(3).

79. Id. § 2710(b)(2)(C).

80. 25 U.S.C. § 2710(b)(2)(D).

81. Id. § 2710(b)(2)(E).

82. The background investigation must be designed to uncover an individual's criminal record, activities, reputation, habits, and associations that may undermine effective regulation of the gaming or add to the danger of illegality or unfairness in the conduct of the gaming, as any person with such a background is ineligible for employment in the casino. Id. §§ 2710(b)(2)(F), 2710(c)(1), (2).

83. Id. §§ 2710(a)(2), 2706(b).

84. As noted above, the NIGC revised its self-regulation rules in 2013. Self-Regulation of Class II Gaming, Final Rule by National Indian Gaming Commission, 78 Fed. Reg. 20236 (Apr. 4, 2013). The revisions streamlined the review process for self-regulation petitions, which are handled through the NIGC's Office of Self-Regulation. 25 C.F.R. §§ 518.2–.8.

counting of revenues, a reputation for safe, fair, and honest games, and minimal instances of crime. Second, the tribe must have adopted and implemented adequate systems of operation, including accounting, employee licensing and monitoring, and enforcement of the tribe's gaming ordinances and regulations. Third, the tribe's casino must be fiscally and economically sound.[85] The tribe bears the burden of proving its eligibility for self-regulation status. Relevant information includes documentation of the effectiveness of the tribe's regulatory body (authority, qualifications, funding), accounting systems, internal controls, recordkeeping, and gaming regulations.[86]

The NIGC's Office of Self Regulation (OSR) reviews submitted petitions for self-regulation status. The OSR's decision to deny the tribe's petition is a final agency action and is appealable in federal district court. An approved petition becomes effective on January 1 of the following year.[87]

Under self-regulation of Class II gaming, the tribe is exempt from the Commission's oversight powers of monitoring the games, inspecting gaming facilities, conducting background investigations, and inspecting and auditing the casino's records of gross revenues, but remains subject to the Commission's other oversight and enforcement powers. A self-regulating tribe must continue to submit annual independent audits of the gaming to the NIGC and also must provide the Commission with résumés for all licensed employees. The tribe also must notify the NIGC of any circumstances that might cause the Commission to reassess the tribe's self-regulation status, such as the casino's financial instability or a new management contract. The NIGC has the power to remove a certificate of self-regulation for failing to meet the eligibility or approval requirements, or for other material factors. The Commission's decision to remove a certificate of self-regulation is reviewable in federal district court.[88]

Class III — Casino-Style Games

Though widely popular at commercial casinos in Las Vegas, Atlantic City, Reno, and on riverboat casinos scattered throughout the United States, casino-style gambling remains controversial to some policymakers and members of the general public, and is the most highly regulated form of gaming. The same is

---

85. 25 U.S.C. § 2710(c)(4).
86. 25 C.F.R. § 518.4.
87. Id. §§ 518.5–.9.
88. 25 U.S.C. § 2710(c); 25 C.F.R. §§ 518.10–.13.

true in the context of tribal casinos. Under IGRA, Class III gaming includes all other games not included in Class I or Class II.[89] These games, typically high-stakes, include slot machines, banked card games such as baccarat, chemin de fer, blackjack, and pai gow poker, lotteries, pari-mutuel betting, jai alai, and other casino games such as roulette, craps, and keno.[90]

Slot machines, the infamous "one-armed bandits"—although today more like video games armed with buttons to mash and graphics to entertain—are played by inserting money (or loyalty cards) and spinning the reels. If a particular combination of symbols lines up after the spin, the player wins.[91] In blackjack, or "21," each card is assigned a numerical value and the object of the game is to build a hand whose total value approaches but does not exceed 21. Each player competes against the dealer: if a player's hand is closer to 21 (without going over) than the dealer's, then the player wins.[92] As in blackjack, the rules of baccarat and chemin de fer assign numerical values to each card. Two hands are dealt according to specific rules, the "banker" hand and the "player" hand. All players bet on either hand to win, or for the hands to tie. The winning hand has the highest point total; hands that total more than nine are reduced by ten, so that the highest possible hand is nine.[93] Banked forms of poker, such as pai gow poker (a card version of the dominos game played with rules similar to poker), also fall under Class III.

An American roulette wheel has 38 slots, numbered one through 36, zero, and double zero, and colored red, black, or green. The dealer spins a ball through the wheel as it turns; when the ball loses momentum, it falls into one of the wheel's slots. Players may make a variety of bets on where the ball will

---

89. 25 U.S.C. §2703(8).

90. 25 C.F.R. §502.4.

91. The modern version of a slot machine contains a random number generator that selects a number within a range of a few billion each millisecond. Each number corresponds to a combination of symbols on the machine's reels. When a player spins the reels, whether by pulling the machine's arm or pressing a button, the number selected by the random number generator in that instant determines the combination of symbols for that spin. Basil Nestor, *The Unofficial Guide to Casino Gambling* (New York: Hungry Minds, 1999), 44. For other accessible descriptions of casino games, see, for example, Stanford Wong and Susan Spector, *The Complete Idiot's Guide to Gambling Like a Pro*, 3rd ed. (Indianapolis: Alpha Books, 2003).

92. In blackjack, two through ten are counted as they are numbered, "face cards" (jacks, queens, and kings) are counted as ten, and aces are counted as either one or 11, according to player preference. Nestor, *Unofficial Guide*, 86–87.

93. In baccarat, two through nine are counted as they are numbered, aces are counted as one, and tens, jacks, queens, and kings are counted as zero. Id. at 161–63.

fall.[94] Craps is a dice game, in which the "shooter" (the person rolling the dice) wins or loses according to the number shown on the dice. Players place bets on the shooter's game.[95] In keno, 20 numbers, from one to 80, are selected randomly. Players win by selecting their own numbers that match the random numbers.

Pari-mutuel betting commonly is offered on horse and dog races and jai alai (a fast-paced ball game, once hugely popular in Florida and famously depicted in the opening credits of the 1980s television show *Miami Vice*, in which players in a three-walled indoor court hurl the ball from wicker "baskets").[96] The total amount wagered is divided among the winning players according to the amount of their bets. Pari-mutuel wagering may be offered "on-track," at the site of the race or game, or "off-track," at a remote location such as a casino, often through a "simulcast" (simultaneous telecast) of the race or game.[97]

IGRA's requirements for Class III gaming mimic, in large part, the requirements for Class II gaming. Thus, a tribe may operate Class III gaming on tribal lands only in states that permit such gaming for any purpose by any person.[98] As with Class II gaming, Class III gaming encompasses only "such gaming [that] is not otherwise specifically prohibited on Indian lands by Federal law."[99] Although many casino games ordinarily are illegal under the Johnson Act, games offered in compliance with IGRA's provisions are exempt from federal proscription.[100]

---

94. Id. at 111–14.

95. Id. at 132–37; 215–20. Keno, though similar to bingo and lotto games, is classified by the NIGC as a Class III game under IGRA. See 25 C.F.R. §502.4(a)(2).

96. Although jai alai has faced dwindling interest and revenue, there may yet be life in it. In April 2013, lender ABC Funding bought out Miami Jai-Alai Casino owner Florida Gaming, which had filed for bankruptcy, for $155 million. ABC outbid the Mohegan Tribal Gaming Authority, among others. "Lender Places Winning Bid for Miami Jai-Alai," *Wall Street Journal*, http://stream.wsj.com/story/latest-headlines/SS-2-63399/SS-2-492257/ (last visited Apr. 1, 2014).

97. See, for example, Robert M. Jarvis et al., *Gaming Law: Cases and Materials* (Newark, NJ: Matthew Bender & Company, 2003), 166–69.

98. 25 U.S.C. §2710(d)(1)(B). We discuss the "permits such gaming" requirement in greater detail in Chapter 4.

99. Id. §2710(d)(1)(A)(ii).

100. Under the Johnson Act, it is illegal to possess or use any gambling device (defined by the Act as any "machine or mechanical device" primarily used for gambling, such as a slot machine or roulette wheel) in Indian country. 15 U.S.C. §§1175(a), 1171(a). IGRA specifically waives application of 15 U.S.C. §1175 to any gaming conducted in accordance with a valid tribal-state compact in a state in which gambling devices are legal. 25 U.S.C. §2710(d)(6); see also 18 U.S.C. §1166. We discuss the Johnson Act further below.

Before opening its Class III casino, a tribe must adopt a regulatory ordinance, approved by the NIGC Chair.[101] The tribal ordinance must incorporate the same specific provisions required for Class II gaming, outlined above.[102] A tribe has "sole discretion" to revoke an ordinance authorizing Class III gaming on its reservation.[103] As with Class II gaming, the tribe may enter into an approved management contract for the operation of a Class III casino.[104] In addition to the Class II requirements, however, for Class III gaming the tribe must enter into an agreement with the state, called a "tribal-state compact."

The Tribal-State Compact Requirement

A valid tribal-state compact is a prerequisite for casino-style tribal gaming. Before a tribe may operate Class III games, it must enter into an agreement with the state in which the games will be located. This requirement created an active role for states in regulating casino-style gaming within their borders by both requiring the tribe to negotiate an agreement with the state and giving the state, along with the tribe, the power to sue in federal court to enforce the provisions of a tribal-state compact by seeking to enjoin any Class III gaming activity that violates the compact.[105]

The State's Duty to Negotiate in Good Faith

If a tribe wants to conduct Class III gaming, it first must formally request that the state enter into compact negotiations. Once the state receives the tribe's compact negotiation request, "the State shall negotiate with the Indian tribe in

---

101. 25 U.S.C. § 2710(d)(1)(A).

102. Id. § 2710(d)(2)(A).

103. A tribe's revocation of an authorizing ordinance must be submitted to the NGIC Chair for publication in the Federal Register and becomes effective upon such publication. Id. § 2710(d)(2)(D).

104. Id. § 2710(d)(9).

105. Id. § 2710(d)(7)(A)(ii). The Court of Appeals for the Eleventh Circuit has held that a state's right of action extends only to gaming activities that violate an existing compact; the state does not have authority to seek to enjoin Class III games conducted *in the absence* of a tribal-state compact. Florida v. Seminole Tribe of Florida, 181 F.3d 1237 (11th Cir. 1999). Of course, as noted above, the NIGC has power to fine or close tribal gaming operations that violate IGRA, including the requirement of a tribal-state compact for Class III gaming.

good faith to enter into such a compact."[106] Which state official or branch of state government has authority to negotiate on behalf of the state is not addressed by IGRA; as a practical matter, it is a question of state law and separation of powers principles.[107] In many states, the governor has power (sometimes formally delegated by the legislature) to negotiate a tribal-state compact, but the legislature retains authority to approve or reject the compact, as the decision to bind the state to the compact's terms invokes the legislative powers of lawmaking or policymaking.[108]

As written, IGRA created a mechanism to enforce the state's duty to negotiate in good faith: if the state failed to negotiate in good faith, the tribe could sue the state in federal court. The U.S. Supreme Court invalidated this cause of action in *Seminole Tribe v. Florida*, which we discuss in detail in Chapter 4. Nevertheless, the statutory cause of action remains relevant for at least two reasons: first, even after *Seminole Tribe*, a state may consent to suit under IGRA, and second, federal regulations promulgated subsequent to *Seminole Tribe* in large part mimic IGRA's original procedures.

The Federal Cause of Action

As enforcement mechanisms, IGRA authorizes three federal causes of action. First, a tribe may sue a state in federal court for failing to negotiate in good faith a tribal-state compact. Additionally, the Secretary of the Interior may sue to en-

---

106. 25 U.S.C. §2710(d)(3)(A). The Court of Appeals for the Sixth Circuit has held that before a state's good-faith duty will be triggered, the tribe requesting compact negotiations must possess qualifying Indian lands; in other words, a state has no duty to negotiate with a tribe that lacks a reservation or other land constituting Indian lands under IGRA. Match-E-Be-Nash-She-Wish Band of Pottawatomi Indians v. Engler, 304 F.3d 616 (6th Cir. 2002). The Ninth Circuit followed suit in Guidiville Band of Pomo Indians v. NGV Gaming, Ltd., 531 F.3d 767 (9th Cir. 2008).

107. See, for example, Florida House of Representatives v. Crist (voiding compact signed by governor without legislative ratification as exceeding governor's authority under state constitution); Panzer v. Doyle (detailing state law concerning governor's authority to negotiate compacts and to agree to certain provisions); Saratoga County Chamber of Commerce v. Pataki, 798 N.E.2d 1047 (N.Y. 2003) (holding that compact negotiations involve policymaking and thus fall within the state legislature's authority).

108. See, for example, Florida House of Representatives v. Crist; Taxpayers of Michigan Against Casinos v. Michigan; Panzer v. Doyle; Saratoga County Chamber of Commerce v. Pataki; State ex rel. Clark v. Johnson, 904 P.2d 11 (N.M. 1995); Narragansett Indian Tribe v. State, 667 A.2d 280 (R.I. 1995); State ex rel. Stephan v. Finney, 836 P.2d 1169 (Kan. 1992); McCartney v. Attorney General, 587 N.W.2d 824 (Mich. Ct. App. 1998). We discuss the roles of state actors in more detail in Chapter 5.

force the compact procedures promulgated through a tribe's suit against the state. Finally, either a tribe or a state may sue to stop a Class III gaming activity that violates the governing tribal-state compact.[109]

IGRA sets forth detailed procedures governing a tribe's cause of action against the state for its failure to negotiate in good faith a tribal-state compact. First, to trigger the state's duty to negotiate in good faith, the tribe must formally request that the state enter into compact negotiations. After the tribe's formal request, if 180 days pass without a response from the state, or without successful negotiation of a compact, then a cause of action accrues and the tribe may file suit against the state in federal district court.[110] To support its claim, the tribe must present evidence showing that the state did not respond to its request to enter into compact negotiations, or that the state and the tribe failed to reach a compact. Upon this prima facie or initial showing, the burden of proof shifts to the state to establish that it in fact negotiated in good faith.[111]

The court then determines whether the state negotiated in good faith, considering the state's public interest as well as concerns about public safety, criminality, financial integrity, and adverse economic impacts on existing gaming. Any of these considerations might indicate that despite the failure to negotiate or to reach a compact, the state nevertheless fulfilled its good-faith duty. If, however, the state sought to tax the tribe, the court must consider that as evidence of bad faith on the part of the state.[112] If the court finds that the state fulfilled its duty to negotiate in good faith, then it must decide the case in favor of the state. If the court finds that the state did not negotiate in good faith, then the court may do only one thing: order the state and the tribe to reach a compact within 60 days.[113]

If, after the court-ordered 60-day negotiation period, the state and the tribe have not successfully negotiated a compact, the court appoints a mediator and directs the state and the tribe each to submit proposed compacts — the state's and the tribe's "last best offer" — to the mediator. The mediator then chooses the proposed compact that "best comports with the terms of [IGRA] and any other applicable Federal law and with the findings and order of the court."[114] After choosing between the state's and the tribe's proposed com-

---

109. 25 U.S.C. §2710(d)(7)(A). IGRA does not, however, provide a general private right of action against a tribe, a state, or the federal government. See Hartman v. Kickapoo Tribe Gaming Commission, 319 F.3d 1230, 1232 (9th Cir. 2003).

110. 25 U.S.C. §2710(d)(7)(B)(I).

111. Id. §2710(d)(7)(B)(ii).

112. Id. §2710(d)(7)(B)(iii).

113. Id.

114. Id. §2710(d)(7)(B)(iv).

pacts, the mediator forwards the selected version to both the state and the tribe, which then have 60 days to consider the mediator's chosen compact. If the state accepts the compact during that 60-day period, the compact is treated as though the state and the tribe successfully negotiated it and is submitted to the Secretary of the Interior for approval.[115] If, however, the state does not agree to the mediator's compact, the mediator must notify the Secretary of the state's disapproval. The Secretary then consults with the tribe to draft a "compact" to govern the tribe's Class III gaming. In so doing, the Secretary takes into account the mediator's compact, IGRA's provisions, and state law.[116] The Secretary has the power to sue in federal court to enforce the provisions of the administrative "compact."[117]

As a compromise between tribal and federal interests on the one hand and state interests on the other, IGRA's compact provisions reflect Congress's attempt to balance those competing interests. IGRA ultimately encourages tribal-state compacts and therefore Class III gaming as a means of reservation economic development, at least in those states where casino-style gambling does not violate state public policy.

The Role of the Secretary of the Interior

The Interior Secretary has the power to approve or disapprove a tribal-state compact, whether reached through amicable negotiations between the state and the tribe or through the tribe's cause of action in federal court. The Secretary may disapprove a compact for any of three reasons: the compact violates one or more of IGRA's provisions; the compact violates federal law, other than the federal law allocating jurisdiction over gambling on reservation lands; or the compact violates the federal government's trust obligation to the tribes.[118]

If the Secretary takes no action on a tribal-state compact within 45 days of its submission, the compact automatically is approved. This "pocket" approval is limited to the extent that the compact's provisions comport with IGRA.[119] Notices of approved tribal-state compacts are published in the *Federal Register*, and a compact becomes effective upon such publication.[120]

---

115. 25 U.S.C. §2710(d)(7)(B)(vi).
116. Id. §2710(d)(7)(B)(vii).
117. Id. §2710(d)(7)(A)(iii).
118. Id. §2710(d)(8).
119. Id. §2710(d)(8)(c)).
120. 25 U.S.C. §§2710(d)(8)(D), 2710(d)(3)(B).

As noted above, the Supreme Court's decision in *Seminole Tribe v. Florida* invalidated the cause of action against a state for failure to negotiate a tribal-state compact in good faith. In the wake of *Seminole Tribe*, the Secretary in 1999 promulgated regulations to effectuate Class III gaming when a state both fails to negotiate in good faith and refuses to submit to federal court jurisdiction.[121] We discuss these regulations in detail in Chapter 4.

Compact Provisions

IGRA enumerates seven areas that may be included in a tribal-state compact. A compact and, by logical extension, the compact negotiations between the state and the tribe, may include provisions concerning (1) application of the state's and the tribe's criminal and civil laws and regulations "that are directly related to, and necessary for, the licensing and regulation" of Class III games, (2) allocation of criminal and civil jurisdiction between the state and the tribe "necessary for the enforcement of such laws and regulations," (3) payments to the state to cover the state's costs of regulating the tribe's Class III games, (4) tribal taxation of Class III gaming, limited to amounts comparable to the state's taxation of similar activities, (5) remedies for breach of contract, (6) operating and facility maintenance standards, including licensing, and (7) "any other subjects that are directly related to the operation of gaming activities."[122] IGRA expressly prohibits states from seeking, through a tribal-state compact, to tax or charge the tribe a fee, other than the reimbursal of the state's regulatory costs. Additionally, "no state may refuse to enter into the negotiations ... based upon the lack of authority ... to impose such a tax, fee, charge, or other assessment."[123]

Although IGRA does not dictate that a tribal-state compact must provide for state regulation of Class III gaming, compacts typically have done so.[124] The tribe retains the right to concurrent regulation of its Class III gaming, so long as tribal regulation is not inconsistent with or less stringent than the state's regulation as provided in the compact.[125]

---

121. 25 C.F.R. pt. 291.

122. 25 U.S.C. § 2710(d)(3)(c).

123. Id. § 2710(d)(4).

124. Carole E. Goldberg et al., "Amici Curiae Brief of Indian Law Professors in the Case of *Hotel Employees and Restaurant Employees International Union v. Wilson*," in Angela Mullis and David Kamper, eds., *Indian Gaming: Who Wins?* (Los Angeles: UCLA American Indian Studies Center, 2000), 62.

125. 25 U.S.C. § 2710(d)(5).

Some states have sought to include in tribal-state compacts provisions not expressly authorized by IGRA, such as restrictions on tribal hunting and fishing treaty rights.[126] Compacts have included, with tribal approval, provisions authorizing direct payments or profit sharing with the states. Some states and tribes have negotiated separate compacts for the state's fee or percentage take of the casino's profits to comply with the letter of IGRA. We discuss these and similar issues in greater detail in Chapters 5 and 6.

Gaming Revenue

Restrictions on Use of Gaming Revenue

Through its required provisions for tribal ordinances authorizing either Class II or Class III games, IGRA limits how tribes may use net revenues from their gaming operations. Specifically, tribes may use net revenues for only five purposes: to fund tribal government operations or programs, to provide for the general welfare of the tribe and its members, to promote tribal economic development, to donate to charitable organizations, and to help fund operations of local government agencies.[127] Net revenues are defined by federal regulation as a casino's gross revenues less prizes paid out and operating expenses (excluding management fees).[128]

Taxation

State tax laws, like other state laws, usually do not apply to tribes or to activities that take place on reservations without the express authorization of Congress. Generally, revenue earned by tribal governments is not subject to federal income tax. Tribes' exempt status, however, has been the result of long-standing practice by the Internal Revenue Service rather than an explicit statutory exemption in the Internal Revenue Code. Congress granted states, on the other hand, a statutory exemption for income earned in connection with essential government functions, including state operation of lotteries.[129]

Arguably, IGRA gave tribes a statutory exemption from federal tax laws by providing that the portions of the Internal Revenue Code "concerning the re-

---

126. See, for example, Steven A. Light and Kathryn R.L. Rand, "Do 'Fish and Chips' Mix? The Politics of Indian Gaming in Wisconsin," *Gaming Law Review* 2 (1998): 129–42.
127. 25 U.S.C. §2710(b)(2)(B), (d)(2)(A).
128. 25 C.F.R. §502.16.
129. See I.R.C. §115.

porting and withholding of taxes with respect to the winnings" from gaming operations would apply to tribal gaming facilities "in the same manner as such provisions apply to State gaming and wagering operations."[130] But in *Chickasaw Nation v. United States*, the U.S. Supreme Court held that IGRA only exempted tribes from reporting and withholding requirements, so that tribes were required to pay gambling-related taxes under the Internal Revenue Code. As a result, although states are exempt from federal wagering excise and related occupational taxes, tribes are not.[131]

Per Capita Payments

Tribes also may decide to distribute gaming profits through per capita payments to tribal members. Before doing so, a tribe must prepare a general plan for use of net revenues in accordance with the five approved expenditures set forth in IGRA. The tribe's plan must be approved by the Secretary of the Interior as adequately affording for tribal government operations and tribal economic development.[132] Only after the Secretary is satisfied that these purposes are adequately funded may the tribe distribute per capita payments to its members. The tribe must also protect the interests of minors and other legal incompetents entitled to per capita payments. All per capita payments to tribal members are subject to federal taxation.[133]

As per capita payments inextricably involve tribal membership determinations, the federal courts have been reluctant to review a tribe's distribution of such payments.[134] Two federal district courts, in *Maxam v. Lower Sioux Indian*

---

130. 25 U.S.C. §2719(d)(1). The argument stemmed from Congress's reference in the provision to the portion of the Internal Revenue Code that deals with the actual imposition of taxes: although the provision explicitly says "the reporting and withholding of taxes," by including a reference to tax-imposing provisions, the argument goes, Congress intended tribes to be exempt from actual taxation in the same manner that states are.

131. 534 U.S. 84 (2001). For a useful and detailed discussion of the applicability of federal and state income taxes to gaming-related income of tribes and tribal members, see Scott A. Taylor, "Federal and State Income Taxation of Indian Gaming Revenues," *Gaming Law Review* 5 (2001): 383–99.

132. The procedures for submission and approval of a tribe's per capita payment plan are detailed in federal regulations promulgated by the Secretary. See 25 C.F.R. pt. 290.

133. 25 U.S.C. §2710(b)(3).

134. See Santa Clara Pueblo v. Martinez, 436 U.S. 49 (1978) (holding that tribal sovereignty includes the authority to determine membership, and that membership determinations generally are exclusively within tribal jurisdiction); see also Kathryn R.L. Rand and Steven A. Light, "Virtue or Vice? How IGRA Shapes the Politics of Native American Gam-

Community and *Ross v. Flandreau Santee Sioux Tribe*, have ruled that the federal court may prevent a tribe from distributing per capita payments in violation of IGRA. In both cases, the tribe's per capita payment plan had not yet been approved by the Secretary. Each court held that engaging in gaming under IGRA was an implicit waiver of tribal sovereign immunity, allowing the court to determine whether the tribe had complied with IGRA's requirements. Because the tribe had not obtained the Secretary's approval of the per capita payment plan, the court enjoined the tribe from making such payments.[135]

In *Smith v. Babbitt*, the district court held that federal jurisdiction under *Maxam* and *Ross* was limited to determining compliance with IGRA's per capita payment requirements and did not extend to examining the legitimacy of a tribe's membership determinations.[136] In *Hein v. Capitan Grande Band of Dieguaeno Mission Indians*, the Court of Appeals for the Ninth Circuit held that because there is no general private right of action to enforce IGRA's provisions, a tribal "splinter group" could not sue in federal court under IGRA to recover their purported share of the tribe's gaming revenue.[137] Instead, the court sug-

---

ing, Sovereignty, and Identity," *Virginia Journal of Social Policy and the Law* 4 (1997): 381–437 (discussing the importance of tribal membership in relation to Indian gaming).

135. Maxam v. Lower Sioux Indian Community, 829 F. Supp. 277 (D. Minn. 1993); Ross v. Flandreau Santee Sioux Tribe, 809 F. Supp. 738 (D.S.D. 1992). The district court in Davids v. Coyhis, 869 F. Supp. 1401 (E.D. Wis. 1994), reached a different conclusion. There, several tribal members challenged a number of tribal government actions related to casino revenue. The district court held that the tribe's sovereign immunity barred the lawsuit, reasoning that because any waiver of tribal sovereign immunity must be unequivocally expressed by the tribe, it did not effectively waive its sovereign immunity simply by engaging in gaming under IGRA. Further, the court held that even if tribal sovereign immunity were waived, IGRA did not create a general private cause of action by, for instance, tribal members or others to enforce its provisions. Instead, IGRA authorizes several specific causes of action, including a state's or a tribe's suit to enjoin Class III gaming in violation of a tribal-state compact. See 25 U.S.C. § 2710(d)(7)(A). Accordingly, the court declined to decide whether tribal government officials' actions complied with IGRA. 869 F. Supp. at 1408–9, 1412.

136. 875 F. Supp. 1353 (D. Minn. 1995), *aff'd*, 100 F. 3d 556 (8th Cir. 1996); see also Lincoln v. Saginaw Chippewa Indian Tribe, 967 F. Supp. 966 (E.D. Mich. 1997) (declining to review the tribe's membership determinations in the context of a duly approved per capita payment plan). Similarly, the Eighth Circuit Court of Appeals declined to review an internal dispute over legitimacy of tribal leadership. In re Sac & Fox Tribe, 340 F.3d 749 (8th Cir. 2003); see also Davids v. Coyhis, 869 F. Supp. 1401 (E.D. Wis. 1994) (involving an internal dispute over tribal government).

137. 201 F.3d 1256 (9th Cir. 2000). "Where IGRA creates a private cause of action," said the court, "it does so explicitly," and thus there was no implied general private right of action. Id. at 1260; see also Tamiami Partners v. Miccosukee Tribe of Indians, 63 F.3d 1030,

gested that the group should seek administrative relief from the NIGC or Interior Secretary.[138]

Criminal Provisions

There are a number of federal criminal statutes of general applicability that may pertain to a tribal gaming operation. For example, the sports bribery law prohibits bribery to influence the outcome of a sporting contest;[139] the lottery statutes prohibit mailing and other interstate transportation of lottery tickets, as well as television and radio advertisements for lotteries (with exceptions for state-authorized lotteries);[140] the Gambling Ship Act prohibits "gambling ships" in U.S. waters;[141] the Wire Act prohibits the use of wire communications, such as telephone calls, to transmit sports bets or wagering information;[142] the Travel Act generally prohibits interstate travel or use of the mail in carrying out illegal activities;[143] the Paraphernalia Act prohibits the interstate distribution of illegal gambling aids;[144] the Antigambling Statute prohibits illegal gambling businesses;[145] and the Racketeer Influenced and Corrupt Organizations Act prohibits racketeering activity, defined to include violations of various federal anti-gambling statutes.[146] Additionally, the Unlawful Internet Gambling Enforcement Act of 2006 prohibits gambling businesses from knowingly accepting payments in connection with a wager that involves the use of the Internet and is unlawful under federal or state law.[147] Because of their specific applicability to Indian gaming, two federal laws, IGRA's criminal provisions and the Johnson Act, merit further discussion.

1049 (11th Cir. 1995) (holding that IGRA does not authorize a direct right of action for every violation of the statute).

138. 201 F.3d at 1260–61.

139. 18 U.S.C. § 224.

140. Id. §§ 1301–1307.

141. Id. §§ 1081–1083. In 1992, Congress amended federal law to allow gambling on U.S. flag vessels in limited circumstances. 15 U.S.C. § 1175. See also, for example, Stardancer Casino, Inc. v. Stewart, 556 S.E.2d 357 (S.C. 2001) (discussing applicable federal law); Jarvis et al., *Gaming Law*, 397–467 (describing various laws applying to shipboard gaming).

142. 18 U.S.C. § 1084.

143. Id. § 1952.

144. Id. § 1953.

145. Id. § 1955.

146. Id. §§ 1961–1968.

147. 31 U.S.C. §§ 5361–67.

IGRA's Criminal Provisions

In addition to its civil regulatory scheme, IGRA also created three federal criminal provisions, found in Title 18 of the United States Code, that are tethered to its general intent and specific provisions.

Section 1166, titled "Gambling in Indian country," generally prohibits gambling in violation of state law on tribal lands. The statute authorizes federal enforcement of state laws "pertaining to the licensing, regulation, or prohibition of gambling,"[148] regardless of whether the gambling activity is authorized by a tribe.[149] Importantly, the statute excludes from its definition of "gambling" Class I, Class II, and Class III gaming conducted in compliance with IGRA's regulatory provisions.[150]

Section 1167 makes it a federal crime to steal money or property from a tribal gaming establishment.[151] Theft of $1,000 or less is punishable by fine and up to one year of imprisonment; theft of more than $1,000 is punishable by fine and up to ten years imprisonment.

Section 1168 applies to officers, employees, and individual licensees of tribal gaming establishments, making it a federal crime for them to embezzle or steal

---

148. Section 1166 provides that "all State laws pertaining to the licensing, regulation, or prohibition of gambling, including but not limited to criminal sanctions applicable thereto, shall apply in Indian country in the same manner and to the same extent as such laws apply elsewhere in the State." 18 U.S.C. § 1166(a). The statute does not expand state criminal jurisdiction over tribal lands, however, as it gives the federal government exclusive jurisdiction to enforce such state laws through section 1166, "unless an Indian tribe pursuant to a Tribal-State compact ... or under any other Federal law, has consented to the transfer to the State of criminal jurisdiction with respect to gambling on the lands of the Indian tribe." Id. § 1166(d).

149. The statute prohibits "any act or omission involving gambling" if it violates state gambling laws, "whether or not conducted or sanctioned by an Indian tribe." Id. § 1166(b). Violations of the statute are subject to "like punishment" as provided by state law. Id.

150. The statute provides, "For the purpose of this section, the term 'gambling' does not include (1) class I gaming or class II gaming regulated by the Indian Gaming Regulatory Act, or (2) class III gaming conducted under a Tribal-State compact approved by the Secretary of the Interior under [25 U.S.C. § 2710(d)(8)] of the Indian Gaming Regulatory Act that is in effect." Id. § 1166(c)).

151. Section 1167 provides, "Whoever abstracts, purloins, willfully misapplies, or takes and carries away with intent to steal, any money, funds, or other property ... belonging to an establishment operated by or for or licensed by an Indian tribe pursuant to an ordinance or resolution approved by the National Indian Gaming Commission shall be" guilty of a crime. Id. § 1167. Similarly, 18 U.S.C § 1163 prohibits theft and embezzlement from tribal organizations.

money from the facility.[152] Theft of $1,000 or less is punishable by a fine of up to $250,000 and imprisonment of up to five years; theft of more than $1,000 is punishable by a fine of up to $1 million and up to 20 years imprisonment.

The Johnson Act

The Johnson Act prohibits the interstate transportation of illegal gambling devices[153] as well as the possession or use of illegal gambling devices in Indian country.[154] The statute broadly defines gambling devices to include slot ma-

---

152. The statute provides, "Whoever, being an officer, employee, or individual licensee of a gaming establishment operated by or for or licensed by an Indian tribe pursuant to an ordinance or resolution approved by the National Indian Gaming Commission, embezzles, abstracts, purloins, willfully misapplies, or takes and carries away with the intent to steal, any moneys, funds, assets, or other property of such establishment" shall be guilty of a crime. Id. §1168.

153. 15 U.S.C. §1172 ("It shall be unlawful knowingly to transport any gambling device to any place in a State ... from a place outside of such State...."). The statute makes exceptions for transportation of such devices to states in which the use of gambling devices is legal. Id. The Johnson Act provides a detailed definition of "gambling device":

(1) any so-called "slot machine" or any other machine or mechanical device an essential part of which is a drum or reel with insignia thereon, and (A) which when operated may deliver, as the result of the application of an element of chance, any money or property, or (B) by the operation of which a person may become entitled to receive, as the result of the application of an element of chance, any money or property; or

(2) any other machine or mechanical device (including, but not limited to, roulette wheels and similar devices) designed and manufactured primarily for use in connection with gambling, and (A) which when operated may deliver, as the result of the application of an element of chance, any money or property, or (B) by the operation of which a person may become entitled to receive, as a result of the application of an element of chance, any money or property; or

(3) any subassembly or essential part intended to be used in connection with any such machine or mechanical device, but which is not attached to any such machine or mechanical device as a constituent part.

Id. §1171(a).

154. This portion of the Johnson Act is sometimes called the Indian Gambling Act. 15 U.S.C. §1175(a) ("It shall be unlawful to manufacture, recondition, repair, sell, transport, possess, or use any gambling device ... within Indian country as defined in section 1151 of Title 18...."). The legal term of art "Indian country" is defined by federal law as

(a) all land within the limits of any Indian reservation under the jurisdiction of the United States Government, notwithstanding the issuance of any patent, and, including rights-of-way running through the reservation, (b) all dependent Indian communities within the borders of the United States whether within the original or subsequently acquired territory thereof, and whether within or without the

chines, roulette wheels, and other devices used in connection with gambling to award prizes based on an element of chance.[155]

Prior to IGRA, the Johnson Act clearly prohibited slot machines and similar casino games on reservations.[156] After the Supreme Court's decision in *Cabazon*, although state gambling regulations would not apply on reservations, presumably federal regulations, including the Johnson Act, would. Thus, although *Cabazon* allowed tribes to conduct bingo and card games, as did the Cabazon and Morongo Bands, the Johnson Act continued to prohibit gambling devices in Indian country. IGRA effectively expanded the types of gambling allowed on reservations by exempting Class III gaming from the Johnson Act.

IGRA provides that the Johnson Act's prohibitions will not apply to any gaming conducted under a tribal-state compact in "a state in which gambling devices are legal."[157] Thus, Class III gaming under a compact will be exempt from the Johnson Act, but similar games conducted without a compact may be subject to the Act's criminal penalties. For example, in *United States v. 1020 Electronic Gambling Machines*, the district court stated that "for the [tribe's] machines to be exempt from [the Johnson Act], the tribe must have a compact with the State of Washington. [I]t does not." Therefore, held the court, the tribe's machines were subject to the Johnson Act's criminal prohibitions.[158]

One question has been whether Class II games that fall under the Johnson Act's definition of gambling device similarly should be exempt from the Act. In *Seneca-Cayuga Tribe v. NIGC*, the Court of Appeals for the Tenth Circuit held that Class II electronic, computer, and technologic aids are shielded from the Johnson Act, reasoning that a contrary conclusion would "expos[e] users of Class II technologic aids to Johnson Act liability for the very conduct authorized

---

limits of a state, and (c) all Indian allotments, the Indian titles to which have not been extinguished, including rights-of-way running through the same. 18 U.S.C. § 1151.

155. 15 U.S.C. § 1171(a).

156. See, for example, United States v. Blackfeet Tribe, 369 F. Supp. 562 (D. Mt. 1973) (upholding Johnson Act against constitutional challenge to its application on tribal lands).

157. 25 U.S.C. § 2710(d)(6). In Citizen Band Potawatomi Indian Tribe v. Green, 995 F.2d 179 (10th Cir. 1993), the court held that whether gaming devices were legal in a particular state should be determined by state law. The court rejected the tribe's argument that the tribal-state compact made the devices legal in the state. "Congress must have meant that gambling devices be legal absent the Tribal-State compact; otherwise it would not have been necessary to require both that gambling devices be legal and that the compact be 'in effect.'" Id. at 181 (citations omitted).

158. 38 F. Supp. 2d 1213, 1216 (E.D. Wash. 1998). The court rejected the tribe's arguments that tribal sovereignty precluded application of the Johnson Act. Id. at 1214–15.

by IGRA."[159] Relying on IGRA's legislative history as well as the need to give effect to Congress's intent in both statutes, the court held that "*if* a piece of equipment is a technologic aid to an IGRA Class II game, its use, sale, possession or transportation within Indian country is then necessarily not proscribed as a gambling device under the Johnson Act."[160] The Eighth Circuit reached a different conclusion in *United States v. Santee Sioux Tribe,* holding that in operating Class II games, a tribe must comply with both IGRA and the Johnson Act. Although the court's reasoning presumes that, at least in theory, some Class II technologic aids may violate the Johnson Act, the court held that the one at issue in *Santee Sioux Tribe* did not qualify as a gambling device.[161]

* * *

IGRA established many of the guidelines and enforcement mechanisms under which Indian gaming is regulated by federal, state, and tribal officials. Subsequent legal developments have further clarified—and complicated—the practical application of IGRA's framework as well as the relationship of tribes to the states and to the federal government.

---

159. 327 F.3d 1019, 1032 (10th Cir. 2003); see also United States v. 162 MegaMania Gambling Devices, 231 F.3d 713, 725 (10th Cir. 2000) (noting that IGRA indicates Congress's intent to exempt Class II games from the Johnson Act); Diamond Game Enterprises, Inc. v. Reno, 230 F.3d 365, 367 n.20 (D.C. Cir. 2000) (stating that IGRA limits "the Johnson Act prohibition to devices that are neither Class II games approved by the [NIGC] nor Class III games covered by tribal-state compacts"); United States v. 103 Electronic Gambling Devices, 223 F.3d 1091, 1101 (9th Cir. 2000) (concluding that "IGRA quite explicitly indicates that Congress did not intend to allow the Johnson Act to reach [Class II] bingo aids"). IGRA includes in its definition of Class II games "electronic, computer, or other technologic aids ... used in connection therewith." 25 U.S.C. §2703(7)(A)(i). The NIGC defined Class III gaming to specifically include "slot machines as defined in [the Johnson Act]." See 25 C.F.R. §502.4(b).

160. 327 F.3d at 1035.

161. 324 F.3d 607, 611–13 (8th Cir. 2003). The court opined, "If, however, the Lucky Tab II [pull-tab dispenser] machines were computer-generated versions of the game of pull-tabs itself, or perhaps, even if it randomly chose which pull-tab from the roll it would dispense, it could fall within [the Johnson Act's proscription]." Id. at 612.

CHAPTER 4

SUBSEQUENT LEGAL DEVELOPMENTS

The statutory framework of the Indian Gaming Regulatory Act of 1988 (IGRA) reflects Congress's attempt to accommodate competing interests, but as many commentators have observed, as a compromise, IGRA may have pleased no one.[1] Yet it is important to note that both states and American Indian tribes benefited from the congressional balancing of interests. Under the U.S. Supreme Court's decision in *California v. Cabazon Band of Mission Indians*, states that allowed gambling had no role in regulating Indian gaming. And, although generally considered a victory for tribes, *Cabazon* left open an important question: whether the federal Johnson Act would prohibit slot machines and other electronic gambling devices on reservations.[2] Congress's regulatory "fix" via IGRA gave states a role in regulating casino-style gaming on reservations through the tribal-state compact requirement and opened the door to tribes' use of lucrative slot machines through the statutory exception to the Johnson Act. Neither states nor tribes were wholly satisfied with IGRA's compromise, however, and the battle of competing interests quickly moved to the courts.

In this chapter, we explore in detail three key areas of formative litigation concerning IGRA's regulatory provisions: state public policy and the scope of gaming, classification of games, and state sovereign immunity. We also address additional challenges to IGRA.

---

1. As one observer put it, "Like most compromises, IGRA has something for everyone to hate." Joseph M. Kelly, "Indian Gaming Law," *Drake Law Review* 43 (1995): 506 (citing 138 Cong. Rec. E1399 (daily ed. May 14, 1992) (statement of Rep. Eni Faleomavaega (American Samoa))).

2. 15 U.S.C. §§ 1171–1178.

State Public Policy and Scope of Gaming

IGRA authorizes tribes to conduct Class II and Class III gaming in states that "permit such gaming for any purpose by any person, organization or entity."[3] The meaning of "permits such gaming" is highly controversial, especially with regard to Class III gaming and its catch-all definition of "all forms of gaming" that do not fall within Class I or Class II. Does a state "permit such gaming" if it regulates gambling generally, rather than prohibiting it entirely? If a state allows some forms of gambling but not others, does it "permit" all gambling, or only those games authorized by state law? Does "such gaming" refer to casino-style gaming in general, so that if a state allows some Class III games, a tribe may conduct any Class III game on its reservation? Or is "such gaming" game-specific, so that a tribe may conduct only those games allowed under state law? How fine a game-specific line may a state draw? Could it allow wagering on horse racing, but not dog racing? Roulette, but not slot machines? Five-card poker, but not seven-card poker? At bottom, these questions go to the scope of gaming allowed under IGRA as well as the scope of the state's duty to negotiate in good faith.

Expansive Interpretations

An expansive interpretation of "permits such gaming" builds off of the Supreme Court's distinction in *Cabazon* between state regulation and state prohibition of gambling. There, the Court examined state law to determine whether the state's intent was to generally prohibit gambling or to generally permit gambling subject to regulation. A state's "criminal/prohibitory" laws could be enforced against a tribe; the state's "civil/regulatory" laws could not. "The shorthand test," said the *Cabazon* Court, "is whether the conduct at issue violates the State's public policy."[4]

Against this dichotomy, a state "permits such gaming" if it regulates gambling in general rather than prohibiting it entirely as a matter of state public policy. The broadest interpretation defines "such gaming" as encompassing the entirety of games within Class II or Class III; a more conservative view focuses on similarity of games—traditional keno and video keno, for example, or blackjack and baccarat. Either way, the expansive interpretation allows for the possibility, through a duly negotiated tribal-state compact for Class III gaming, that a tribe may operate games that otherwise would be illegal under state law.[5]

---

3. 25 U.S.C. §§2710(b)(1)(A), 2710(d)(1)(B).
4. 480 U.S. 202, 209 (1987).
5. See Rumsey Indian Rancheria of Wintun Indians v. Wilson, 64 F.3d 1250, 1253 (9th

Early on, some states took the position that "permits such gaming" included only those games expressly allowed under state law and conducted in accordance with state limitations. In *United States v. Sisseton-Wahpeton Sioux Tribe*, the Court of Appeals for the Eighth Circuit rejected South Dakota's argument that the tribe's Class II card games must comply with state wager limits, reasoning that "Congress intended to permit a particular gaming activity, even if conducted in a manner inconsistent with state law, if the state law merely regulated, as opposed to completely barred, that particular activity."[6] The Court of Appeals for the Second Circuit reached a similar conclusion with regard to Class III gaming in *Mashantucket Pequot Tribe v. Connecticut*. Although state law allowed charities to conduct a number of casino-style games at "Las Vegas nights" fundraisers, Connecticut argued that Class III gaming nevertheless was contrary to state public policy. The court disagreed. Relying on *Cabazon*'s distinction between state laws that are "criminal/prohibitory" and those that are "civil/regulatory," the court concluded that Connecticut law permitted, "albeit in a highly regulated form," the casino-style games allowed under the "Las Vegas nights" law.[7]

Both *Sisseton-Wahpeton Sioux Tribe* and *Mashantucket Pequot Tribe* interpreted IGRA's legislative history as adopting *Cabazon*'s criminal/prohibitory-civil/regulatory dichotomy. In reference to Class II gaming, the Senate Report accompanying the bill eventually passed as IGRA stated,

> [T]he Committee anticipates that Federal courts will rely on the distinction between State criminal laws which prohibit certain activities and the civil laws which impose a regulatory scheme upon those activities to determine whether Class II games are allowed in certain States. This distinction has been discussed by the Federal courts many times, most recently and notably by the Supreme Court in *Cabazon*....
>
> ....
>
> If such gaming is not criminally prohibited by the State in which tribes are located, then tribes, as governments, are free to engage in such gaming.[8]

Cir. 1996) (Canby, J., dissenting from the denial of rehearing en banc) ("[U]nder IGRA a compact may permit the tribe to operate games that state law otherwise prohibits.") (citing 18 U.S.C. § 1166(c)(2)).

6. 897 F.2d 358, 365 (8th Cir. 1990).

7. 913 F.2d 1024, 1029–32 (2d Cir. 1990).

8. S. Rep. No. 100-446, 100th Cong. 2d Sess., 1998 U.S.C.C.A.N. 3071, 3076, 3082.

The *Sisseton-Wahpeton Sioux Tribe* court reasoned that IGRA's acknowledgment of tribal sovereignty and the general inapplicability of state law on reservations required that state public policy, rather than specific state laws, should constrain the scope of gaming "permitted" by the state.[9] The *Mashantucket Pequot Tribe* court was persuaded that the same rationale should apply to Class III gaming, as Congress had employed the identical "permits such gaming" language with regard to Class II and Class III.[10]

Neither case, however, directly addressed the more difficult issue of whether "such gaming" should be defined categorically as extending to all Class II or Class III games, or limited to those expressly allowed by state law. In *Mashantucket Pequot Tribe*, for example, the court's decision left open the question of whether the tribe could operate slot machines, which were not specifically allowed under Connecticut's "Las Vegas nights" law.[11]

In *Lac du Flambeau Band v. Wisconsin*, the district court held that "such gaming" was not limited to the particular games expressly allowed under state law. At the time, Wisconsin's constitution permitted pari-mutuel on-track betting and a state lottery, which the court interpreted as authorizing any state-operated game involving prize, chance, and consideration. The state argued that it permitted only those games in actual operation: on-track betting and the state lottery. The district court disagreed, drawing a distinction between games expressly approved by the state and games expressly prohibited by state law. Because the broad definition of "lottery" allowed the state to operate any game of chance, the state constitution "permitted such gaming" in theory even if the state chose not to operate any games beyond a lottery in practice. As the court determined, "It is not necessary for [the tribe] to show that the state formally authorizes the same activities [the tribe] wish[es] to offer. The inquiry is whether Wisconsin prohibits those particular gaming activities. It does not."[12]

---

9. 897 F.2d at 365–66.

10. 913 F.2d at 1030 (noting identical language in 25 U.S.C. §§ 2710(b)(1)(A) (Class II) and 2710(d)(1)(B) (Class III)). See also Yavapai-Prescott Indian Tribe v. Arizona, 796 F. Supp. 1292 (D. Ariz. 1992) (discussing the "scope of gaming" issue and declining to decide whether the state was required to negotiate certain types of gaming, as the ongoing tribal-state compact negotiations were designed to resolve such disputes).

11. The state law authorized a number of casino games for charitable fundraisers, including blackjack, poker, dice, roulette, and baccarat, but did not allow slot machines. In determining that the state permitted Class III gaming generally, the court somewhat ambiguously directed the state to negotiate "the conduct of casino-type games of chance" with the tribe. 913 F.2d at 1032. The resulting tribal-state compact reached a compromise on the issue, in that it included slot machines, as well as the state's 25% take of slot revenue.

12. 770 F. Supp. 480, 487 (W.D. Wis. 1991).

The *Lac du Flambeau Band* court's holding turned on the broad definition of lottery under state law, rather than the conclusion that if a state allows one form of Class III gaming, it "permits" all Class III games under IGRA. In other words, one possible reading of the cases thus far is that "such gaming" includes all games in Class II or Class III that are not expressly prohibited under state law. Nevertheless, the courts' reliance on the criminal/prohibitory-civil/regulatory distinction in *Sisseton-Wahpeton Sioux Tribe*, *Mashantucket Pequot Tribe*, and *Lac du Flambeau Band* seemed to provide support for the idea that a state that allows one Class III game must negotiate with tribes over Class III games in general, regardless of whether specific games might be prohibited.[13]

In perhaps the most expansive interpretation of "permits such gaming," the Court of Appeals for the Ninth Circuit in *Sycuan Band of Mission Indians v. Roache* adopted a categorical approach, asking not whether the Class II electronic games at issue were permitted under California law, but whether California permitted Class II gaming generally. Citing the *Cabazon* Court's conclusion that the state "regulates rather than prohibits gambling in general and bingo in particular," the court used a generalized, rather than game-specific, inquiry. Because California generally permitted Class II gaming, it could not credibly argue that some Class II games, but not others, violated its public policy. "[T]he state cannot regulate and prohibit, alternately, game by game and device by device, turning its public policy off and on by minute degrees."[14] The dissent in a later Ninth Circuit case set out this interpretation in the context of Class III gaming:

> But the proper question is not what Congress meant by "permits," but what Congress meant by "such gaming." Did it mean the particular game or games in issue, or did it mean the entire category of Class III gaming? The structure of IGRA makes clear that Congress was dealing categorically, and that a state's duty to bargain is not to be determined game-by-game. The time to argue over particular games is during the negotiation process. The only natural reading of [IGRA] is that, when Congress says "Class III gaming activities shall be lawful ... if located in a State that permits such gaming," then "such gam-

---

13. See, for example, Kevin K. Washburn, "Recurring Problems in Indian Gaming," *Wyoming Law Review* 1 (2001): 442–43; Anthony J. Marks, Note, "A House of Cards: Has the Federal Government Succeeded in Regulating Indian Gaming?" *Loyola Los Angeles Entertainment Law Journal* 17 (1996): 192–93. But see Coeur d'Alene Tribe v. Idaho, 842 F. Supp. 1268, 1276–77 (D. Idaho 1994) (construing cases as examining legality of specific games under state law rather than the legality of Class III gaming generally).

14. 54 F.3d 535, 539 (9th Cir. 1995).

ing" refers back to the category of "Class III gaming," which is the next prior use of the word "gaming." ... Congress allows a tribe to conduct Class III gaming activities (pursuant to a compact) if the State allows Class III gaming by anyone.[15]

Restrictive Interpretations

In contrast, other courts have interpreted "permits such gaming" as referring to only the specific games authorized by state law. In *Rumsey Indian Rancheria of Wintun Indians v. Wilson*, several tribes sought to negotiate with the state for operation of electronic gaming machines, including video poker and video keno, and banked card games. The state argued that because each of the proposed games was illegal under California law, the tribes were precluded from offering the games on their reservations. Relying on *Cabazon* and *Mashantucket Pequot Tribe*, the tribes contended that the games did not violate state public policy, as the state permitted gambling generally. Further, the tribes argued that California specifically authorized video lottery terminals and some banked casino games that were similar to the proposed games.

The Court of Appeals for the Ninth Circuit read "permits such gaming" narrowly, requiring that state law must allow a specific game. Because California law did not allow electronic gaming machines or banked card games, the court held that the state did not "permit such gaming" and thus the tribes could not operate the games.[16] Nor was the court persuaded that state law authorized sufficiently similar games. "The fact that California allows games that share some characteristics" — notably, state law permitted both nonbanked card games and other banked casino games— "is not evidence that the State permits the proposed gaming activities." The court explained,

> IGRA does not require a state to negotiate over one form of Class III gaming activity simply because it has legalized another, albeit similar form of gaming.... [A] state need only allow Indian tribes to operate

---

15. Rumsey Indian Rancheria, 64 F.3d at 1254 (Canby, J., dissenting from denial of rehearing en banc); see also Yavapai-Prescott Indian Tribe, 796 F. Supp. at 1296 (declining to decide whether state was required to negotiate video gaming because Congress intended negotiation process to "facilitate the elimination of some areas of disagreement ... as to what forms of ... Class III gaming could be conducted under a compact").

16. 64 F.3d 1250, 1257–58 (9th Cir. 1994). The court noted a "possible exception" for video lottery terminals, which the state operated in connection with its lottery. Id. On remand, the district court held that state law disallowed all "slot machines," broadly defined to include the lottery terminals. 39 F. Supp. 2d 1227 (E.D. Cal. 1998).

games that others can operate, but need not give tribes what others cannot have.[17]

Distinguishing its treatment of Class II gaming in *Sycuan Band of Mission Indians*, the *Rumsey Indian Rancheria* court reasoned that a more restrictive interpretation of "permits such gaming" was appropriate for Class III gaming, as Congress intended a significant role for state law in regulating casino-style gaming.[18]

Another version of a restrictive interpretation employs *Cabazon*'s criminal/prohibitory-civil/regulatory distinction, but with regard to specific games. In *Coeur d'Alene Tribe v. Idaho*, for example, the district court construed the state constitutional limits on gambling as a public policy against casino-style gambling generally, with a handful of exceptions including a state lottery and parimutuel betting on horse, mule, and dog races. The court concluded that all other games violated state public policy.[19] In *Cheyenne River Sioux Tribe v. South Dakota*, the Court of Appeals for the Eighth Circuit took a similarly narrow view. South Dakota allowed video keno; the tribe wanted to offer traditional keno at its casino. The court held that the state had no obligation to negotiate over traditional keno:

> The "such gaming" language of [IGRA] does not require the state to negotiate with respect to forms of gaming it does not presently permit. Because video keno and traditional keno are not the same and video keno is the only form of keno allowed under state law, it would be illegal, in addition to being unfair to the other tribes, for the tribe to offer traditional keno to its patrons.[20]

The restrictive interpretation of "permits such gaming" requires a careful examination of state law to determine which games are allowed and which are not. Some courts have held that the terms of a tribal-state compact are irrelevant to this inquiry; that is, whether a state "permits such gaming" must be determined according to state constitutional and statutory law. If not specifically authorized by state law, a particular form of gaming is, as one court termed it, "uncompactable."[21]

---

17. 64 F.3d at 1258.

18. Id. at 1259.

19. 842 F. Supp. 1268, 1270–81 (D. Idaho 1994).

20. 3 F.3d 273, 279 (8th Cir. 1993).

21. United States v. Santa Ynez Band of Chumash Mission Indians, 33 F. Supp. 2d 862, 863 (C.D. Cal. 1998).

In *Panzer v. Doyle*, the Wisconsin Supreme Court held that the state constitution precluded the state from allowing a tribe, through a tribal-state compact, to conduct any game other than those specifically authorized by state law. Because IGRA, according to the court, does not "authorize *any* state actor to create a monopoly for Indian tribes by superseding, disregarding, or violating fundamental state law," IGRA essentially created two categories of Class III games: those specifically allowed under state law, "over which a state *must* negotiate with a tribe," and those that are not specifically authorized by state law, which "are illegal to negotiate."[22]

Alternative Interpretations

The issue of the scope of gaming allowed under state law is important for at least three reasons. First, if a state does not "permit such gaming," then a tribe may not conduct that form of gaming on its reservation. Second, courts have uniformly linked the scope of Class III gaming to the determination of whether the state negotiated in good faith during the compacting process: if a state does not "permit such gaming," then the state has no obligation to negotiate that form of gaming for purposes of a tribal-state compact. Third, some courts have construed "such gaming" as a limit on a state's ability to negotiate specific types of Class III games: if a game is not allowed under state law, then a state may not authorize a tribe to conduct the game.

Plainly, the two general interpretations—expansive and restrictive—reach very different results. Under an expansive interpretation, a tribe operating Class II games in a state that allows some bingo likely will be entitled to oper-

---

22. 680 N.W.2d 666, 695 (Wis. 2004). See also, for example, Hotel Employees and Restaurant Employees Int'l Union v. Davis, 981 P.2d 990 (Cal. 1999) (holding that voter initiative could not authorize casino-style tribal gaming when state constitution prohibited casinos); American Greyhound Racing, Inc. v. Hull, 146 F. Supp. 2d 1012, 1067–68 (D. Ariz. 2001) ("[A] compact cannot make legal class III gaming not otherwise permitted by state law. The State must first legalize a game, even if only for tribes, before it can become a compact term."), *vacated on other grounds*, 305 F.3d 1015 (9th Cir. 2002).

In Artichoke Joe's California Grand Casino v. Norton, 353 F.3d 712 (9th Cir. 2003), the Ninth Circuit Court of Appeals considered whether a state law that allowed only tribes to conduct certain types of gaming "permit[ted] such gaming for any purpose by any person, organization, or entity" under 25 U.S.C. §2710(d)(1)(B). The plaintiffs argued that IGRA's "permits such gaming" provision necessarily required that the state permit such gaming for non-tribal persons, organizations, or entities. Although it found the provision ambiguous, the court construed it as encompassing state law that allows only tribal gaming, "not because it is necessarily the better reading, but because it favors Indian tribes and the statute at issue is both ambiguous and intended to benefit those tribes." Id. at 730.

ate all Class II games, regardless of whether state law, for example, allows pull-tabs.[23] A state that permits some Class III games will have to negotiate at least all games similar to those permitted under state law and perhaps all Class III games. The expansive interpretation envisions the games allowed under state law as a "floor" for compact negotiations; a state may agree to games that are not specifically allowed under state law.

The restrictive interpretation, on the other hand, limits both negotiations and compact terms to only those Class III games expressly authorized by state law, drawing distinctions between, for example, video keno and traditional keno. If a state does not permit a specific game, then it has no good-faith duty to negotiate whether the tribe may offer the game and, depending on state law, it may be precluded from including the game in a tribal-state compact.

Neither approach, perhaps, is completely satisfactory in its extreme form in the context of casino-style games—that permitting one Class III game means that no Class III game violates state public policy, or that state public policy appropriately is determined game by game. As Kevin Washburn, current Assistant Secretary for Indian Affairs and former general counsel for the National Indian Gaming Commission (NIGC), pointed out:

> [I]t seems clear that it is possible to divide the broad range of Class III gaming into portions that the state prohibits and portions that do not violate state policy. For example, if a state prohibits gambling on cockfighting, it is doubtful that any court would hold the state liable for failing to negotiate in good faith regarding that activity. On the other hand, what if the state bans seven-card poker but allows five-card poker, or bans single-deck blackjack, but allows blackjack that is dealt out of a six-deck shoe? In such circumstances, it seems that the proper approach is a negotiation process in which the state can explain its concerns about the particular evil that accompanies a particular game.[24]

Legal scholar Alex Tallchief Skibine proposed a similar alternative, grouping specific games into distinct forms of gaming that may have different public policy implications. Under this approach, "such gaming" refers to gaming activity, "understood to mean more than a specific form of game but as en-

---

23. This outcome appears to be nearly uniformly adopted by courts in light of the clear legislative history indicating Congress's intent to apply *Cabazon*'s criminal/prohibitory-civil/regulatory distinction to Class II gaming. But see Rumsey Indian Rancheria, 64 F.3d at 1257–59 (relying on "plain meaning," without resort to legislative history, to conclude that state does not "permit" any game not specifically authorized under state law).

24. Washburn, "Recurring Problems," 443.

compassing all games sharing enough similarities so that players engaging in them can be considered to be engaged in the same type of gaming action." For example,

> if a state allowed any kind of casino games where the player bets against the house, it should be considered to have allowed all these types of casino games. If it allowed off-track parimutuel betting, it should be considered to allow all off-track parimutuel betting whether on horses, dogs, boxing matches or sports games. If any kind of lottery is allowed, all lottery-type games should be subject to negotiations.[25]

And so on. A state could demonstrate that a form of gaming activity violated state public policy. For example, if a state allowed pari-mutuel betting on horse races, it could show that slot machines, though falling within the same class of gaming under IGRA, were a distinct gaming activity that violated state public policy. But a state should not be able to refuse to negotiate pari-mutuel betting on dog races unless it demonstrated that the distinction between dog and horse racing was necessary to its public policy. Using state public policy, rather than simply the particulars of state law, would allow a state to justify prohibiting pari-mutuel betting on dog races but not horse races while preventing lesser, merely regulatory state law distinctions, such as between five-card and seven-card poker, from controlling compact negotiations and terms.[26] Under Skibine's alternative approach, a state would be obligated to negotiate all gaming activities permitted under state law, and the resulting tribal-state compact could include specific games within those groups of gaming activities, even if the specific game were not allowed under state law.

As it stands, what is the scope of gaming encompassed by IGRA's reference to whether a state "permits such gaming" has no clear or definitive answer. It therefore remains a controversial and often contentious legal and, more often, political issue in many jurisdictions.

---

25. Alex Tallchief Skibine, "Scope of Gaming, Good Faith Negotiations and the Secretary of Interior's Class III Gaming Procedures: Is IGRA Still a Workable Framework After *Seminole?*" *Gaming Law Review* 5 (2001): 409–10.

26. Id. at 410–11.

CLASSIFICATION OF GAMES

Under IGRA, Class III gaming is defined as a residual category that includes "all forms of gaming" that fall into neither Class I nor Class II.[27] Class II gaming, commonly referred to as "bingo," is defined as:

> the game of chance commonly known as bingo (whether or not electronic, computer, or other technologic aids are used in connection therewith)—
> (I) which is played for prizes, including monetary prizes, with cards bearing numbers or other designations,
> (II) in which the holder of the card covers such numbers or designations when objects, similarly numbered or designated, are drawn or electronically determined, and
> (III) in which the game is won by the first person covering a previously designated arrangement of numbers or designations on such cards, including (if played in the same location) pull-tabs, lotto, punch boards, tip jars, instant bingo, and other games similar to bingo....[28]

In addition to the statutory definitions, the NIGC promulgated regulations meant to clarify the distinctions between Class II and Class III gaming. The current regulations in large part mimic the statutory language, but also provide "plain English" definitions and additional guidance, as discussed in more detail below. The NIGC also issues advisory opinions on whether a specific game is Class II or Class III.[29]

---

27. 25 U.S.C. § 2703(8).

28. Id. § 2703(7)(A)(i). Class II also includes nonbanked card games, but only under relatively stringent accord with state law:

> [Class II gaming means] card games that—
> (I) are explicitly authorized by the laws of the State or,
> (II) are not explicitly prohibited by the laws of the State and are played at any location in the State,
> but only if such card games are played in conformity with those laws and regulations (if any) of the State regarding hours or periods of operation of such card games or limitations on wagers or pot sizes in such card games.

Id. § 27103(7)(A)(ii).

29. Many of the NIGC's advisory opinions are collected and easily accessible on its web site. See National Indian Gaming Commission (NIGC), "Game Classification Opinion," http://www.nigc.gov/Reading_Room/Game_Classification_Opinions.aspx (last visited Apr. 1, 2014). The NIGC's advisory opinions are not given the same force as its regulations; the informal opinions are persuasive rather than binding on the courts. Under principles of

Whether a game falls within the catch-all of Class III or qualifies as a Class II game has significant impact. The legality of Class II games depends only on whether "such gaming" is permitted in the state and the tribe retains exclusive regulatory jurisdiction (with limited federal oversight) over the games. Class III games, on the other hand, are allowed only under the terms of a valid tribal-state compact, which must be negotiated with the state and typically includes a role for the state in regulating the games.[30] A dispute over whether a particular game is Class II or Class III usually arises when there is no tribal-state compact in place; a determination that the game falls within Class II effectively means that the tribe may operate it without state interference, while a determination that it is a Class III game precludes the tribe from offering the game unless and until a valid compact is negotiated and approved.

Other Games Similar to Bingo

In addition to bingo, Class II includes pull-tabs, lotto, punch boards, tip jars, instant bingo, and "other games similar to bingo," if played at the same location. Federal regulations clarify that a game similar to bingo is a variant of bingo, as described by IGRA, and "is not a house banked game," meaning that the game is not one that is "played with the house as a participant in the game, where the house takes on all players, collects from all losers, and pays all winners, and the house can win."[31]

---

administrative law, an agency's opinion statements are, as the U.S. Supreme Court has held, "entitled to respect." The weight given an informal interpretation "will depend upon the thoroughness evident in its considerations, the validity of its reasoning, its consistency with earlier and later pronouncements, and all those factors which give it power to persuade, if lacking power to control." Skidmore v. Swift & Co., 323 U.S. 134, 140 (1944); see also, for example, United States v. 162 MegaMania Gambling Devices, 231 F.3d 713, 719 (10th Cir. 2000) (discussing weight to be given NIGC advisory opinion under Skidmore).

Recent classification opinions are scarce; the NIGC held several requests for advisory opinions in abeyance during its efforts to promulgate new classification regulations. As of this writing, the most recent advisory opinion considered a card game called "WhoopAss Poker," concluding that the house-banked version was a Class III game. NIGC, "WhoopAss Poker Game Classification Decision," Aug. 6, 2012, available at NIGC, "Game Classification Opinion." For additional background on advisory opinions, see generally Heidi McNeil Staudenmaier and Andrew D. Lynch, "The Class II Gaming Debate: The Johnson Act vs. the Indian Gaming Regulatory Act," Gaming Law Review 8 (2004): 234–35 (describing current NIGC administrative routes for game classification).

30. 25 U.S.C. §2710(d)(1)(C) (requiring that Class III gaming must be "conducted in conformance with a Tribal-State compact entered into by the Indian tribe and the State").

31. 25 C.F.R. §§502.9, 502.11; see also 25 U.S.C. 2703(7)(A)(i) and 25 C.F.R. §502.3(a)

In cases decided prior to the NIGC's regulatory definitions, both the U.S. Courts of Appeals for the Seventh and Ninth Circuits held that lottery games were not "lotto" nor were they similar to bingo. Relying on the types of games included in Class II under IGRA as well as the statute's legislative history, the courts concluded that large-stake lotteries such as those operated by state governments were Class III games.[32] In *Shakopee Mdewakanton Sioux Community v. Hope*, the tribe challenged a federal regulation that classified keno not as a Class II bingo variant, but as a Class III casino game.[33] The district court upheld the regulation, on the basis that keno was sufficiently dissimilar to bingo, particularly because it was a house-banked game.[34]

The Ninth Circuit examined the game played on "MegaMania" machines in *United States v. 103 Electronic Gambling Devices*, and concluded that it constituted bingo or a game similar to bingo over a number of objections raised by the federal government. The machines allowed players to compete against each other in a common game interlinked through individual terminals at multiple locations. A player bought electronic bingo "cards," which were displayed on the machine's video screen, and the game commenced when at least 12 people had bought cards. As the numbers were drawn in the common game by a bingo blower in Oklahoma, they were transmitted via computer to the individual terminals and displayed on the machines' video screens. Each player had to press a "daub" button to cover the numbers on their video cards that matched the drawn numbers. As the court explained,

> When a player covers a straight line either horizontally, vertically or diagonally and declares "bingo" (by pressing the daub button) on one or more cards, every player in every facility nationwide is notified of the bingo. Once a player (or players) gets bingo, this straight-line game

---

(both describing the essential components of bingo).

32. Oneida Tribe of Indians v. Wisconsin, 951 F.2d 757, 760–63 (7th Cir. 1991); Spokane Indian Tribe v. United States, 972 F.2d 1090, 1093–95 (9th Cir. 1992). The NIGC subsequently included lotteries in its definition of Class III gaming. See 25 C.F.R. § 502.4(d).

33. See 25 C.F.R. § 502.4(a)(2) (defining Class III games as including "casino games such as roulette, craps, and keno"). Keno is similar to bingo, lotto, and lotteries, in that it is played by attempting to predict randomly drawn numbers. Typically, a player chooses one or more numbers on which to bet. A blower or similar device randomly selects 20 numbers ranging from one to 80. If a player's numbers match the selected numbers, the player wins. In each game of keno, there may be many winners, or no winner at all. See, for example, Basil Nestor, *The Unofficial Guide to Casino Gambling* (New York: Hungry Minds, 1999), 215–20.

34. 798 F. Supp. 1399 (D. Minn. 1992); see also Sisseton-Wahpeton Sioux Tribe v. United States, 804 F. Supp. 1199 (D.S.D. 1992) (reaching same conclusion).

ends. Each player with bingo wins a monetary prize.... In addition to the traditional straight-line game, there is a "corners game" (dubbed "CornerMania"). In the corners game, each player who covers two, three, or four corners of a card gets a prize. The corners game is played continuously until the straight-line game ends, so there can be one or more CornerMania winners on each draw after the first.[35]

The court rejected the government's efforts to limit bingo and "other games similar to bingo" to bingo in its "classic form." "Whatever nostalgic inquiry into the vital characteristics of the game as it was played in our childhoods or hometowns might discover, IGRA's three explicit criteria, we hold, constitute the sole *legal* requirements for a game to count as Class II bingo." Further, IGRA's explicit inclusion of "other games similar to bingo" in Class II "preclud[ed] any reliance on the exact attributes of the children's pastime."[36]

The government contended that MegaMania's "continuous win" feature, which paid out to CornerMania winners prior to the game-ending straight-line win, did not comply with the statutory definition of bingo, as it could be won by more than one person, rather than only "by the first person covering a previously designated arrangement of numbers" on the bingo card.[37] The court construed "win" as different than "beat," so that the statute did not preclude multiple winners. "[T]he IGRA requirement that a 'bingo' game be 'won' by the 'first player' covering a pre-designated pattern does not mean that the game must *end* when one player does so, so that everyone else wins nothing."[38] The government also argued that CornerMania was a house-banked game, in that it was not played against other players, but the court disagreed: "[T]he house is not a participant in the game the way it is in blackjack, for example, where the house plays a hand, and the success of the players depends on the success of the house." The fact that a mathematical formula governing the corner game ensured the house a 15% net of the players' antes did not change the court's conclusion. "Just because the house turns a profit on players' deposits doesn't make the house 'a participant in the game' that 'takes on all players' and that 'can win.'" After all, noted the court, the "house" nets a portion of the players' money in every church-hall bingo game.[39]

---

35. 223 F.3d 1091, 1093–94 (9th Cir. 2000).

36. Id. at 1096.

37. See 25 U.S.C. §2703(7)(A)(I).

38. 223 F.3d at 1097–99. The court also noted that "there is no indication that the straight-line game is a mere sham supporting CornerMania." Id. at 1098 n.9.

39. Id. at 1099 (quoting regulatory definition of "house banking game," 25 C.F.R. §502.11); see also United States v. 162 MegaMania Gambling Devices, 231 F.3d 713 (10th Cir. 2000) (reaching same conclusion).

Technologic Aid or Electronic Facsimile?

Class II gaming specifically excludes "electronic or electromechanical facsimiles of any game of chance or slot machines of any kind," which fall within Class III's residual category. But IGRA also allows some Class II games to be played with "electronic, computer, or other technologic aids."[40] With an expanding gambling market that inspires technological innovation, a significant and highly controversial issue arising under IGRA's gaming classification scheme is whether a particular gaming machine is merely a Class II technologic aid or a Class III electronic facsimile requiring a valid tribal-state compact.[41]

Congress included IGRA's Class II "technologic aid" provision to ensure that tribes "have maximum flexibility to utilize games such as bingo and lotto for tribal economic development." Tribes' Class II games should not be limited to "existing game sizes, levels of participation, or current technology," but should "take advantage of modern methods" of conducting games. According to the Senate Report,

> [T]ribes may wish to join with other tribes to coordinate their class II operations and thereby enhance the potential of increasing revenues. For example, linking participant players at various reservations whether in the same or different States, by means of telephone, cable, television or satellite may be a reasonable approach for tribes to take. Simultaneous games participation between and among reservations can

---

40. 25 U.S.C. §27103(7)(A), (B).

41. As we discuss in Chapter 3, courts generally have held that Class II technologic aids are exempt from the Johnson Act's criminal prohibitions, but Class III electronic facsimiles likely would fall within the Johnson Act's definition of a "gambling device" and, without a valid tribal-state compact, would expose the tribe to criminal charges. See Seneca-Cayuga Tribe v. NIGC, 327 F.3d 1019, 1032 (10th Cir. 2003) (holding that technologic aids are shielded from the Johnson Act and reasoning that a contrary conclusion would "expos[e] users of Class II technologic aids to Johnson Act liability for the very conduct authorized by IGRA"); United States v. 162 MegaMania Gambling Devices, 231 F.3d 713, 725 (10th Cir. 2000) (noting that IGRA indicates Congress's intent to exempt Class II games from the Johnson Act); Diamond Game Enterprises, Inc. v. Reno, 230 F.3d 365, 367 n.20 (D.C. Cir. 2000) (stating that IGRA limits "the Johnson Act prohibition to devices that are neither Class II games approved by the [NIGC] nor Class III games covered by tribal-state compacts"); United States v. 103 Electronic Gambling Devices, 223 F.3d 1091, 1101 (9th Cir. 2000) (concluding that "IGRA quite explicitly indicates that Congress did not intend to allow the Johnson Act to reach [Class II] bingo aids"). But see United States v. Santee Sioux Tribe, 324 F.3d 607, 611–13 (8th Cir. 2003) (stating that in operating Class II games, a tribe must comply with both IGRA and the Johnson Act).

> be made practical by use of computers and telecommunications tech-
> nology as long as the use of such technology does not change the fun-
> damental characteristics of the bingo or lotto games and as long as
> such games are otherwise operated in accordance with applicable Fed-
> eral communications law. In other words, such technology would
> merely broaden the potential participation levels and is readily dis-
> tinguishable from the use of electronic facsimiles in which a single
> participant plays a game with or against a machine rather than with
> or against other players.[42]

Thus, Congress encouraged tribes' use of technology "as long as the use of such
technology does not change the fundamental characteristics" of the Class II games.

Although Congress's intent in authorizing the use of Class II technologic
aids may have been clear, the line between a technologic aid and an electronic
facsimile was not. The statute itself did not define either term. Until it amended
its regulations in 2002, the NIGC offered only the following definitions: a technologic aid is "a device … that when used … is not a game of chance but merely
assists a player or the playing of a game [and] is readily distinguishable from
the playing of a game of chance on an electronic or electromechanical facsimile," while an electronic facsimile is "any gambling device" under the Johnson Act's broad and detailed definition.[43] As one court noted, "Boiled down
to their essence, the regulations tell us little more than that a Class II aid is
something that is not a Class III facsimile."[44] Not surprisingly, the issue found
its way into the courts, typically in the context of a specific disputed machine.

In one of the first cases to apply the distinction between a technologic aid
and an electronic facsimile, the U.S. Court of Appeals for the Ninth Circuit
held that a video lottery game, Pick Six Lotto, was a Class III facsimile. In Pick
Six, the player selected six numbers ranging from one to 45. The machine then
displayed six randomly selected numbers. If two or more of the player's numbers matched those selected by the machine, the player won. The court readily concluded that "Pick Six is an electronic facsimile in which a single participant
plays against the machine."[45]

In *Cabazon Band of Mission Indians v. NIGC*, the Court of Appeals for the
D.C. Circuit held that a computerized version of pull-tabs was an electronic fac-

---

42. S. Rep. 100-446, 100th Cong. 2d Sess., 1988 U.S.C.C.A.N. 3071, 3079.

43. See Diamond Game Enterprises, Inc. v. Reno, 230 F.3d 365, 367 (D.C. Cir. 2000)
(quoting then-existing NIGC regulations).

44. Id. at 369.

45. Spokane Indian Tribe v. United States, 972 F.2d 1090, 1091–93 (9th Cir. 1992).

simile of the paper pull-tabs game. As described by the court, "The computer randomly selects a card for the gambler, pulls the tab at the gambler's direction, and displays the result on the screen. The computer version, like the paper version, has a fixed number of winning cards in each deal." Relying on the plain meaning of "facsimile," the court reasoned that because the traditional pull-tabs game was "wholly incorporated into an electronic or electromechanical version," the machine "exactly replicates the paper version of the game, and if that is not sufficient to make it a facsimile, we doubt … that anything could qualify."[46]

Similarly, in *Sycuan Band of Mission Indians v. Roache*, the Ninth Circuit held that the "Autotab Model 101 electronic pull-tab dispenser" was an electronic facsimile. Based on a computer chip containing a pull-tab "deck," the machine displayed a video reproduction of a pull-tab ticket, revealing the numbers under the tab to determine whether it was a winning ticket. The player had the option of printing out a winning ticket for redemption by a cashier or using the winning amount for further play. Again relying on the common definition of "facsimile," the court concluded that the machine was a self-contained electronic game that exactly copied the paper version of pull-tabs.[47] The court opined that in contrast, Congress intended a technologic aid "as a device that offers some sort of *communications* technology to permit broader participation in the basic game being played, as when a bingo game is televised to several rooms or locations."[48]

The Ninth Circuit considered whether "MegaMania" machines, video terminals at which players competed in a linked live bingo game, were technologic aids to playing bingo or electronic facsimiles of the game. The court distinguished MegaMania from the pull-tabs machine in *Sycuan Band of Mission Indians* on the basis that the MegaMania machine was neither a self-contained game with a single player nor a facsimile of bingo. "MegaMania is in truth being played outside the terminal; the terminal merely permits a person to connect to a network of players comprising each MegaMania game, and without a network of at least twelve other players playing at other terminals, an individual terminal is useless." Thus, according to the court, the machine squarely satisfied Congress's intention to allow technologic aids that broaden potential participation levels of Class II games.[49] In *United States v. 162 MegaMania Gambling Devices*, the Court of Appeals for the Tenth Circuit also examined Mega-

---

46. 14 F.3d 633, 635–36 (D.C. Cir. 1994).
47. 54 F.3d 535, 542 (9th Cir. 1994).
48. Id. at 542–43.
49. United States v. 103 Electronic Gambling Devices, 223 F.3d at 1100.

Mania machines and reached the same conclusion. In the context of the bingo game played on the machines, the court summarized the requirements for a technologic aid: it must operate to broaden participation in a common game and must be distinct from an electronic facsimile in which a single participant plays with the machine rather than other players.[50]

In *Diamond Game Enterprises, Inc. v. Reno*, the Court of Appeals for the D.C. Circuit held that "Lucky Tab II," another electronic pull-tabs game, was a Class II technologic aid. The machine, which contained an actual paper pull-tabs roll, cut a player's tab from the roll and dropped it into a tray. At the same time, the machine scanned a bar code on the paper tab and displayed a video image of the tab. A disclaimer on the machine warned that "video images may vary from actual images on pull tabs" and instructed players to open the paper tab to verify its contents. To collect on a winning ticket, the player was required to present the paper tab to a cashier. The court distinguished the Lucky Tab II from the video pull-tabs game at issue in *Cabazon Band of Mission Indians v. NIGC*:

> To begin with, the Lucky Tab II is not a "computerized version" of pull-tabs. Although the Lucky Tab II has a video screen, the screen merely displays the contents of a paper pull-tab. Instead of using a computer to select patterns, the Lucky Tab II actually cuts tabs from paper rolls and dispenses them to players.... [P]layers must peel and display [the tab] to a clerk before they can obtain prizes.

In short, the machine was "little more than a high-tech dealer," rather than a facsimile of pull-tabs.[51] The court rejected the argument that IGRA required a technologic aid to operate to broaden player participation, noting that "nothing in the Senate Report [accompanying IGRA] suggests that an electronic device *must* link players on different reservations to qualify as a Class II aid."[52]

In 2002, the NIGC amended its regulations defining technologic aids and electronic facsimiles. Under the new definition,

> (a) *Electronic, computer or other technologic aid* means any machine or device that:
>   (1) Assists a player or the playing of a game;
>   (2) Is not an electronic or electromechanical facsimile; and
>   (3) Is operated in accordance with applicable Federal communications law.

---

50. 231 F.3d 713, 724 (10th Cir. 2000).
51. 230 F.3d 365, 367–70 (D.C. Cir. 2000).
52. Id. at 370–71.

(b) Electronic, computer or other technologic aids include, but are not limited to, machines, or devices that:
    (1) Broaden the participation levels in a common game;
    (2) Facilitate communication between and among gaming sites; or
    (3) Allow a player to play with or against other players rather than with or against a machine.
(c) Examples of electronic, computer or other technologic aids include pull tab dispensers and/or readers, telephones, cables, televisions, screens, satellites, bingo blowers, electronic player stations, or electronic cards for participants in bingo games.[53]

An electronic or electromechanical facsimile, on the other hand,

> means a game played in an electronic or electromechanical format that replicates a game of chance by incorporating all of the characteristics of the game, except when, for bingo, lotto, and other games similar to bingo, the electronic or electromechanical format broadens participation by allowing multiple players to play with or against each other rather than with or against a machine.[54]

Two federal appellate courts have applied the amended version of the NIGC's regulations. In *United States v. Santee Sioux Tribe*, the tribe operated Lucky Tab II machines, the same game at issue in *Diamond Game*. The Court of Appeals for the Eighth Circuit agreed with the *Diamond Game* court's reasoning and held that the machine was a Class II technologic aid.[55] The court also stated that the NIGC regulations supported its conclusion, as the amended regulatory definition of technologic aid includes the specific example of a pull-tab dispenser and reader.[56]

---

53. 25 C.F.R. § 502.7.

54. Id. § 502.8. At the same time, the NIGC amended its definition of "other games similar to bingo" to mean "any game played in the same location as bingo [as defined in IGRA] constituting a variant on the game of bingo, provided that such game is not house banked and permits players to compete against each other for a common prize or prizes." Id. § 502.9.

55. 324 F.3d 607, 613–15 (8th Cir. 2003).

56. Id. at 615. The court noted that because the NIGC "merely *amended*" its regulations in 2002, the definitions were not "newly promulgated." As the new definitions tracked prior case law, the court indicated that applying the definitions retroactively was not impermissible. Id. at 615 n.4; see also Seneca-Cayuga Tribe v. NIGC, 327 F.3d 1019, 1036 (10th Cir. 2003).

In *Seneca-Cayuga Tribe v. NIGC*, the Court of Appeals for the Tenth Circuit examined the "Magical Irish Instant Bingo Dispenser System," another pull-tabs machine containing a paper pull-tabs roll:

> When a player inserts money into the Machine and presses the button marked "DISPENSE," the Machine cuts the next pull-tab card from the pre-printed roll within its dispenser compartment and drops the tab into a tray for the player to receive. The Machine has a "verify" feature that allows players to see the results for a given pull-tab posted on a video display. When this feature is enabled, the Machine's display screen scans a bar code that has been previously printed on the back of a paper tab. After the tab is dispensed, the screen displays the contents of the paper tab on a video screen approximately six seconds later. The video screen depicts a grid that is similar in appearance to that of a slot machine. Whether or not the "verify" function is enabled, any winning tabs dispensed by the Machine must be presented for in-person inspection by a gaming hall clerk before the player receives payment. The clerk must confirm that the paper pull-tab contains a winning prize, and only then may the clerk award the appropriate (pecuniary) prize. The game played with the Machine can be a high-stakes, high-speed affair. A winning ticket pays up to $1,199.00 per one-dollar play. When working properly, the Machine completes one play every seven seconds.[57]

Applying the NIGC's amended definitions, the court concluded that the machine, as a pull-tab dispenser and reader, was a Class II technologic aid. Citing the Tenth Circuit's previous decision in *162 MegaMania Gambling Devices* as well as the Ninth Circuit's decision in *Sycuan Band of Mission Indians*, the government argued that because the machine did not broaden participation in the game of pull-tabs, it could not qualify as a technologic aid. The court reasoned that the NIGC definition, along with the prior cases, did not require that an aid broaden participation in a game, but merely "identified the broadening of participation as a factor favoring a finding that a device is a Class II aid."[58] In line with the regulatory definition of a technologic aid, the machine assisted in the playing of pull-tabs and was not an electronic facsimile of the game, as it contained and dispensed tabs from a paper roll. The court explained,

---

57. 327 F.3d 1019, 1025 (10th Cir. 2003).
58. Id. at 1042.

Like the Lucky Tab II [in *Diamond Game*], the Machine (1) cuts tabs from paper rolls and dispenses them to players, and when its "verify" feature is enabled, displays the contents of the paper pull-tab on the video screen; (2) does not use a computer to select the patterns of the pull-tabs it dispenses; and (3) requires players to peel each pull-tab to confirm the result and provide the pull-tab to a clerk for inspection prior to receiving any prize.... [T]he Machine is not the game of pull-tabs; rather, the Machine facilitates the playing of pull-tabs, "the game is in the paper rolls." As such, the Machine is not a "computerized version" of pull-tabs.[59]

Attempted Federal Regulations

In both *Santee Sioux Tribe* and *Seneca-Cayuga Tribe*, the U.S. Department of Justice took a position contrary to that of the NIGC, contending that both games at issue were Class III electronic facsimiles or, alternatively, even if Class II technologic aids, the games violated the federal Johnson Act's criminal prohibitions against gambling devices.[60] Although the government sought review of both decisions, supported by a number of states as amici, the U.S. Supreme Court denied certiorari.[61]

Despite the amended regulatory definitions, nearly every new electronic gaming machine purported to be a Class II aid generates controversy along with considerable administrative and legal expense. The line between technologic aids and what many would consider to be a slot machine is less than clear, despite IGRA and NIGC regulations, and is purposely blurred by game manufacturers attempting to expand the Class II gaming market. As one commentator put it, current law defining Class II gaming is confusing and controversial, and therefore costly.[62]

Recognizing the ongoing issues in classifying specific games, and particularly in applying the line between Class II technologic aids and Class III electronic facsimiles, the NIGC in 2004 formed a Class II Game Classifications Standards Advisory Committee. The Committee was charged with assisting the NIGC in developing definitive classification and technical standards for

---

59. Id. at 1042–44 (quoting Diamond Game, 230 F.3d at 369–70).

60. We discuss both courts' opinions in Chapter 3.

61. Santee Sioux Tribe v. United States, 540 U.S. 1229 (2004); Ashcroft v. Seneca-Cayuga Tribe, 540 U.S. 1218 (2004).

62. Marcus Webb, "Wanted: Clarity," *Casino Enterprise Management* (Mar. 2005), 35.

distinguishing Class II aids from Class III facsimiles.[63] As the NIGC explained at the time,

> The Commission is concerned that accelerating changes in gaming technology and methods threaten to obscure the distinction between Class II and Class III gaming under IGRA. To address this concern, the Commission believes that clear, precise, objective, and verifiable uniform classification and technical standards, distinguishing permissible Class II technologic gaming aids from Class III technologic game facsimiles and slot machines, must be developed and implemented as Commission regulations. Such standards must be amenable to impartial, objective and definitive laboratory testing, measurement, and findings, sufficient to provide Tribes, States, the NIGC, and gaming manufacturers and vendors with clear guidance regarding the required technical and operational characteristics of gaming technology that is utilized in connection with the operation and play of Class II game of chance....[64]

The draft regulations included detailed technical specifications for Class II technologic aids and amended definitions of "electronic or electromechanical facsimile" and "other games similar to bingo," as well as extensive "question and answer" explanations.[65]

The proposed regulations inspired a "blistering dispute," as described in one account, with tribes and games manufacturers challenging the specific technical requirements as drafted as well as the necessity of any additional regulation.[66] In particular, tribes argued that any additional regulation of Class II games would have the unintended effect of diminishing tribal gaming revenue. After an unsuccessful reception to its 2006 proposed regulations, the NIGC issued a revised, less stringent set of draft regulations in October 2007. The NIGC commissioned a 2008 economic impact study, conducted by economist Alan

---

63. NIGC, "Development of Class II Game Classification and Technical Standards," http://www.nigc.gov/nigc/documents/announcements/devclass2105.jsp (last visited Mar. 23, 2005).

64. Id.

65. See NIGC, "Fourth Preliminary Working Draft of Proposed Rule Definition Changes and Class II Game Classification Standards," http://www.nigc.gov/nigc/documents%5Cannouncements%5Cclass2standfourthdraft.jsp (last visited Mar. 23, 2005); NIGC, "Second Preliminary Working Draft of Proposed Class II Game Technical Standards," http://www.nigc.gov/nigc/documents%5Cannouncements%5Ctechstdsver.jsp (last visited Mar. 23, 2005).

66. Virginia W. Boylan, "Reflections on IGRA 20 Years After Enactment," *Arizona State Law Journal* 42 (2010): 1, 7.

Meister, to gauge the effect of the revised regulations. Meister's study predicted that the proposed regulations would have "a significant negative impact on Indian tribes … [that] would vary widely" among tribal gaming operations, including decreases in gaming and non-gaming revenue and available jobs for tribal members. In all, the regulations would cause a loss of approximately $1.2 billion in tribal gaming revenue, $127 million in non-gaming revenue, and more than 3,300 tribal member jobs.[67]

After extended public comment and debate, the NIGC withdrew the draft regulations in June 2008. Then-chair Philip Hogen indicated that while the NIGC was "putting aside what have become the more controversial portions" of the proposed regulations, it would continue to consider new regulations setting technical standards for Class II games.[68] In 2012, the NIGC successfully promulgated Class II minimum internal control standards (MICS), found in 25 C.F.R. pt. 543, and minimum technical standards for Class II gaming systems and equipment, including technologic aids, found in 25 C.F.R. pt. 547.

Despite a seemingly steady spread of Class III gaming in states that formerly allowed only Class II gaming, including California and Oklahoma, Class II gaming remains an important and lucrative market for many tribes.[69] As such, the distinctions between Class II and Class III games likely will continue to garner attention and controversy.

State Sovereign Immunity

A key part of Congress's attempt to accommodate both tribal and state interests in IGRA was the state's role in regulating casino-style Indian gaming through the tribal-state compact requirement. Early on in post-IGRA tribal gaming, some states resisted entering into compacts to allow Class III gaming on reservations.[70] Without a compact, a tribe could not legally conduct casino-style gaming.

---

67. Alan Meister, "The Potential Economic Impact of the October 2007 Proposed Class II Gaming Regulations" (2008), http://www.nigc.gov/Portals/0/NIGC%20Uploads/lawsregulations/proposedamendments/MeisterReport2FINAL2108.pdf (last visited Apr. 1, 2014).

68. NIGC, "NIGC Sets Aside Class II Classification, Definition Regulations," Press Release PR-92 06-2008, June 5, 2008, http://www.nigc.gov/Media/Press_Releases/2008_Press_Releases/PR-92_06-2008.aspx (last visited Dec. 28, 2012).

69. See Webb, "Wanted: Clarity," 34–42.

70. Alex Tallchief Skibine, "Gaming on Indian Reservations: Defining the Trustee's Duty in the Wake of *Seminole Tribe v. Florida*," *Arizona State Law Journal* 29 (1997): 122.

State resistance to tribal gaming was, of course, the impetus for Congress to enact a companion provision to the tribal-state compact requirement: IGRA imposes a duty on states to negotiate in good faith with tribes toward reaching a tribal-state compact. Congress was concerned both that states might simply refuse to negotiate a tribal-state compact, thus effectively precluding Class III tribal gaming, and that states might use the compacting process to demand inappropriate concessions from tribes. To give teeth to the state's good-faith duty, Congress created an enforcement mechanism in the form of a federal cause of action: if a state failed to negotiate in good faith, the tribe could sue the state in federal court.[71] According to the Senate Report,

> This section is the result of the Committee balancing the interests and rights of tribes to engage in gaming against the interests of States in regulating such gaming. Under this act, Indian tribes will be required to give up any legal right they may now have to engage in class III gaming if: (1) they choose to forgo gaming rather than to opt for a compact that may involve State jurisdiction; or (2) they opt for a compact and, for whatever reason, a compact is not successfully negotiated. In contrast, States are not required to forgo any State governmental rights to engage in or regulate class III gaming except whatever they may voluntarily cede to a tribe under a compact. Thus, given this unequal balance, the issue ... was how best to encourage States to deal fairly with tribes as sovereign governments. The Committee elected, as the least offensive option, to grant tribes the right to sue a State if a compact is not negotiated and chose to apply the good faith standards as the legal barometer for the State's dealings with tribes in class III gaming negotiations.[72]

Some states challenged IGRA's cause of action to enforce the good-faith duty as an unconstitutional infringement of state sovereignty. In its landmark decision in *Seminole Tribe v. Florida*, the U.S. Supreme Court sided with the states, holding that the Eleventh Amendment prevents Congress from authorizing such suits by tribes against states.[73]

Seminole Tribe v. Florida

The Eleventh Amendment provides that "[t]he judicial power of the United States shall not be construed to extend to any suit in law or equity, commenced

---

71. 25 U.S.C. § 2710(d)(3)(A), (d)(7)(A)(I).
72. S. Rep. 100-446, 100th Cong., 2d Sess., 1988 U.S.C.C.A.N. 3071, 3084.
73. 517 U.S. 44 (1996).

or prosecuted against one of the United States by Citizens of another State, or by Citizens or subjects of any Foreign State."[74] The Supreme Court has interpreted the Eleventh Amendment broadly to generally proscribe suits against the states, including against state officials acting in their official capacity, without the state's consent. This general rule has a few exceptions, including Congress's limited ability to abrogate states' immunity from suit and what is commonly known as the "*Ex parte Young* exception": state sovereign immunity does not extend to state officials acting unconstitutionally or contrary to federal law, so that they may be sued for prospective injunctive relief despite the state's immunity from suit.[75]

In 1991, the Seminole Tribe filed a suit against Florida and Republican Governor Lawton Chiles under IGRA, alleging that the state had refused to negotiate a tribal-state compact allowing the tribe to offer Class III games on its reservation. Florida moved to dismiss the tribe's action, asserting its state sovereign immunity under the Eleventh Amendment. Essentially, the case raised two questions: first, whether Congress's authorization, through IGRA, of a suit against the state violated the Eleventh Amendment, and second, whether the tribe's suit against the governor of Florida fell within the *Ex parte Young* exception.

Congress's power to abrogate state sovereign immunity is limited and must be "exercised with unmistakable clarity."[76] IGRA's provisions creating the cause of action against a state for failing to negotiate in good faith were an unequivocal expression of Congress's intent to abrogate state sovereign immunity.[77] But Congress must possess the power to effect its intent. Prior to *Seminole Tribe*, the Supreme Court had held that only the Fourteenth Amendment and Article I's Interstate Commerce Clause[78] provided sufficient constitutional authorization for Congress to override the Eleventh Amendment. Congress did not enact IGRA under either the Fourteenth Amendment or the Interstate Commerce Clause, instead relying on its presumed power to regulate tribes under the Indian Commerce Clause.[79]

In a prior case, *Pennsylvania v. Union Gas Co.*, the Supreme Court had held, through a plurality opinion, that the Interstate Commerce Clause gave Con-

---

74. U.S. Const., amend. XI.

75. See Ex parte Young, 209 U.S. 123 (1908).

76. Blatchford v. Native Village of Noatak, 501 U.S. 775, 785 (1991).

77. Seminole Tribe, 517 U.S. at 56–57.

78. "The Congress shall have Power ... to regulate commerce ... among the several States...." U.S. Const., art. I, § 8, cl. 3.

79. "The Congress shall have Power ... to regulate commerce ... with the Indian tribes...." U.S. Const., art. I, § 8, cl. 3.

gress power to abrogate state sovereign immunity.[80] If the Interstate Commerce Clause authorized congressional abrogation of state immunity, the tribe argued, then it logically followed that the Indian Commerce Clause should grant Congress similar power since both the Interstate and Indian Commerce Clauses stem from the same delegation of congressional authority. Indeed, the Supreme Court's construction of Congress's so-called plenary power over tribes under the Indian Commerce Clause arguably is of greater scope than its authority under the Interstate Commerce Clause.[81]

The *Seminole Tribe* Court, however, expressly overruled *Union Gas* and held that neither the Interstate Commerce Clause nor the Indian Commerce Clause authorized Congress to abrogate state sovereign immunity. State sovereignty, said the Court, "is not so ephemeral as to dissipate when the subject of a suit is an area, like the regulation of Indian commerce, that is under the exclusive control of the Federal Government."[82] In other words, despite its exclusive authority to deal with tribes, Congress may not create a cause of action against the states under the Indian Commerce Clause, as it attempted to do through IGRA.

The tribe also argued that the *Ex parte Young* exception allowed the suit against Florida's governor for prospective injunctive relief based on a violation of federal law, namely IGRA's provision requiring the state to negotiate in good faith. The Court, however, disagreed. Although a state official who violates federal law sheds the cloak of state sovereign immunity, the remedies afforded for such a violation may be limited by the federal law itself. Where Congress chooses a specific remedial scheme to enforce a statutory right, other more general remedies—such as a cause of action under the *Ex parte Young* exception—may be precluded. Under IGRA, upon a finding that the state failed to negotiate in good faith, the district court only has authority to take certain steps specified in the statute and meant to effect the negotiation of a tribal-state compact. In contrast, a suit under the *Ex parte Young* exception would allow the district court to exercise a broad range of judicial powers, including imposing sanctions on the state.[83] Thus, the Court held that because IGRA's cause

---

80. 491 U.S. 1 (1989).

81. Seminole Tribe, 517 U.S. at 59–62 ("If anything, the Indian Commerce Clause accomplishes a greater transfer of power from the States to the Federal Government than does the Interstate Commerce Clause.").

82. Id. at 72.

83. Id. at 73–76. Ironically, under the Court's reasoning, the same comprehensive remedial scheme in IGRA that precludes an *Ex parte Young* cause of action also violates the Eleventh Amendment, thus invalidating the statute's own preclusive remedy.

of action against the state is narrower that the general remedy allowed under the *Ex parte Young* doctrine, the exception does not apply to suits under IGRA.

Accordingly, the *Seminole Tribe* Court held that a state could not be sued in federal court by a tribe under IGRA without the state's consent. In effect, the Court invalidated Congress's statutory compromise between state interests and tribal and federal interests over Indian gaming. Without the enforcement mechanism against the states, the states' duty to negotiate compacts in good faith lacked teeth. In the wake of the Court's decision in *Seminole Tribe*, a state effectively could prevent a tribe from engaging in Class III gaming simply by refusing to negotiate a tribal-state compact. Indeed, no Class III tribal-state compact was finalized for over two years following *Seminole Tribe*, as states took advantage of the Court's holding.[84]

Tribal-State Compact Negotiations after Seminole Tribe

The Supreme Court's decision in *Seminole Tribe v. Florida* left open the question of what should happen when a state fails to negotiate in good faith with a tribe toward reaching a tribal-state compact. One possibility, of course, was that the state could waive its sovereign immunity and consent to be sued in federal court under IGRA's cause of action. More likely, though, was that the state would invoke its Eleventh Amendment immunity under *Seminole Tribe* and the suit would be dismissed, leaving the tribe without a remedy for the state's alleged breach of the good-faith duty.

Because IGRA contains a severability clause, to the extent that the *Seminole Tribe* Court held that IGRA's enforcement mechanism—the federal cause of action to enforce the state's good-faith duty—was unconstitutional, that portion should be severed from the rest of the statute, allowing the remainder of the federal regulatory scheme to remain in effect.[85] But exactly what provision

---

84. See Washburn, "Recurring Problems," 430.

85. 25 U.S.C. § 2721 ("In the event that any section or provision of this chapter, or amendment, made by this chapter, is held invalid, it is the intent of Congress that the remaining sections or provisions or this chapter, and amendments made by this chapter, shall continue in full force and effect."). A statute's severability clause creates a presumption that the remaining provisions are valid, unless there is "strong evidence" that Congress did not mean for the rest of the statute to remain in effect without the invalid provision. See Alaska Airlines, Inc. v. Brock, 480 U.S. 678 (1987). Put another way, "the unconstitutional provision must be severed unless the statute created in its absence is legislation that Congress would not have enacted." Id. at 685.

Most courts and commentators agree that IGRA's severability clause protects IGRA's remaining provisions, so that *Seminole Tribe* invalidates only the tribe's cause of action against

or provisions to sever? In other contexts, the Supreme Court has directed that the remainder of a statute must function independently of the invalidated portion and in accord with congressional intent, but it offered little concrete guidance on the issue in *Seminole Tribe*.[86]

As explained by law professor Alex Tallchief Skibine, three alternatives exist. First is to strike section 2710(d) in its entirety, which would include not only the state's good-faith duty and the federal cause of action, but also the entire section governing Class III gaming, including the tribal-state compact requirement. Under this alternative, the law governing casino-style Indian gaming would revert to the Supreme Court's decision in *Cabazon*.[87] The second possibility is to sever sections 2710(d)(7)(A)(i) (the provision creating the federal cause of action to enforce the state's good-faith duty) and 2710(d)(7)(B)(i) to (vii) (the provisions describing the cause of action and the federal court's role, as well as the role of the court-appointed mediator and the Interior Secretary in resolving an impasse between the tribe and the state). Under this approach, a tribal-state compact still would be a requirement for Class III gaming, but the tribe would be left without any means of legally conducting casino-style gaming when a state refused to negotiate in good faith and invoked its sovereign immunity.[88] The third alternative is a variation on the second approach in which 2710(d)(7)(B)(vii) is omitted from the severed provisions,

---

the state, rather than the entire Act or the entire section addressing Class III gaming. As the Eleventh Circuit noted, "IGRA contains an explicit severability clause and we find no 'strong evidence' to ignore that plain congressional directive." Seminole Tribe v. Florida, 11 F.3d 1016, 1029 (11th Cir. 1994), *aff'd*, 517 U.S. 44 (1996). But see United States v. Spokane Tribe of Indians, 139 F.3d 1297 (9th Cir. 1998) (suggesting in dicta that because Congress would not have required tribal-state compacts without the tribal cause of action against the state for failing to negotiate in good faith, the Supreme Court's invalidation of that provision may call into question the entire regulatory scheme for Class III gaming).

86. As discussed below, in the lower court decision in the case, the Eleventh Circuit suggested that if IGRA's cause of action violated the Eleventh Amendment, then a tribe would have the option to asking the Secretary of the Interior to issue regulations governing the tribe's Class III gaming when the state failed to negotiate in good faith a tribal-state compact. See Seminole Tribe v. Florida, 11 F.3d 1016, 1029 (11th Cir. 1994). The Supreme Court sidestepped the issue, stating, "we do not consider, and express no opinion upon, that portion of the position of the decision below that provides a substitute remedy to a Tribe bringing suit." Seminole Tribe, 517 U.S. at 76 n.18.

87. As Professor Skibine explained, "This option would not invalidate compacts which are already in operation.... [and] would sever section [2710(d)] only in those cases in which a state has invoked its sovereign immunity." Skibine, "Gaming on Indian Reservations," 141 (footnotes omitted).

88. See id. at 138–41.

thus preserving the Secretary's power to issue an administrative "compact" governing the tribe's Class III gaming.

Skibine persuasively contended that neither the first nor second alternatives is consistent with congressional intent, as the balance between state and tribal interests in the compact requirement is, in many ways, IGRA's centerpiece. Congress plainly did not intend *Cabazon* to govern casino-style gaming; at the same time, in light of IGRA's legislative history, "it is difficult to believe that Congress would have passed an Act providing the tribes with no recourse" for a state's refusal to negotiate a compact.[89] As the Court of Appeals for the Ninth Circuit put it, "Congress meant to guard against this very situation when it created IGRA's interlocking checks and balances."[90] Commenting on state claims of sovereign immunity arising soon after IGRA's passage, U.S. Senator Daniel Inouye (D-Haw.), one of IGRA's architects, said,

> I believe that if we had known at the time we were considering the bill—if we had known that this proposal of tribal-state compacts that came from the States and was strongly supported by the States, would later be rendered virtually meaningless by the action of those States which have sought to avoid entering into compacts by asserting [state sovereign immunity] to defeat federal court jurisdiction, we would not have gone down this path.[91]

Most courts addressing the severability issue after *Seminole Tribe* agreed that not only did the tribal-state compact requirement survive, but that the Interior Secretary's power to issue an administrative "compact" provides a tribe recourse when a state fails to negotiate in good faith and refuses to consent to suit. Before the Supreme Court decided *Seminole Tribe*, the Court of Appeals

---

89. Id. at 140. Skibine acknowledges that the third approach is not without its problems: "[C]lause (vii) is so intertwined with the rest of section [2710(d)(7)(B)] that it cannot survive on its own if the rest of the section is severed.... [I]t is questionable whether clause (vii) can survive on its own when its very language refers to the lawsuits filed by the tribe. If the tribe cannot file the lawsuit, there can never be a mediator's report and, therefore, clause (vii) technically does not even take effect." Id. at 139.

90. Spokane Tribe, 139 F.3d at 1301.

91. Implementation of the Indian Gaming Regulatory Act: Oversight Hearings Before the U.S. House Subcommittee on Native American Affairs of the Committee on Natural Resources, 103rd Cong., 1st Sess. (Apr. 2, 1993). Without the statute's enforcement mechanism to bring states to the bargaining table over Class III gaming, said Senator Inouye, IGRA is "a piece of paper." Implementation of the Indian Gaming Regulatory Act: Hearing Before the U.S. Senate Select Committee on Indian Affairs, 102d Cong., 2d Sess. (Mar. 18, 1992).

for the Eleventh Circuit had endorsed the third severability alternative, opining that if a tribe's suit to enforce the state's good-faith duty were dismissed on the basis of state sovereign immunity, then the tribe could petition the Interior Secretary to issue regulations governing the tribe's Class III gaming.

> [W]e are left with the question as to what procedure is left for an Indian tribe faced with a state that not only will not negotiate in good faith, but also will not consent to suit. The answer, gleaned from the statute, is simple. One hundred and eighty days after the tribe first requests negotiations with the state, the tribe may file suit in district court. If the state pleads an Eleventh Amendment defense, the suit is dismissed, and the tribe, pursuant to 25 U.S.C. §2710(d)(7)(B)(vii), then may notify the Secretary of the Interior of the tribe's failure to negotiate a compact with the state. The Secretary then may prescribe regulations governing class III gaming on the tribe's lands. This solution conforms with IGRA and serves to achieve Congress' goals....[92]

The Ninth Circuit seemed to agree, commenting in *United States v. Spokane Tribe of Indians* that the Eleventh Circuit's approach "is a lot closer to Congress' intent than mechanically enforcing the IGRA against tribes even when states refuse to negotiate."[93]

---

92. 11 F.3d at 1029. Skibine argued that this position finds support in *Seminole Tribe*, as the Court's reliance on IGRA's detailed remedial scheme in rejecting the tribe's argument under the *Ex parte Young* exception suggests that the Court believed that the remedial scheme would still have some effect:

> If the *Seminole* Court thought that by pleading its now reinstated sovereign immunity, the state could just make the tribe and its gaming plans go away, its justification for what amounts to an exception to the *Ex parte Young* doctrine would be really disingenuous if not altogether dishonest.... Therefore, one must assume that the Court was of the opinion that the 'detailed remedial scheme' could still be used by the tribes in order to enforce their statutory right under IGRA.

Skibine, "Scope of Gaming," 406–7.

93. Spokane Tribe, 139 F.3d at 1301–2. In *Spokane Tribe*, the Ninth Circuit addressed the issue in the context of whether the tribe could be enjoined under IGRA from operating Class III games without a tribal-state compact. The court noted that the compact negotiations between the state and the tribe had completely broken down after two years, that the state had refused to consent to suit, and that the tribe had appealed to the Interior Secretary to no avail. "Under the circumstances," said the court, "IGRA's provisions governing class III gaming may not be enforced against the tribe." Id. at 1302; see also United States v. 1020 Electronic Gambling Machines, 38 F. Supp. 2d 1219, 1223 (E.D. Wash. 1999) (interpreting *Spokane Tribe* to mean that "the government may not enforce IGRA against Indian tribes unless circumstances have occurred that cause IGRA to function as Congress intended"). The Ninth Circuit disavowed its earlier statement in Spokane Tribe of Indians

In *Chemehuevi Indian Tribe v. Wilson*, the district court adopted a different, more far-reaching approach, holding that when a state failed to negotiate in good faith and refused to consent to suit, the federal government has a duty to sue the state on the tribe's behalf under IGRA.

> A duty on behalf of the United States to sue the State to bring it to the bargaining table can certainly be implied from IGRA, since it appears that that is the only legal remedy available to the plaintiff Tribes to seek the benefits Congress intended them to have and to preserve the balance Congress carefully struck between the interests of the state and the tribes…. Whatever the full extent of the fiduciary relationship [between tribes and the federal government], it certainly should include a duty to represent the plaintiffs in a situation where, absent representation, the Tribes will have no legal remedy with which to bring the state to the bargaining table and obtain the benefits of IGRA as Congress intended.[94]

But in *United States v. 1020 Electronic Gambling Machines*, the district court disagreed, holding that there was no specific trust duty created by IGRA that would obligate the federal government to sue a recalcitrant state on behalf of a tribe. The court's conclusion was bolstered by the politics at play and the "absolute discretion" generally afforded to agency enforcement decisions. "This case illustrates the wisdom of that rule," said the court:

> Indian gaming raises a number of complicated issues [and] *Seminole [Tribe]* has not made the resolution of those issues any easier. Confronted with a difficult situation, neither the [Interior] Secretary or the Attorney General wants to bring an action against the State of Washington…. This court is in no position to second guess that decision.[95]

Despite the potential impact of the severability issue and the states' upper hand after *Seminole Tribe*, only a few cases address the issues. It appears that

---

v. Washington, 28 F.3d 991 (9th Cir. 1994), that allowing a tribe to appeal directly to the Interior Secretary when a state and a tribe failed to reach a compact "would pervert the congressional plan," turning the Secretary into "a federal czar." "[T]hat was in the context of our (incorrect) assumption that tribes could sue states," explained the court. 139 F.3d at 1301.

94. 987 F. Supp. 804, 808–9 (N.D. Cal. 1997). See also Spokane Tribe, 139 F.3d at 1302 (listing as a post-*Seminole Tribe* fix the possibility that "the Department of Justice might resuscitate the statute by prosecuting tribes only when it determines that the state has negotiated in good faith, or by suing states on behalf of tribes when it determines that the states are refusing to comply with their obligations under IGRA").

95. 38 F. Supp. 2d 1213, 1217 (E.D. Wash. 1998).

states and tribes primarily have sought resolution through channels other than the federal courts.

Federal Regulations in Response to Seminole Tribe

Although severability and the validity of the Secretary's role remained open questions, the Court's decision in *Seminole Tribe* and the resulting legal uncertainty prompted the Secretary of the Interior to initiate the administrative rule-making process. The regulations, which took effect in 1999, set forth the procedure for the Secretary's promulgation of Class III gaming regulations in the absence of a valid tribal-state compact.[96]

The regulations essentially follow the mediated negotiation process set forth in IGRA. First, the tribe must initiate the compact negotiations with the state as required by IGRA.[97] If the state refuses to negotiate, or if the state and the tribe cannot agree on a compact, then the tribe must sue the state in federal court in accordance with IGRA's cause of action provision. The federal regulations are triggered only after the state asserts its immunity from suit under the Eleventh Amendment and the case is dismissed.[98]

The tribe then may ask the Interior Secretary to issue procedures for conducting Class III gaming by submitting a detailed proposal containing documentation of the tribe's suit against the state as well as draft administrative "compact" provisions mandated by IGRA and other federal law.[99] The Secretary reviews the proposal for completeness and determines whether the tribe

---

96. 25 C.F.R. pt. 291.

97. Id. §291.3; 25 U.S.C. §2710(d)(3)(A) (providing that the tribe "shall request the State in which such lands are located to enter into negotiations for the purpose of entering into a Tribal-State compact governing the conduct of gaming activities").

98. 25 C.F.R. §291.3.

99. The tribe's proposal must include background information (including the tribal ordinance authorizing Class III gaming and the tribe's organic documents), documentation of the tribe's suit against the state (including the tribe's written request initiating compact negotiations and the tribe's complaint and other court documents), factual and legal support for the type of games proposed by the tribe, and the proposed procedures for conduct of the games (including certification of the tribe's accounting procedures, a reporting system for taxes and fees, financial statements of the tribe's gaming enterprises, internal control standards, a record retention plan, provisions for the conduct and integrity of the games, rules governing the licensing of casino employees, health and safety policies, surveillance and security, procedures for resolving disputes between the casino and its patrons and employees, the tribal liquor ordinance, tribal enforcement and investigatory mechanisms, and "[a]ny other provisions deemed necessary by the Indian tribe"). Id. §291.4.

is eligible to seek Class III gaming regulations short of a tribal-state compact.[100] A copy of the tribe's proposal is provided to the state's governor and attorney general, who have 60 days to submit comments on the tribe's proposal and an alternate proposal to the Secretary.[101]

If the state does not submit an alternative proposal, the Secretary may approve or disapprove the tribe's proposal. The Secretary must consider whether the tribe's proposal meets the requirements of the federal regulations, the tribe has appropriate jurisdiction over the location of the casino, the games are consistent with state public policy, and the proposal is consistent with state law, the federal trust obligation to the tribe, IGRA, and any other applicable federal law.[102] If the tribe's proposal is approved, the Secretary notifies the state. If the tribe's proposal is disapproved, the Secretary must identify "unresolved issues and areas of disagreements" and invite the tribe and the state's governor and attorney general to negotiate solutions. The Secretary considers the results of the negotiation and makes a final decision whether to approve the proposal.[103]

If the state submits an alternative proposal, the Secretary appoints a mediator to resolve the differences between the tribe's original proposal and the state's alternative proposal. Both the tribe and the state submit their "last best offer" to the mediator, and the mediator convenes a process that includes an opportunity for the tribe and the state "to be heard and present information supporting their respective positions."[104] The mediator's decisional role is limited to "select[ing] from the two proposals the one that best comports with the terms of IGRA and any other applicable Federal law."[105] Once the mediator selects a proposal, the Secretary may approve or disapprove the proposal. In deciding whether to approve the mediator's proposal, the Secretary must consider the same four factors relevant to the tribe's original proposal.[106] If the Secretary disapproves the proposal selected by the mediator, the Secretary must promulgate regulations for the tribe to conduct Class III gaming "that comport with the mediator's selected proposal as much as possible, the provisions of IGRA, and the relevant provisions of the laws of the State."[107]

---

100. Id. § 291.6.
101. Id. § 291.7.
102. Id. § 291.8.
103. 25 C.F.R. § 291.8.
104. Id. §§ 291.9, 291.10.
105. Id. § 291.10(b).
106. Id. § 291.11.
107. Id. § 291.11(c)).

A few commentators have questioned the constitutionality of the Secretary's power to promulgate regulations allowing Class III gaming in the absence of a tribal-state compact.[108] One argument is that the Secretary's role under the regulations exceeds the role envisioned by Congress. Because IGRA authorizes the Secretary's promulgation of an administrative "compact" only after a federal court determines that the state failed to negotiate in good faith and the court-mandated mediation process fails to produce a mutually acceptable compact, the Secretary's action in absence of these statutory prerequisites goes beyond the authority granted by Congress.[109] The federal regulations, however, do not rely solely on the Secretary's power under IGRA, but also invoke the Secretary's broad general authority to manage Indian affairs under 25 U.S.C. §§ 2 and 9.[110] Even so, the argument goes, the federal regulations create a power for the Secretary that contravenes federal law, specifically IGRA's requirement that a tribe may operate Class III gaming only under a valid tribal-state compact. At least one commentator would read the requirement as allowing only the narrow exception created by the statute itself.[111] Skibine, on the other hand, has defended the Secretary's regulations as a reasonable interpretation of the ambiguity created by the confluence of the Secretary's specific and narrowly defined role under IGRA and the Secretary's broad power under sections 2 and 9.[112]

Another argument is that because the Secretary is charged with effecting the federal government's trust obligation to the tribes, the Secretary is not a sufficiently impartial referee to decide disputes between a tribe and a state over

---

108. See, for example, Joe Lexague, Note, "Indian Gaming and Tribal-State Negotiations: Who Should Decide the Issue of Bad Faith?," *Journal of Legislation* 25 (1999): 77–94; Rebecca S. Lindner-Cornelius, Comment, "The Secretary of the Interior as Referee: The States, the Indian Nations, and How Gambling Led to the Illegality of the Secretary of the Interior's Regulations in 25 C.F.R. § 291," *Marquette Law Review* 84 (2001): 685–99.

109. See, for example, Lexague, "Indian Gaming and Tribal-State Negotiations," 85–87.

110. 63 Fed. Reg. 3290–91; see also Skibine, "Gaming on Indian Reservations." Section 2 provides, "The Commissioner of Indian Affairs shall, under the direction of the Secretary of the Interior, and agreeably to such regulations as the President may prescribe, have the management of all Indian affairs and of all matters arising out of Indian relations." 25 U.S.C. § 2. Section 9 provides, "The President may prescribe such regulations as he may think fit for carrying into effect the various provisions of any act relating to Indian affairs, and for the settlement of the accounts of Indian affairs." Id. § 9.

111. Lexague, "Indian Gaming and Tribal-State Negotiations," 87 ("The plain words of the IGRA make it clear that Class III gaming may only take place under a valid tribal-state compact. Despite the Secretary of the Interior's broad authority in the area of Indian affairs, the clear command of the statute is unavoidable.").

112. Skibine, "Scope of Gaming;" see also Skibine, "Gaming on Indian Reservations," 142–62.

casino-style gaming. "Logically, it appears difficult, if not impossible, for the Secretary to faithfully pursue the tribe's best interests while fairly adjudicating the conflicting interests of the state."[113] Of course, a state could avoid the issue of the Secretary as "judge and jury"[114] by consenting to suit in federal court under IGRA.

The U.S. Court of Appeals for the Fifth Circuit examined the constitutionality of the federal regulations in 2007. The case arose out of the Kickapoo Traditional Tribe of Texas' unsuccessful efforts to negotiate a Class III gaming compact with the state. Following the dismissal of the tribe's lawsuit on state sovereign immunity grounds, the tribe filed an application for an administrative "compact" under 25 C.F.R. pt. 291. After determining that the tribe was eligible for an administrative "compact," the Interior Secretary invited Texas to provide comments on the proposed administrative rules or to submit an alternative proposal for rules governing the tribe's Class III gaming. Instead, the state filed suit in federal court challenging the Secretary's authority to issue administrative rules. The district court dismissed the state's challenge on ripeness grounds, but opined that it appeared the regulations were an appropriate exercise of the Secretary's authority under IGRA as well as 25 U.S.C. §§2 and 9.[115]

The Fifth Circuit reversed. After determining that the issue was ripe for review, the court first reasoned that Congress, through IGRA, intended to "permit[] limited secretarial intervention only as a last resort, and only after the statute's judicial remedial procedures have been exhausted." The court stated that in fact, "the Secretarial Procedures stand in direct violation of IGRA … insofar as they may authorize Class III gaming without a compact."[116] Nor did 25

---

113. Lexague, "Indian Gaming and Tribal-State Negotiations," 91; see also Lindner-Cornelius, "Secretary of the Interior as Referee," 696 ("[I]n the new regulations, when a state claims it has negotiated in good faith to no avail, the only recourse it is left with is a biased factfinder who can do what it wants without any state input."). Skibine disagreed:

> There is, however, something not right in arguing that the Secretary will be unequivocally biased in favor of tribes because of the trust relationship when one realizes that the tribes could never bring a successful lawsuit against the Secretary for breach of trust if she made a determination about lack of good faith or scope of gaming which ran counter to the tribal position.

Skibine, "Scope of Gaming," 408.

Further, Skibine notes that there is little empirical evidence to suggest that the Secretary has exercised power under the regulations in a manner unfair to the states. Id. at 408–9 & n.63.

114. 144 Cong. Rec. S50 (daily ed. Jan. 27. 1998) (statement of Sen. Richard Bryan (D-Nev.)).

115. Texas v. U.S., 362 F. Supp. 2d 765, 770–71 (W.D. Tex. 2004).

116. Texas v. U.S. 497 F.3d 491, 503–07 (5th Cir. 2007).

U.S.C. §§ 2 and 9 provide sufficient support for the regulations, as those statutes only delegated authority to the Secretary to promulgate "regulations that ... are consistent with other relevant federal legislation." Because the court saw the regulations as inconsistent with IGRA, sections 2 and 9 could not provide authority. As the court concluded, IGRA "does not guarantee and Indian tribe the right to conduct Class III gaming," but only "grants tribes the right to negotiate the terms of a tribal-state compact."[117]

A "Seminole *Fix*"?

Meanwhile, in Florida, the Seminole Tribe's continued efforts to secure a Class III gaming compact underscored the real-world impact of the U.S. Supreme Court's 1996 decision.

In 2007, after some 16 years of negotiation, the tribe and Republican Governor Charles Crist signed a compact permitting the tribe to operate slot machines and house-banked card games, in exchange for $375 million in revenue sharing payments to the state over the first three years of the compact's 25-year term.[118] On the heels of the compact, however, the Florida House of Representatives filed suit, challenging the Governor's authority to authorize banked card games, which were otherwise illegal under state law. (At the time, state law allowed counties to legalize slot machines, but casino card games such as blackjack were prohibited.) The Florida Supreme Court sided with the legislators, concluding, "The Governor has no authority to change or amend state law. Such power falls exclusively to the Legislature. Therefore, we hold that the Governor lacked authority to bind the State to a compact that violates Florida law as this compact does."[119]

---

117. Id. at 509–11. The dissenting opinion noted that the state's "stonewalling" by refusing to negotiate effectively blocked the application of IGRA as Congress intended. Id. at 511 (Dennis, J., dissenting).

118. The tribe and state agreed to minimum annual revenue sharing payments of $100 million over the life of the compact, with set amounts in the first three years of operation: $50 million upon the compact taking effect, $175 million over the first two years, and $150 million in the third year. See Fla. House of Representatives v. Crist, 999 So. 2d 601, 603 (Fla. 2008) (a copy of the compact is reprinted in the court's decision); Robert M. Jarvis, "The 2007 Seminole-Florida Gambling Compact," *Gaming Law Review* 12 (2008): 13.

119. Crist, 999 So.2d at 616. As is usually the case in challenges to tribal gaming on state constitutional grounds, the tribe was not party to the suit, although its material impacts clearly would affect the tribe. See Kathryn R.L. Rand, "Caught in the Middle: How State Politics, State Law, and State Courts Constrain Tribal Influence Over Indian Gaming," *Marquette Law Review* 90 (2007): 971.

The Florida court's decision produced a standoff: the tribe continued to operate its card games, despite the state's and commercial competitors' efforts to enforce state law, and deposited the agreed-upon revenue-sharing payments in an account.[120] A few months later, the state legislature approved compact terms for fewer games and more revenue sharing.[121] The tribe and Governor Crist further negotiated and signed a compact in April 2010. The legislature ratified the modified compact but imposed a 2015 expiration date. Under the terms of the 2010 compact, the tribe has exclusive rights to operate blackjack and other banked card games at four of its casinos, and the state will collect at least $1 billion from the tribe.[122] In 2012, Florida lawmakers considered ways to expand commercial gaming, including a possible $3.8 billion casino resort on Miami's Biscayne Bay, while preserving its revenue under the compact with the Seminole Tribe.[123]

Despite calls for legislation to "fix" the Supreme Court's decision in *Seminole Tribe*,[124] it is politically unlikely that Congress will take any action on this issue in the foreseeable future. As we note above, it appears that disputes between tribes and states over Class III gaming are more likely to be resolved in the political arena than through resort to adjudication by the federal courts or the Secretary.[125]

---

120. See Allison Sirica, "A Great Gamble: Why Compromise Is the Best Bet to Resolve Florida's Indian Gaming Crisis," *Florida Law Review* 61 (2009): 1201, 1220–24.

121. Under the new compact, the Tribe was authorized to offer blackjack and other banked card games at only four of its seven casinos, and the Tribe's initial revenue-sharing payment to the state was increased to $600 million with minimum annual payments of $150 million thereafter for the 15-year term of the new compact. See id. at 1223–24.

122. The 2010 compact is downloadable through the Florida Department of Business and Professional Regulation at www.myfloridalicense.com/dbpr/pmw/documents/2010_Compact-Signed1.pdf (last visited Apr. 1, 2014).

123. See, e.g., Michael C. Bender, "Genting Boost as Florida Casino Plan Clears First Senate Hurdle," *Bloomberg Businessweek*, Jan. 10, 2012, http://www.businessweek.com/news/2012-01-10/genting-boost-as-florida-casino-plan-clears-first-senate-hurdle.html (last visited Apr. 1, 2014).

124. See, e.g., Kathryn R.L. Rand and Steven Andrew Light, "How Congress Can and Should 'Fix' the Indian Gaming Regulatory Act: Recommendations for Law and Policy Reform," *Virginia Journal of Social Policy & the Law* 13 (2006): 396, 445–49; Matthew L.M. Fletcher, "Bringing Balance to Indian Gaming," *Harvard Journal on Legislation*, 44 (2007): 39.

125. For a detailed account of compact negotiations and state constitutional law challenges in Wisconsin, see Rand, "Caught in the Middle." In Dairyland Greyhound Park Inc. v. Doyle, 719 N.W.2d 408 (Wis. 2006), the Wisconsin Supreme Court held that the tribes' and state's contractual right to renew and amend the Class III compacts "is constitutionally protected by the Contract Clauses of the Wisconsin and United States Constitutions."

OTHER CONSTITUTIONAL CHALLENGES

Two additional legal challenges to IGRA are worth brief discussion here: another challenge based on state sovereignty, this time rooted in the Tenth Amendment, and challenges based on equal protection.[126] Neither approach has seen much success in the courts.

Tenth Amendment Challenges

A separate constitutional challenge to IGRA also derives from state sovereignty, this time under the Tenth Amendment, which reserves to the states "powers not delegated to the United States by the Constitution, nor prohibited by it to the States."[127] Along with the Eleventh Amendment's recognition of state sovereign immunity, the Tenth Amendment reflects the balance of power between the federal government and state governments. In its cases grounded in issues of federalism, or the division of authority between the states and the federal government, the U.S. Supreme Court has interpreted the Tenth Amendment as prohibiting "coercion" and "commandeering" of state governments. The federal government may not require states to adopt a particular law or to implement federal law, but it may provide strong incentives for states to do so, including conditional federal funds and the threat of federal preemption.[128]

Some states have argued that IGRA's tribal-state compact requirement and the accompanying duty of the state to negotiate in good faith violate the Tenth Amendment. By forcing states to negotiate compacts, the argument goes, IGRA

---

126. A few courts have addressed other, more limited constitutional claims related to IGRA. See, for example, American Greyhound Racing, Inc. v. Hull, 146 F. Supp. 2d 1012 (D. Ariz. 2001) (claim that compact is a treaty); Crow Tribe of Indians v. Racicot, 87 F.3d 1039 (9th Cir. 1996) (due process claim stemming from tribe's asserted property interest in slot machines); Forest County Potawatomi Community v. Doyle, 828 F. Supp. 1401 (W.D. Wis. 1993) (due process claims based on tribe's asserted property and liberty interests in conducting gaming under tribal-state compact and IGRA), *aff'd*, 45 F.3d 1079 (7th Cir. 1995); Red Lake Band of Chippewa Indians v. Swimmer, 740 F. Supp. 9 (D.D.C. 1990) (due process claim based on IGRA's alleged infringement of tribal sovereignty and self-government).

127. U.S. Const. amend. X ("The powers not delegated to the United States by the Constitution, nor prohibited by it to the States, are reserved to the States respectively, or to the people.").

128. See generally Printz v. United States, 521 U.S. 898 (1997); New York v. United States, 505 U.S. 144 (1992); South Dakota v. Dole, 483 U.S. 203 (1987).

either requires the state to adopt a specific law, namely the tribal-state compact, or requires it to give effect to federal law, namely IGRA, by mandating that the state regulate Class III gaming through the compact.[129]

In *Ponca Tribe v. Oklahoma*, the Court of Appeals for the Tenth Circuit rejected the arguments of New Mexico and Oklahoma that IGRA's good-faith duty violated the Tenth Amendment:

> IGRA merely directs the state to negotiate in good faith, and stops well short of imposing a requirement on the states to enact or enforce a federal regulatory program.... In essence, the states' duty ... to negotiate with the Indian tribe in good faith is nothing more than a requirement that the states make a good faith attempt to craft a voluntary agreement with the Indian tribe pertaining to Class III gaming on Indian land that is consistent with state policy. IGRA reflects Congress' attempt to encourage, but not mandate, cooperative rulemaking between the Indian tribes and the states.[130]

A handful of other courts have reached similar conclusions.[131]

---

129. The Tenth Amendment also has been invoked to challenge the gubernatorial concurrence requirement in the context of gaming on newly acquired lands under 25 U.S.C. §2719(b)(1)(A). See Lac Courte Oreilles Band of Lake Superior Chippewa Indians v. United States, 367 F.3d 650, 663–65 (7th Cir. 2004) (holding that IGRA does not "commandeer[] the Governors of the 50 States into federal service or ... interfer[e] with the functioning of Wisconsin state government").

130. 37 F.3d 1422, 1434 (10th Cir. 1994), *judgment vacated by* 517 U.S. 1129 (1996), *and rev'd on other grounds*, 89 F.3d 690 (10th Cir. 1996). The Tenth Circuit also reasoned that "IGRA preserves state governmental accountability in the field of Indian gaming" and does not "impose an onerous burden on state financial resources." Id.

131. See Cheyenne River Sioux Tribe v. South Dakota, 3 F.3d 273, 281 (8th Cir. 1993) ("IGRA does not force states to compact with Indian tribes regarding Indian gaming and does not violate the tenth amendment."); Yavapai-Prescott Indian Tribe v. Arizona, 796 F. Supp. 1292, 1297 (D. Ariz. 1992) ("If IGRA attempted to force the State to regulate by compact all gaming activities on tribal lands it might indeed run afoul of the Tenth Amendment.... [But] IGRA's terms do not force the State to enter into a compact, it only demands good faith negotiation in order to meet state, as well as tribal and federal, interests."); Dalton v. Pataki, 780 N.Y.S.2d 47, 65 (N.Y. App. Div. 2004) ("IGRA does not force New York to accept a particular compact. It simply affords the state the opportunity to assert authority over gaming on Indian lands, a power that the state otherwise lacks."). But see Neil Scott Cohen, Note, "In What Often Appears to be a Crapshoot Legislative Process, Congress Throws Snake Eyes When It Enacts the Indian Gaming Regulatory Act," *Hofstra Law Review* 29 (2000): 277–308 (arguing that IGRA violates the Tenth Amendment).

Equal Protection Challenges

The Fourteenth Amendment's Equal Protection Clause prohibits a state from "deny[ing] to any person within its jurisdiction the equal protection of the laws." The Fifth Amendment's Due Process Clause has been construed as similarly limiting the federal government.[132] Under the U.S. Supreme Court's equal protection jurisprudence, classifications based on racial groups are "suspect;" that is, the government ordinarily cannot treat people differently based on race, absent a compelling justification.[133]

In *Morton v. Mancari*, the Supreme Court held that distinctions between Indians and non-Indians were not suspect, as they were rooted not in race but in Indians' political status as members of federally recognized tribes. Rather than requiring a compelling justification under "strict scrutiny" review, such classifications need only satisfy ordinary and highly deferential "rational basis" review:

> As long as the special treatment can be tied rationally to the fulfillment of Congress' unique obligation toward the Indians, such legislative judgments will not be disturbed.... [W]here the preference is reasonable and rationally designed to further Indian self-government, we cannot say that Congress' classification violates due process.[134]

Equal protection challenges related to Indian gaming, although more prevalent in public discourse alleging "unfairness" or "special rights" than in lawsuits, have taken two forms: first, to IGRA itself, in that it allows tribes, but not others, to engage in gaming on Indian lands with only limited applicability of state laws governing gambling; and second, to a tribal-state compact or state law that allows tribes to engage in forms of gaming not available to others in the state. In *Artichoke Joe's California Grand Casino v. Norton*, the Court of Appeals for the Ninth Circuit addressed both arguments in the context of California's rather convoluted state laws relating to Indian gaming.[135]

---

132. U.S. Const., amends. V & XIV.

133. The Court applies "strict scrutiny" to race classifications, requiring them to be "narrowly tailored" to a "compelling" government interest. See, e.g., Adarand Constructors, Inc. v. Pena, 515 U.S. 200, 227 (1995).

134. 417 U.S. 535, 555 (1974); see also United States v. Antelope, 430 U.S. 641 (1977) ("[S]uch regulation is rooted in the unique status of Indians as 'a separate people' with their own political institutions. Federal regulation of Indian tribes, therefore, is governance of once-sovereign political communities; it is not to be viewed as legislation of a 'racial group consisting of Indians'....").

135. 353 F.3d 712 (9th Cir. 2003).

Following the Ninth Circuit's decision in *Rumsey Indian Rancheria* that California was not obligated to negotiate over all forms of Class III gaming, Republican Governor Pete Wilson refused to include casino-style games and slot machines in compact negotiations.[136] The tribes turned to California's voter initiative process to pursue passage of a state law that would authorize such games. California voters passed Proposition 5 in 1998, which required the state to enter into compacts allowing the tribes to operate casino-style games and slot machines. The California Supreme Court, however, invalidated Proposition 5 on the ground that it violated the state constitution's prohibition against "casinos of the type currently operating in Nevada and New Jersey."[137] In the meantime, Democratic Governor Gray Davis negotiated compacts that included the disputed games. The compacts were conditioned on the passage of Proposition 1A, which would amend the state constitution to allow the tribes to operate the games. In 2000, California voters ratified Proposition 1A, which provided:

> [T]he Governor is authorized to negotiate and conclude compacts, subject to ratification by the Legislature, for the operation of slot machines and the conduct of lottery games and banking and percentage card games by federally recognized Indian tribes on Indian lands in California in accordance with federal law. Accordingly, slot machines, lottery games, and banking and percentage card games are hereby permitted to be conducted and operated on tribal lands subject to those compacts.[138]

Soon after Proposition 1A's passage, the compacts took effect and tribes began operating casino-style gaming in California.[139]

Under California law, only tribes may conduct the games authorized by Proposition 1A. State law also generally allows charitable organizations and commercial enterprises to conduct a few other games, such as bingo and player-banked card games. In *Artichoke Joe's*, non-tribal casinos operating under the confines of state law challenged both IGRA and Proposition 1A, arguing that allowing only tribes to conduct the more lucrative casino-style gaming was an impermissible race-based distinction that violated equal protection. The Ninth Circuit reasoned that because IGRA governs tribes as sovereign entities, rather

136. See Rumsey Indian Rancheria of Wintun Indians v. Wilson, 64 F.3d 1250 (9th Cir. 1994).

137. See Hotel Employees and Restaurant Employees Int'l Union v. Davis, 981 P.2d 990 (Cal. 1999).

138. Cal. Const. art. IV, §19(f).

139. See Artichoke Joe's, 353 F.3d at 715–18.

than individual American Indians based on race, it "falls squarely within the rule of *Mancari*" requiring only a rational basis to uphold the statute. Similarly, Proposition 1A, as a state law enacted pursuant to IGRA, also triggered only minimal scrutiny.[140] The court readily found that both IGRA and Proposition 1A were rationally related to legitimate government interests. IGRA, said the court, served the federal government's interests of fostering tribal self-government and encouraging tribal autonomy and economic development, while Proposition 1A served California's interests in regulating gambling and promoting a cooperative, government-to-government relationship with tribes. Neither law, then, violated equal protection.[141]

* * *

As the evolution of state law in California and the circumstances giving rise to a number of other cases discussed in this chapter show, litigation in federal and state court is not the only channel through which Indian gaming law and policy is shaped. Moreover, litigation itself is subject to the mediating variables of judicial interpretation and ideology. Equally significant in influence, and even less predictable, we turn next to the politics of Indian gaming.

---

140. Id. at 734–36. The court explained,

IGRA pertains to Indian lands and to tribal self-government and tribal status of federally recognized tribes. Accordingly, under *Mancari*, rational-basis review applies.... Proposition 1A was enacted in response to IGRA, a federal law explicitly designed to readjust the regulatory authority of various sovereigns over class III gaming on the lands of federally recognized Indian tribes. The classifications in Proposition 1A echo those made in IGRA. In ratifying Proposition 1A, the people of California were legislating with reference to the authority that Congress had granted the State of California in IGRA. Accordingly, rational-basis review applies to Proposition 1A as well.

Id. at 736.

141. Id. at 736–42.

CHAPTER 5

THE ROLE OF POLITICS AND POLICY

Within the legal and regulatory boundaries established by the Indian Gaming Regulatory Act of 1988 (IGRA), the numerous actors who negotiate and implement public policy drive the politics of Indian gaming. Tribal gaming is the only form of legalized gambling in the United States that is regulated at three governmental levels: under IGRA, tribal, federal, and state agencies determine the regulatory environment in which tribal gaming occurs. Inside this complex regulatory framework, policymakers often weigh the social and economic impacts of Indian gaming while industry associations and community and other organizations seek to influence policy outcomes, including the tribal-state compacts that govern tribal gaming. In the aftermath of the U.S. Supreme Court's decision in *Seminole Tribe v. Florida*, the political terrain for compact negotiations has shifted to include tribal treaty rights, land claims, and revenue-sharing agreements. These and other political developments demonstrate the interaction of the law and policy governing Indian gaming. Many issues related to tribal gaming may be raised and resolved through political processes, either in conjunction with or rather than litigation or law reform.

In this chapter, we first identify the various governmental regulatory agencies with authority over tribal gaming. We then turn to the most politicized aspect of Indian gaming, casino-style gaming and IGRA's tribal-state compact requirement. We describe the diverse political players who may influence tribal-state compact negotiations and discuss the particular issues and strategies developed in the post-*Seminole Tribe* political environment.

GOVERNMENT REGULATION OF
INDIAN GAMING

IGRA assigns regulatory authority over Indian gaming according to the type of gaming involved. Tribes maintain exclusive regulatory jurisdiction over Class I gaming, or traditional tribal social or ceremonial games of chance, while Class II bingo and other similar games fall under tribal regulatory jurisdiction with National Indian Gaming Commission (NIGC) oversight.[1] Class III casino-style gaming requires both tribal regulation and a tribal-state compact, thus giving the state regulatory authority, as well.[2] The NIGC and the Secretary of the Interior also have regulatory roles regarding Class III gaming. Assorted other tribal, state, and federal agencies enforce applicable laws.

Federal Agencies

Department of the Interior

The Interior Department's mission includes fulfilling the federal government's trust responsibilities, as well as enhancing the quality of life and promoting economic opportunity for American Indians and tribes. The Assistant Secretary of the Interior for Indian Affairs heads the Bureau of Indian Affairs (BIA) and supervises other divisions and programs within the Department pertaining to tribes. The BIA is responsible for managing over 55 million acres of tribal land held in trust by the federal government and administers numerous federal programs that provide services to 1.9 million Native Americans.[3] The Interior Department also houses the Special Trustee for American Indians.[4]

---

1. See 25 U.S.C. §§ 2710(a)–(c), 2705, 2706.
2. See id. § 2710(d)(1).
3. See U.S. Department of the Interior, Bureau of Indian Affairs, "Who We Are," http://www.bia.gov/WhoWeAre/index.htm (last visited Sept. 19, 2013).
4. U.S. Department of the Interior, "Office of the Special Trustee for American Indians," http://www.doi.gov/ost/index.cfm (last visited Sept. 19, 2013). The Special Trustee is responsible for ensuring that all Interior Department functions related to the federal government's trust responsibility are coordinated and consistent. The Trustee also has fiduciary duty over and accounts for the balance of all funds held in trust for the benefit of tribes. At the time of this writing, the Special Trustee office was vacant.
   The federal government's fulfillment of these duties was the subject of the landmark class-action lawsuit in *Cobell v. Salazar*, which after years of contention resulted in a $3.4 billion settlement in favor of the more than 300,000 individual American Indian plaintiffs. The *Cobell* settlement was approved by Congress through the Claims Resolution Act of 2010.

A number of the Department's functions and responsibilities directly relate to Indian gaming.

Under IGRA, only federally acknowledged tribes may conduct tribal gaming, and then only on federally defined Indian lands.[5] As the Interior Department has what many consider to be primary federal authority over the tribal recognition process, it plays a fundamental role in controlling which groups qualify as acknowledged Indian tribes and therefore may conduct gaming on their reservations.[6] The BIA administers the Department's administrative recognition process through the Office of Federal Acknowledgement. Some perceive the Department as a gatekeeper for Indian gaming and assert that tribal groups seeking recognition are doing so merely to "cash in" on the sovereign right to own and operate casinos.[7]

The Interior Secretary has primary authority to take lands into trust for the benefit of tribes, and thus has power to execute the acquisition of Indian lands under IGRA. (However, as discussed in Chapter 3, the U.S. Supreme Court's decision in *Carcieri v. Salazar* largely invalidated the Secretary's authority to take land into trust for tribes not federally recognized in 1934.) Although IGRA generally prohibits gaming on lands acquired by a tribe after 1988, it allows for several exceptions, including when the Secretary determines that gaming on newly acquired lands is "in the best interest of the tribe and its members, and would not be detrimental to the surrounding community."[8] The Secretary's authority to place land in trust and its determinations under IGRA's newly acquired lands exceptions have become increasingly contentious legal and political issues.[9]

Through the settlement, $1.5 billion will be distributed to compensate class members for their historical accounting, trust fund, and asset mismanagement claims against the federal government. See Order Granting Final Approval to Settlement, *Cobell v. Salazar*, No. 1:96CV01285 (D.D.C. July 27, 2011), *aff'd*, 679 F.3d 909 (D.C. Cir. 2012).

5. Indian Gaming Regulatory Act, 25 U.S.C. §§ 2703(5), 2703(4); see also 25 C.F.R. § 502.12.

6. Federal acknowledgment of tribal groups may occur through other means, such as treaties or statutes, but the Interior Department's recognition process is the most common route pursued by tribal groups today.

7. See, for instance, Iver Peterson, "Would-Be Tribes Entice Investors," *New York Times*, Mar. 29, 2004 (describing financial backing of groups seeking recognition); William Yardley, "A Split Tribe, Casino Plans and One Little Indian Boy in the Middle," *New York Times*, Feb. 15, 2004 (discussing criticism of BIA's decision to recognize the Schaghticoke Tribal Nation in Connecticut). We discuss the politics of tribal recognition in Chapter 6.

8. 25 U.S.C. § 2719(b)(1)(A).

9. We discuss the politics of "off-reservation" gaming and gaming on newly acquired lands in Chapter 6.

IGRA charges the Interior Secretary with other specific duties related to Indian gaming, including, for example, the authority to approve a tribe's plan for
per capita distribution of gaming revenue.[10] With regard to IGRA's compact requirement for Class III gaming, the Secretary has power to approve tribal-state
compacts and to adopt an administrative "compact" when a state fails to negotiate in good faith.[11]

Within the BIA is the Office of Indian Gaming (OIG), charged with implementation of the responsibilities assigned by IGRA to the Interior Secretary. The OIG develops policies and procedures for review and approval of
tribal-state compacts, per capita distributions of gaming revenue, and requests
by tribes to take land into trust for the purpose of conducting gaming. The
OIG coordinates with the NIGC as well as state, local, and tribal governments.[12]

National Indian Gaming Commission

Also located within the Interior Department, the NIGC is the federal agency
empowered by IGRA to regulate Indian gaming.[13] The Commission's three
members are appointed by the President and the Interior Secretary.[14] As we
describe in detail in Chapter 3, the NIGC has expansive authority to promulgate rules and regulations to implement IGRA.[15] The Commission exercises
wide-ranging oversight of tribal regulation of gaming operations, including
the power to approve tribal regulatory ordinances and to oversee tribal licensing of key employees and management officials.[16] Through its authority to
close Indian gaming operations and to impose civil fines, the Commission is
further empowered to enforce IGRA's provisions, federal regulations promulgated by the NIGC, and the tribes' own gaming regulations, ordinances, and
resolutions.[17]

---

10. 25 U.S.C. § 2710(b)(3); see also 25 C.F.R. pt. 290.
11. 25 U.S.C. § 2710(d)(8); 25 C.F.R. pt. 291. The Secretarial alternative compacting
procedures in 25 C.F.R pt. 291 were developed in response to the Supreme Court's decision in *Seminole Tribe v. Florida*, 517 U.S. 44 (1996). Only rarely has the Secretary invoked
the procedures. We discuss the political and legal contexts of the Secretary's authority in
Chapter 4.
12. See U.S. Department of the Interior, Bureau of Indian Affairs, "Office of Indian
Gaming," http://www.bia.gov/WhoWeAre/AS-IA/OIG/index.htm (last visited Sept.19, 2013).
13. 25 U.S.C. § 2702.
14. Id. § 2704.
15. Id. § 2706(b)(10).
16. Id. § 2710(b)(2), (c), (d)(1)(A).
17. Id. § 2713(a)(3). The Commission also has authority to conduct inspections of tribal
gaming operations and demand access to tribal records, as well as to subpoena witnesses,

Both despite and because of its broad authority, the NIGC has been accused of being underfunded, understaffed, and underempowered to regulate tribal gaming. The Commission, some say, has overlooked numerous regulatory problems and created opportunities for the possible infiltration of organized crime in some casino operations. It has been accused of granting too much deference to inadequate tribal regulatory authorities or improperly serving as a guardian for tribal sovereignty more generally.[18] Others see the Commission as overzealous, asserting that it uses its powers under IGRA to promulgate regulations that effectively remove or override tribal authority over Indian gaming and thus undercut tribal sovereignty.[19] Regardless of where the truth lays, tribal advocates also point out that tribal gaming, with three layers of governmental regulation, is the most heavily regulated form of legalized gambling in the United States.[20]

Department of Justice

As the executive official charged with enforcing federal laws, the U.S. Attorney General plays a role in ensuring compliance with IGRA and other applicable federal laws related to gaming. The Attorney General heads the U.S. Department of Justice, which includes federal law enforcement agencies, such as the Federal Bureau of Investigation (FBI) and the nation's prosecutors, the U.S. Attorneys. Also within the Department of Justice is the Office of Tribal Justice, which advises the Department on legal and policy issues regarding Native Americans and serves as the point of contact within the Department for tribes.

The FBI exercises federal jurisdiction in investigating criminal activity on tribal lands, including crimes related to Indian gaming. Located within federal judicial districts in each state, the U.S. Attorneys serve as the principal prosecu-

---

hold hearings, and receive testimony and evidence. Id. §§ 2706(b)(4), (8), 2715. NIGC regulations further detail the execution of the Commission's investigative and enforcement powers. See 25 C.F.R. pts. 571, 573.

18. See, for instance, Donald L. Barlett and James B. Steele, "Wheel of Misfortune," *Time* (Dec. 16, 2002), 47–48 (labeling the Commission "the impotent enforcer").

19. The Commission's protracted attempt to adopt "bright line" rules to distinguish between Class II and Class III gaming devices illustrates both sides of the criticism. See, e.g., Ezekiel J.N. Fletcher, "Negotiating Meaningful Concessions from States in Gaming Compacts to Further Tribal Economic Development," *South Dakota Law Review*, 54 (2009): 419, 430–31.

20. See National Indian Gaming Association (NIGA), "Regulation of Indian Gaming," http://www.indiangaming.org/info/pr/presskit/REGULATION.pdf (last visited Mar. 31, 2014) ("Indian gaming is already subject to more stringent regulation and security controls than any other type of gaming in the United States.").

tors on behalf of the United States and at the direction of the Attorney General. Working in conjunction with federal law enforcement agencies, including the FBI, the U.S. Attorneys prosecute criminal and related cases involving Indian gaming. The U.S. Attorneys have power to initiate criminal prosecutions and forfeiture actions under IGRA's criminal provisions, the Johnson Act, and other federal statutes.

Department of the Treasury

The Treasury Department's Financial Crimes Enforcement Network (FinCEN) regulates financial transactions and assists in investigation of money laundering under the federal Bank Secrecy Act.[21] Tribal casinos, like commercial casinos, are subject to the Act's money-laundering controls, including recordkeeping and reporting requirements for large transactions.[22] Besides FinCEN's regulatory role, the Internal Revenue Service (IRS) enforces civil regulations under the Bank Secrecy Act, as well as federal tax laws and regulations that apply to tribal gaming operations.[23] The Treasury Department's law enforcement agencies, including the Secret Service and the IRS's Criminal Investigation Division, coordinate with the U.S. Attorneys in bringing appropriate enforcement actions in federal court.

Tribal Gaming Commissions

Before a tribe may operate either Class II or Class III gaming, IGRA requires that the tribe adopt a gaming ordinance that must be approved by the NIGC

---

21. 31 U.S.C. §§ 5311–5330; 12 U.S.C. §§ 1818(s), 1829(b), 1951–1959.

22. 31 C.F.R. pt. 103. The requirements of the Bank Secrecy Act apply to casinos, tribal or commercial, that earn at least $1 million in gross gaming revenue. 31 C.F.R. § 103.11(n)(5)(i). Casinos are required to report cash transactions of more than $10,000 and to record a number of other financial transactions. Additionally, casinos must adopt a program, in accord with federal regulations, to ensure compliance with the Act. See 31 C.F.R. pt. 103. See also generally Jeanne M. Rubin, "A Tribal Approach to Gaming Enforcement," available at International Institute for Indigenous Resource Management, http://www.iiirm.org/publications/Articles%20Reports%20Papers/Self%20Determination/GaminingEnforce.pdf (last visited Mar. 31, 2014).

23. For an accessible list of applicable tax laws and regulations, see Internal Revenue Service, "Tax Information for Indian Tribal Governments," http://www.irs.gov/GovernmentEntities/Indian-Tribal-Governments (last visited Nov. 1, 2013). See also Scott A. Taylor, "Taxation in Indian Country after *Carcieri v. Salazar*," *William Mitchell Law Review* 36 (2010): 590–620; Scott A. Taylor, "Federal and State Income Taxation of Indian Gaming Revenues," *Gaming Law Review* 5 (2001): 383–99.

Chair. The ordinance must address a number of issues, including the tribe's proprietary interest in and responsibility for gaming, use of gaming revenues, audits, vendor contracts, facility maintenance, and background checks and licensing.[24] Typically, tribes create gaming commissions to implement the tribal gaming ordinance and to ensure compliance with IGRA, tribal-state compacts, and other relevant tribal laws. A tribe's certificate of self-regulation, issued by the NIGC under IGRA, creates additional tribal responsibility for regulating Class II gaming, while a tribal-state compact may further detail the tribe's obligations with regard to Class III gaming.[25] Tribes, of course, also are free to adopt additional ordinances and regulations governing their gaming operations.

Tribal gaming commissioners are either elected or appointed. Although commissions are funded through tribal budgetary allocations, they usually are otherwise independent of other tribal political or governmental bodies. A Gaming Commissioner typically serves as chief administrative and enforcement officer, with responsibilities that include monitoring and enforcement of employee background checks, surveillance, inspection, auditing, compliance, licensing, and rule promulgation. Tribal ordinances authorize the hiring of professional commission staff and may establish appointive gaming review boards that approve regulations and hear appeals concerning licensing, fines, and patron disputes.[26]

As regulatory, rather than managerial, agencies, tribal gaming commissions are empowered to promulgate regulations and to hold hearings. Commissions monitor compliance with tribal internal control standards (ICS) and the NIGC's mandatory minimum internal control standards (MICS). They have unrestricted access to the tribe's gaming facility and its records, and have authority to enforce regulatory provisions through such means as license suspension or revocation.[27]

Tribal regulators interact with tribal, state, and federal law enforcement agencies, tribal casino surveillance and security operations, and tribal court systems, as well as with state and federal regulatory authorities. New regulators may receive on-the-job training from current commissioners, take courses, or enroll in a formal training program. In 2000, the National Indian Gaming

---

24. 25 U.S.C. §2710(b)(2), (d)(2).

25. See id. §2710(c) (outlining the requirements for a certificate of self-regulation).

26. See, for instance, Confederated Tribes of Siletz Indians, "Siletz Tribal Gaming Commission," http://www.ctsi.nsn.us/siletz-tribal-gaming-commission/stgc (last visited Nov. 1, 2013); Viejas Band of Kumeyaay Indians (California), "Viejas Gaming Regulation," http://www.viejasbandofkumeyaay.org/html/tribal_gaming/viejas_gaming_regulation.html (last visited Nov. 1, 2013).

27. See Tracy Burris, "How Tribal Gaming Commissions Are Evolving," *Gaming Law Review* 8 (2004): 243–46.

Association (NIGA) created a commissioner certification program at which tribal regulators receive training on such topics as jurisdiction, human resource management, due process of law, MICS, compliance auditing, avoiding scams, budgeting, and rule promulgation.[28] Commissioners may belong to such organizations as the National Tribal Gaming Commissioners and Regulators, the North American Gaming Regulators Association, or similar state-level organizations, such as the Oklahoma Tribal Gaming Regulators Association.[29]

According to NIGA, tribes in 2012 spent more than $309 million on regulatory activities by 2,900 regulators, including commissioners as well as compliance and audit staff, and reimbursed states nearly $78 million for their regulatory costs. Through IGRA-mandated fees, tribes funded the NIGC with more than $20 million.[30]

State Gaming Commissions

The scope and extent of state regulatory authority concerning tribal gaming is defined and limited by IGRA. Because both Class II and Class III gaming is allowed only in states that permit such gaming, state gaming commissions play a role in determining the overall regulatory environment of legalized gambling within a state's borders. With NIGC and Interior Secretary oversight, Class III gaming falls under state as well as tribal jurisdiction as set forth in the negotiated tribal-state compact.[31]

Tribes' sovereign status, according to the U.S. Supreme Court's decision in *California v. Cabazon Band of Mission Indians*, rendered state gaming commissions absent regulatory authority over tribal gaming independent of congressional delegation.[32] Under IGRA, however, Congress authorized states, through the tribal-state compact requirement, to regulate casino-style gaming. Typically, state gaming commissions are responsible for monitoring compliance with governing tribal-state compacts in concert with state law and public policy as well as IGRA.

---

28. NIGA, "Commissioner Certification Series," http://www.indiangaming.org/events/seminar/commissioners.shtml (last visited Nov. 1, 2013).

29. National Tribal Gaming Commissions and Regulators, http://www.ntgcr.com (last visited Nov. 1, 2013); North American Gaming Regulators Association, http://www.nagra.org (last visited Nov. 1, 2013).

30. See NIGA, *2013 Annual Report*, 33 (2013), http://www.indiangaming.org/info/2013_Annual_Report.PDF (last visited Mar. 31, 2014).

31. See §§ 2710(d), 2705, 2706.

32. 480 U.S. 202 (1987).

State gaming commissions implement, monitor, and enforce state law and public policy regarding all types of legalized gambling allowed in a state. State commissions (or variously, agencies, departments, divisions, and gaming control or racing and wagering boards) often are composed of officials appointed by the governor and confirmed by the state legislature. Commissioners may be required by state law to have different political and professional backgrounds. Commissions are supported by a professional staff that may include auditing, compliance, inspections, law enforcement, legal, licensing, and taxation personnel or divisions. Some commissions report directly to the governor or to the state's attorney general. Commissions may interact with tribal regulatory or law enforcement agencies, state public safety, law enforcement, or other regulatory agencies, local regulatory and law enforcement agencies, and the NIGC or other federal agencies concerning regulatory and enforcement issues related to Indian gaming.

Although the responsibilities and authority of state gaming commissions vary with the type and scope of legalized gaming within a state, there are several similarities. State lotteries, for example, usually are administered and regulated either by the state's general gaming commission or by a separate, lottery-specific agency. Responsibilities of the regulatory agency include advertising, ensuring fairness and accuracy, collection and distribution of funds, and supervision of sales. With regard to pari-mutuel wagering, state gaming commissions ensure integrity of races and events, oversee licensing of tracks and operators, guard against organized crime, and assist in collection of state taxes.[33] State regulation of commercial casinos typically follows one of two models: the "Nevada" model, which encourages maximization of economic benefits to the state, or the "New Jersey" model, which focuses on addressing or mitigating negative social and economic impacts associated with gambling. Both approaches include developing and overseeing minimum internal control standards, conducting audits, issuing licenses, and so on.[34] State regulation of Indian gaming, of course, varies under individual tribal-state compacts, but similar requirements typically apply to tribal casinos.

Although governmental regulatory agencies at the federal, state, and tribal levels have primary responsibility over promulgating regulations and ensur-

---

33. See National Gambling Impact Study Commission (NGISC), *Final Report* (1999), 3-1 to 3-17, http://govinfo.library.unt.edu/ngisc/index.html (last visited Mar. 27, 2005).

34. See, for example, Cory Aronovitz, "The Regulation of Commercial Gaming," *Chapman Law Review* 5 (2002): 181–208. For in-depth coverage of gaming regulation, see Anthony N. Cabot & Keith C. Miller, *The Law of Gambling and Regulated Gaming: Cases and Materials* (Durham, NC: Carolina Academic Press, 2011); Kevin K. Washburn, *Gaming and Gambling Law: Cases and Materials* (New York: Aspen, 2010).

ing that gaming facilities comply with applicable law, they are not the only political actors with sway over Indian gaming. Indeed, a host of political influ-
entials, from community organizations to state governors, have a hand in
shaping tribal gaming. This is particularly true in the context of highly politicized tribal-state compact negotiations after *Seminole Tribe.*

The Political Players

Congressional debate over the bills leading to IGRA's passage in 1988 reflected some members' concerns about unchecked state power over tribal gaming. The tribal-state compact requirement for Class III gaming was Congress's
attempt to balance competing interests and to encourage cooperation between
tribal and state governments. IGRA's legislative history indicates that Congress
concluded that the compact requirement was "the best mechanism to assure that
the interests of both sovereign entities are met with respect to the regulation
of complex gaming enterprises," such as casinos. The "practical problem," as Congress recognized, was "the need to provide some incentive for states to negotiate with tribes in good faith." According to Congress, the appropriate incentive
was the state's role in regulating Class III gaming through the compact requirement with its accompanying good-faith duty, enforceable through IGRA's
legal cause of action; that is, the tribes' right to sue the state in federal court.
Congress recognized that if a state simply refused to negotiate a compact, the
tribe effectively would lose its right to conduct gaming, while the state's rights
would not be lessened. "[G]iven this unequal balance," Congress chose the
cause of action against the state as "the least offensive option" to encourage
fair dealing with tribes.[35] As Senator Daniel Evans (R-Wash.) described it,

> We intend that the two sovereigns—the tribes and the States—will sit
> down together in negotiations on equal terms and come up with a
> recommended methodology for regulation of class III gaming on In-
> dian lands. Permitting the States even this limited say in matters that
> are usually in the exclusive domain of tribal government has been per-
> mitted only with extreme reluctance.[36]

From the start, however, states asserted Eleventh Amendment immunity
from such suits, and several lower courts refused to reach the merits of the

---

35. S. Rep. 100-446, reprinted in 1988 U.S.C.C.A.N. 3071, 3083–84.
36. 134 Cong. Rec. S12643 (Daily ed. Sept. 15, 1988) (statement of Sen. Daniel Evans
(R-Wash.)).

disputes, instead dismissing the cases on the basis of state sovereign immunity. As we discuss in Chapter 4, the U.S. Supreme Court held in *Seminole Tribe v. Florida* that tribes could not sue states without their consent under IGRA and, as a result, the referee role of the federal courts was available to tribes only if the state consented to suit. Tribes no longer could force states to negotiate tribal-state compacts in good faith, or at all.[37] Post-*Seminole Tribe*, tribes and states have continued to negotiate compacts in a complicated political environment in which many players are at the table.

Tribes

Through the exercise of tribal sovereignty—tribes' inherent pre-constitutional and extra-constitutional powers of self-governance and self-determination—tribes decide whether or not to pursue gaming. The outcome may result from an electoral referendum of tribal members or be debated and codified by the governing body in the form of a tribal resolution or ordinance.

Tribal governments are varied, influenced not only by overarching federal Indian law and policy, but also by each tribe's unique history, traditions, and culture. As sovereigns, tribes have the inherent right to choose their own form of government. Typically, though, a tribal government will include the political branches of an executive and legislative body, albeit usually with, to western eyes, a relatively weak separation of powers.[38] A tribal legislative body might take the form of a council, business committee, board of directors, or a legislature. Tribal legislative officials generally are elected for a set term, usually two to four years. Tribal legislative bodies enact laws, manage tribal business enterprises, regulate tribal economic affairs, levy taxes, and generally provide for tribal welfare. A tribal executive might be called a president, chair, chief, or governor. Tribal executives may be elected by the tribe's legislative body or by the tribal electorate and typically serve a four-year term. Tribal executives oversee the daily administrative functions of the tribe, execute and

---

37. In 1999, the Secretary of the Interior promulgated federal regulations meant to mitigate states' ability to stonewall compact negotiations after *Seminole Tribe*. The regulations allow a tribe to invoke the Secretary's power to issue a "compact" governing Class III gaming when a state fails to negotiate in good faith and refuses to consent to suit in federal court. See 25 C.F.R. pt. 291. We discuss these regulations in detail in Chapter 4.

38. Nearly every tribe has a legislative and executive body; fewer tribes have developed formal judiciaries. Recently, however, many tribes have initiated the creation of tribal court systems. See David E. Wilkins and Heidi Kiiwetinepinesiik Stark, *American Indian Politics and the American Political System*, 3rd ed. (Lanham, MD: Rowman & Littlefield, 2010), 70–82.

enforce tribal laws, preside over the legislative body, and represent the tribe in intergovernmental relations with the federal government, state and local governments, and other tribes.[39]

A tribe's eligibility to operate gaming within a state in the first place is determined by IGRA's categorization of gaming classes in concert with the legality of such gaming under state public policy. For Class I and Class II gaming, tribal governments have exclusive and primary regulatory authority, respectively.[40] For Class III gaming, IGRA requires the tribe to enter into a tribal-state compact and also requires the state to engage in good-faith compact negotiations with the tribe.[41] Tribal governments are responsible for implementing a tribe's decision to pursue casino-style gaming by initiating and conducting compact negotiations with the state. After a compact is reached, the tribe also is responsible for ensuring tribal compliance with the compact, applicable tribal ordinances, and IGRA and other federal laws.

As we have discussed, however, IGRA's good-faith requirement lacks teeth as a result of the U.S. Supreme Court's decision in *Seminole Tribe*. The absence of a tribal cause of action against states in federal court has made it difficult, if not impossible, for tribes to compel states to come to the table for compact negotiations. Moreover, during such negotiations, the weakened political posture of tribes in relation to states has created opportunities for states to wrest concessions from tribes on a number of issues ranging from treaty hunting, fishing, or water rights to revenue sharing with the state, as tribes may perceive they have little choice if they wish to arrive at a compact agreement. We describe some of the political matters up for negotiation in Chapter 6.

States

According to IGRA, the legality of Class II or Class III gaming in a state is determined by state law and public policy. This fact in the first place conditions Indian gaming on the state's political posture toward legalized gambling.[42] Assuming casino-style or Class III gaming is legal in a state, IGRA grants to states the authority to negotiate compacts with tribes governing tribal operation of casino-style gaming. With statutory reference only to the "State," IGRA does not, however, establish which branch of state government is responsible for

---

39. Id., 140–45.
40. 25 U.S.C. §§ 2703(6), 2710(a)(1), 2710(b)(1).
41. Id. § 2710(d)(3)(A).
42. We discuss case law on this issue in Chapter 4.

the negotiations. In most states, this authority is exercised by the governor.[43] State legislatures and state courts, especially through the interpretation of the appropriate authority of political branches under state law, increasingly have asserted their influence over state policy toward Indian gaming.

The Governor

Congress intended IGRA's good-faith requirement to level the playing field for tribes and states by encouraging the negotiation of a gaming compact. Post-*Seminole Tribe*, the political culture of a state became a key factor in these negotiations. The invalidation of IGRA's legal cause of action against a state greatly hindered federal courts' ability to interpret IGRA's good-faith requirement and to develop a legal standard to determine whether a state has fulfilled its duty to negotiate in good faith. As a practical result, for a state that refuses to consent to suit, "good faith" may equate to nothing more than what the governor is willing to negotiate. The attitudes of a sitting governor toward legalized gambling generally or Indian gaming specifically may determine the governor's posture toward the compacting process and thus, drive compact negotiations. The governor also may size up the state's political environment and pursue a hardball negotiation strategy, seeking to limit the types of games or quantity of gaming devices allowed by a compact, to require the tribe to make revenue-sharing payments with states or localities, or to abrogate treaty or other rights in return for a compact agreement.

By extension, the transition to a new governing regime may change the state's position on an existing compact. Recent examples of this phenomenon include Wisconsin's and Florida's transitions among gubernatorial administrations with differing stances on tribal gaming.[44]

Although IGRA generally prohibits gaming on newly acquired lands, it provides a number of exceptions, as we describe in Chapter 3. One of these exceptions requires the Interior Secretary to determine that gaming on the newly acquired lands is in the best interest of the tribe and tribal members and is not detrimental to the surrounding communities. For the exception to apply, the state's governor must concur in the Secretary's determination.[45] Thus, the gov-

---

43. Kelly B. Kramer, "Current Issues in Indian Gaming: Casino Lands and Gaming Compacts," *Gaming Law Review* 7 (2003): 331.

44. See Kathryn R.L. Rand, "Why State Law Matters: Indian Gaming and Intergovernmental Relations in Wisconsin," in Kenneth N. Hansen and Tracy A. Skopek, eds., *The New Politics of Indian Gaming* (Reno: University of Nevada Press, 2011), 160–84; Kathryn R.L. Rand, "Caught in the Middle: How State Politics, State Law, and State Courts Constrain Tribal Influence over Indian Gaming," *Marquette Law Review* 90 (2007): 971.

45. 25 U.S.C. § 2719(b)(1)(A).

ernor has "veto" power to foreclose both Class II and Class III gaming on newly acquired lands under this exception. At least two governors, of Oregon and Wisconsin, have exercised their veto power following the Secretary's favorable determination, ending the tribes' efforts to locate gaming facilities on newly acquired lands.[46]

The Legislature

IGRA does not grant any formal authority over tribal-state compacting to state legislatures. State law therefore varies, and may require legislative approval before a tribal-state compact takes effect. Legislative activity at the state level reflects a range of influence over the politics of tribal gaming.

Some state legislatures have passed laws specifically intended to limit the scope or extent of Indian gaming. For example, in Connecticut, after the Second Circuit Court of Appeals decided in *Mashantucket Pequot Tribe v. Connecticut* that the state's "Las Vegas nights" law evidenced a permissive stance on casino-style gaming, the state legislature repealed the law in an effort to foreclose any additional tribal casinos in the state.[47] Lawmakers also regularly participate in the policy debates over Indian gaming's social and economic effects on tribal and non-tribal communities. Some legislators have become strong advocates for more stringent regulation of Indian gaming or for tribal payment of additional impact-mitigation fees to compensate for traffic congestion, higher rates of crime, or treatment of problem and pathological gambling.

As state budgetary shortfalls became more severe, even before the national economic recession that began in 2008, legislators in several states encouraged governors to pressure tribes to renegotiate existing tribal-state compacts and incorporate revenue-sharing agreements to "level the playing field" and "spread the wealth" with state and local governments.[48] Legislators or candidates for office in California, Minnesota, and elsewhere increasingly have publicized their positions on existing Indian gaming policy (both state and federal), tribal sovereignty more generally, or on referenda and ballot initiatives that take

---

46. See Confederated Tribes of Siletz Indians v. United States, 110 F.3d 688 (9th Cir. 1997); Lac Courte Oreilles Band v. United States, 367 F.3d 650 (7th Cir. 2004).

47. See 913 F.2d 1024 (2d Cir. 1990); Conn. Gen. Stat. §§7-186a to 7-186l (repealed 2003); see also "Connecticut Governor Admits New Law Barring More Indian Casinos May Not Hold Up," Jan. 7, 2003, http://www.foxnews.com/story/0,2933,74904,00.html (last visited Apr. 2, 2005).

48. See Steven Andrew Light, Kathryn R.L. Rand, and Alan P. Meister, "Spreading the Wealth: Tribal-State Revenue-Sharing Agreements," *North Dakota Law Review* 80 (2004): 657–79.

compact-related policy questions straight to the voters.[49] In a notable recent example, Democratic Massachusetts Governor Deval Patrick took a lead role in advocating for the legalization of gambling statewide, in part by generating support for the Mashpee Wampanoag Tribe's casino project in Taunton.[50]

State Courts

Presumably out of respect for state sovereignty, IGRA's requirements for tribal-state compacting left it to state governments to decide how to negotiate and approve compacts. As a matter of state law, in most states, the governor negotiates a compact that the legislature ratifies. The sometimes contentious politics of legislative delegation of the authority to negotiate compacts to the executive branch, or a governor's unilateral assumption of that power, have resulted in litigation.[51] State courts have been asked to answer important questions related to the separation of powers and other dimensions of state constitutional law.[52]

Because compacts create new law and policy related to gaming, the courts have held that they "incorporate policy choices reserved for the Legislature."[53] State legislators successfully sued the governor of New Mexico for entering into tribal-state compacts without consulting the legislature.[54] The Supreme Court of Kansas agreed with the state attorney general's contention that the governor lacked the authority to unilaterally negotiate compacts that added to the functions of the state lottery agency.[55] IGRA's lack of direction on the appropriate

49. In California, for example, before the 2003 recall election, Republican gubernatorial candidate Arnold Schwarzenegger ran campaign ads asserting that "it's time for [tribes] to pay their fair share.... Their casinos make billions, yet pay no taxes and virtually nothing to the state." See "AdWatch: Schwarzenegger on Indian Donations, Casino Money," *KCRA News* (Sacramento, CA), May 3, 2004, http://www.thekcrachannel.com/politics/25125701/detail.html (last visited Apr. 2, 2005).

50. See, e.g., George Brennan, "Patrick Stands Firm on Backing Tribe Casino," *Cape Cod Times,* Apr. 3, 2013, http://www.capecodonline.com/apps/pbcs.dll/article?AID=/20130410/NEWS/304100343/-1/SPECIAL05 (last visited Nov. 1, 2013).

51. See, for example, Florida House of Representatives v. Crist, 990 So.2d 1035, (Fla. 2008); Taxpayers of Michigan Against Gambling v. Michigan, 685 N.W.2d 221 (Mich. 2004); Panzer v. Doyle, 680 N.W.2d 666 (Wis. 2004); Saratoga County Chamber of Commerce v. Pataki, 798 N.E. 2d 1047 (N.Y. 2003).

52. Kevin Washburn, "Recurring Problems in Indian Gaming," *Wyoming Law Review* 1 (2001): 437–40; see also Rand, "Why State Law Matters."

53. Saratoga County Chamber of Commerce v. Pataki, 798 N.E.2d 1047 (N.Y. 2003); Kramer, "Current Issues," 332.

54. New Mexico ex rel. Clark v. Johnson, 904 P.2d 11 (N.M. 1995).

55. Kansas ex rel. Stephan v. Finney, 836 P.2d 1169 (Kan. 1992).

and legitimate role of state government in negotiating and enacting compacts has led to litigation of otherwise valid compact agreements. In one case, *Panzer v. Doyle*, the Wisconsin Supreme Court invalidated tribal-state compacts negotiated by the governor on state constitutional law grounds.[56] The Florida Supreme Court followed suit, ruling that the governor's unilateral execution of a compact with the Seminole Tribe usurped the legislature's authority.[57] As the courts decide questions of state constitutional and statutory law, tribes, who may not even be party to a state lawsuit, have been forced to forgo casino revenue to avoid coming under federal scrutiny for illegal gaming operations.[58]

Localities

Local governments do not have any direct role in the tribal-state compacting process under IGRA. Nevertheless, non-tribal communities on or near reservations may experience costs associated with tribal casinos, such as road maintenance and increased demands on law enforcement and emergency services, as well as benefits, such as funding for local government agencies and local economic development. Accordingly, local officials may pressure the state to include compact provisions that address such costs or ensure such benefits, or, in some cases, may encourage the state to disallow tribal gaming altogether.[59]

"Off-reservation gaming" is receiving considerable attention at the state and local levels, as we discuss in Chapter 6. Under the most controversial exception to IGRA's general prohibition against gaming on newly acquired lands, IGRA requires the Interior Secretary to make a determination that gaming is in the best interest of the tribe and tribal members and would not harm surrounding communities. The Secretary makes this determination after consulting with the

---

56. 680 N.W.2d 666 (Wis. 2004). The court's decision included a detailed examination of the state legislature's statutory delegation of authority to the governor to negotiate and enter into tribal-state compacts. Although the delegation itself was not unconstitutional under state law, the court concluded that a number of the compact's provisions exceeded the authority of either the governor or the legislature under the state constitution. Id. at 686–71.

57. Florida House of Representatives v. Crist, 999 So. 2d 601 (Fla. 2008); see also Erik L. Coccia, Note, "The Governor Lacks the Authority to Unilaterally Bind the State to a Compact in Contravention of State Public Policy," *Rutgers Law Journal* 40 (2009): 841.

58. Washburn, "Recurring Problems in Indian Gaming," 430–31. See also Matthew L.M. Fletcher, "The Comparative Rights of Indispensable Sovereigns," *Gonzaga Law Review* 40 (2004– 2005): 1–126 (discussing several tribal gaming cases in the context of the compulsory joinder rule).

59. IGRA authorizes tribes to use gaming revenue "to help fund operations of local government agencies." 25 U.S.C. § 2710(b)(2)(B).

tribe, officials of nearby tribes, the state, and local officials.[60] Local governments, therefore, play an important role in generating the political support necessary for tribes to acquire trust land under this exception, with regard to both the Secretary's determination and the governor's concurrence.[61]

Federal Government

Executive Officials

Under IGRA, the Secretary of the Interior plays an integral role in determining the outcome of tribal-state compact negotiations. IGRA authorizes a tribe to sue in federal court if the state fails to negotiate a compact in good faith.[62] If court-imposed negotiation between the tribe and the state does not result in a settlement, the court will appoint a mediator to draft a compact. If the state rejects that compact, the Secretary will draft an administrative "compact."[63] Whether a tribal-state compact in the first place is negotiated amicably or as a result of mediation pursuant to legal action, it is submitted to the Secretary for approval.[64] IGRA also authorizes the Interior Secretary to sue in federal court to enforce compact provisions emplaced through a tribe's suit against a state.[65] After *Seminole Tribe*, the Secretary promulgated regulations that mimic IGRA's process for the issuance of an administrative compact.[66] The Secretary's power to formally recognize tribes and to take land into trust for the benefit of a tribe also may come into play in compact negotiations, whether as bargaining chips used by either side or as necessary prerequisites.

As with other responsibilities assigned to the Interior Secretary under IGRA, and as with other federal officials charged with enforcing Indian gaming laws, the stance of the current presidential administration toward legalized gambling in general and Indian gaming in particular, and toward tribes as a matter of federal Indian policy, may influence outcomes related to tribal-state compacts and Class III gaming. Not only is the Secretary appointed by the

60. See id. §2719(b)(1)(A); see also Office of Indian Gaming Management, "Checklist for Gaming Acquisitions, Gaming-Related Acquisitions, and IGRA Section 20 Determinations" (Mar. 2005) (describing considerations relevant to determination of whether gaming on newly acquired lands would be detrimental to surrounding communities).

61. Light and Rand, "Are All Bets Off?"

62. 25 U.S.C. §2710(d)(7)(B)(I).

63. Id. §§2710(d)(7)(B)(iv)–(vii).

64. See id. §2710(d)(8).

65. Id. §2710(d)(7)(A).

66. 25 C.F.R. pt. 291. We discuss the regulations, as well as challenges to the Secretary's role, in Chapter 4.

President, as are the U.S. Attorney General, the U.S. Attorneys, and the NIGC Chair, but executive policy may directly or indirectly affect executive officials' actions concerning compacts and casino-style gaming. The Bureau of Indian Affairs, led by an Assistant Secretary within the Interior Department, plays a significant role in shaping and executing tribal gaming policy.[67]

Congress

In recent years, the Senate Committee on Indian Affairs has held numerous hearings regarding Indian gaming. The general focus of the hearings has centered on the effective regulation of tribal gaming, the potential impacts of legalizing online gaming, and the operations and authority of the National Indian Gaming Commission.[68] Beyond hearings, Congress has exercised little formal oversight over the NIGC; however, Indian gaming has been the object of close scrutiny by a number of senators and representatives who have introduced proposed amendments to IGRA. Some bills would have imposed additional fees or taxes on tribal gaming operations.[69] Many proposals would have increased state and local authority over the tribal-state compacting process. Several bills mandated local participation in compact negotiations.[70] Other proposals would have imposed additional restrictions on determinations of whether newly acquired trust land can be used for Indian gaming.[71] Although no at-

---

67. The current Assistant Secretary for Indian Affairs is Kevin K. Washburn. His recent significant decisions include approvals of off-reservation casinos in Kenosha, Wisconsin, for the Menominee Indian Tribe, and in Braman, Oklahoma, for the Kaw Nation; and the disapproval of the initial compact negotiated by Democratic Massachusetts Governor Deval Patrick and the Mashpee Wampanoag Tribe. See Office of Indian Gaming, http://www.bia.gov/WhatWeDo/ServiceOverview/Gaming/index.htm (last visited Nov. 1, 2013).

68. For example, in the last two years, the Senate's Indian Affairs Committee has held oversight hearings on Regulation of Tribal Gaming: From Brick & Mortar to the Internet (July 26, 2012); The U.S. Department of Justice Opinion on Internet Gaming: What's at Stake for Tribes (Feb. 9, 2012); The Future of Internet Gaming: What's at Stake for Tribes (Nov. 17, 2011); and Enforcing the Indian Gaming Regulatory Act: The Role of the National Indian Gaming Commission and Tribes as Regulators (July 28, 2011). The Indian Affairs Committee also has taken up related issues with impacts beyond gaming, such as the impact of the *Carcieri* decision on tribal trust lands. See generally United States Senate Committee on Indian Affairs, "Hearings & Meetings," http://www.indian.senate.gov/hearings/hearing.cfm (last visited Mar. 31, 2014).

69. See S. 1529, 108th Congress (July 31, 2003).

70. See, for instance, H.R. 1364, 104th Congress (Mar. 30, 1995) (requiring community approval for Class III gaming).

71. See, for example, S. 477, 113th Congress (Mar. 6, 2013); S. 711, 112th Congress (Apr. 8, 2011); H.R. 2353, 109th Congress (May 17, 2005); H.R. 2323, 103d Congress (May 27,

tempt to amend IGRA has yet been successful, such bills regularly are introduced and debated.

Federal Courts

As we discuss in Chapter 3, IGRA authorizes three federal causes of action in relation to compacting: a tribe may sue a state for failing to negotiate in good faith, the Interior Secretary may sue to enforce compact provisions resulting from a tribe's suit, and either a tribe or a state may sue to halt casino-style gaming that violates an existing compact.[72] A U.S. Attorney also may initiate a criminal prosecution or forfeiture action related to Class III gaming, such as confiscating slot machines operated by a tribe without a valid tribal-state compact. Through these causes of action, as we detail in Chapter 4, the federal courts have handed down numerous decisions interpreting IGRA's tribal-state compact provisions, including the scope of negotiations and the state's good-faith duty. Even after *Seminole Tribe*, the federal courts continue to influence compact negotiations by deciding cases brought by tribes to enforce the state's good-faith duty in which the state has consented to federal jurisdiction, as well as the other types of actions authorized under IGRA and other federal law. These cases have had the practical effect of establishing the parameters for compact negotiations and resultant compacts.

Associations and Organizations

The high stakes of Indian gaming, as well as IGRA's framework for tribal-state compact negotiations, have created a political environment in which non-governmental associations and organizations play critical lobbying, advocacy, and educational roles. As tribal gaming has grown and spread, both critics and proponents have disseminated information about Indian gaming's costs and benefits and sought to influence policy outcomes.

Industry Associations and Corporations

As a peak or umbrella advocacy organization, the National Indian Gaming Association (NIGA) represents the interests of gaming tribes throughout the United States. Founded in 1985—before *Cabazon* was decided or IGRA was

---

1993). Senate Bill 477, introduced by Senator Dianne Feinstein (D-CA) and titled the "Tribal Gaming Eligibility Act," would have required a tribe to demonstrate both "direct modern" and "direct aboriginal" connections to land on which the tribe intends to conduct gaming.

   72. 25 U.S.C. §2710(d)(7)(A).

enacted—NIGA is an information clearinghouse and a legislative and policy resource for its 184 tribal nation members, other tribes, policymakers, and the general public. NIGA also monitors legislative and regulatory activity, sponsors and conducts research, including annual reports on tribal gaming's economic impacts, and facilitates sharing of information and experience among tribes and tribal gaming facilities. Its associate members from the industry include vendors, advertisers, publishers, architecture and engineering firms, and tax, insurance, auditing, accounting, and business planning firms. With particular emphasis on Indian gaming policy, NIGA's mission focuses on advancing general tribal welfare, economic self-sufficiency, and self-determination, with the goal of maintaining and protecting tribal sovereignty.[73]

Throughout the United States, a number of state and regional Indian gaming associations, such as the California Nations Indian Gaming Association, whose membership represents more than 60 gaming tribes, or the Great Plains Indian Gaming Association, representing 24 tribes in a seven-state region, similarly serve as information clearinghouses, engage in public relations, lobby policymakers, and advise or represent gaming tribes as they negotiate or renegotiate gaming compacts.[74]

Commercial gaming interests find some common cause with tribes as they disseminate information to the public and policymakers about gambling's economic or social benefits, seek to dispel perceived myths about its costs, and lobby for favorable regulatory environments and policy outcomes. For example, the American Gaming Association (AGA), the trade organization for the commercial casino industry, represents casino operators, equipment manufacturers, suppliers, and vendors. Its mission is to educate and advocate on behalf of commercial casino gaming interests. The release of the AGA's annual report on the state of the gaming industry is an event keenly anticipated by insiders. The AGA's former director characterized the association as "a truth squad of sorts" in its efforts to fend off anti-gaming advocates and lobby federal regulators and policymakers.[75] While the AGA represents the interests of the entire commer-

---

73. National Indian Gaming Association (NIGA), "All About NIGA," http://www.indiangaming.org/info/index.shtml (last visited Mar. 31, 2014). Ernest L. Stevens, Jr., is the current Chair of NIGA. Stevens, an enrolled member of the Oneida Nation of Wisconsin, serves as NIGA's official spokesperson. Id. His predecessor, Rick Hill, also a member of the Oneida Nation of Wisconsin, served as NIGA Chair from 1993 to 2001.

74. See California Nations Indian Gaming Association, http://www.cniga.com/ (last visited Nov. 13, 2013); Great Plains Indian Gaming Association, http://www.gpiga.com (last visited Nov. 13, 2013).

75. See Frank J. Fahrenkopf, Jr., "The Status of Gaming in the United States," reprinted in Robert M. Jarvis et al., *Gaming Law Cases and Materials* (Newark, NJ: Matthew Bender

cial gaming industry, publicly traded companies such as MGM Resorts International and Caesars Entertainment seek to maximize investor return and shareholder value in a highly competitive marketplace.[76] Caesars, for instance, uses market research, public relations, and lobbying to distribute its views on gambling and responsible gaming to the public and policymakers. Casino magnates, such as Sheldon Adelson (Sands Hotel and Casino, Venetian Las Vegas, and Venetian Macau), Kirk Kerkorian (Las Vegas' Caesars Palace and MGM Grand), and Steve Wynn (Las Vegas' Mirage, Bellagio, Treasure Island, rebuilt Golden Nugget, and luxury Wynn and Encore Las Vegas and Wynn Macau), also maintain a high profile and their own lobbying and public relations operations.

The corporate governance structures, investor and shareholder profit motivations, and legal, political, and regulatory environments for commercial casino operations dramatically differ from those of tribal governments and tribally run casinos. Although they share similar educational and advocacy goals with tribes and tribal gaming associations, commercial gambling interests see tribal casinos as economic competitors and act accordingly in the marketplace as well as in political and policymaking arenas.[77]

Organizations and Citizen Groups

National and state organizations, along with citizen and community groups, socialize political conflicts over Indian gaming by bringing them into the public eye and making policymakers aware of constituent viewpoints. Such groups shape the political environment in which tribal-state compacts are negotiated and enforced. As a practical matter, such groups typically oppose gambling; fewer groups, especially citizen or community groups, organize in support of gaming.

Some organizations focus on education and addressing the negative effects generally associated with legalized gambling, particularly problem and pathological gambling.[78] A number of national or state advocacy groups, organized

---

& Company, 2003), 9–15; see also generally American Gaming Association (AGA), http://www.americangaming.org/ (last visited Nov. 13, 2013).

76. See MGM Resorts International, http://www.mgmresorts.com/ (last visited Nov. 13, 2013); Caesars Entertainment, http://www.caesars.com/corporate/ (last visited Nov. 13, 2013).

77. See, for example, Mark Arsenault, "Suffolk Downs, Revere Set to Reopen Casino Talks," *Boston Globe,* Nov. 12, 2013 (describing competition among Wynn Resorts, Hard Rock International, Caesars Entertainment, and the Mashantucket Pequots' Foxwoods Resort Casino to obtain a gaming license for the Suffolk Downs racetrack, part of the newly legalized Massachusetts gaming market).

78. See, for example, National Center for Responsible Gaming, "About NCRG," http://www.ncrg.org/about-ncrg (last visited Nov. 13, 2013) (focusing, as the American Gaming

around broader policy issues, adopt anti-gambling stances.[79] Other groups oppose the expansion of gaming generally and often tribal gaming specifically as a manifestation of state public policy. The California Coalition Against Gambling Expansion, for example, "seeks to prevent the moral, economic, scientific and social problems caused by gambling," while the Granite State Coalition Against Expanded Gambling is "dedicated … to a single mission: halt gambling expansion in New Hampshire."[80] California's largest and most powerful gaming-related citizens group, Stand Up for California!, takes specific policy stances with regard to tribal gaming:

> In Tribal State compacts we seek stringent regulations, patron and employee protections, environmental concerns and judicially enforceable mitigation agreements with affected local governments. At the federal level we are seeking amendments to the Indian Gaming Regulatory Act and changes in policy and administrative rules that enhance regulatory oversight and give voice to affected parties in the location, size and scope of tribal gaming developments.[81]

Some groups couch their resistance to Indian gaming in the allegation that tribal sovereignty unfairly disadvantages state and local governments. Upstate Citizens for Equality, for instance, opposes the proposed expansion of Indian gaming in New York State on the basis that "there is no reference to absolute Indian sovereignty in the U.S. Constitution."[82]

Ad hoc citizen groups may form in response to tribal efforts to open or expand a specific casino; other anti-gambling organizations have more permanent foundations and funding. Although not all citizen or community

---

Association's affiliated charity, on funding scientific research on pathological and youth gambling); National Council on Problem Gambling, "About NCPG," http://www.ncpgambling.org/ (last visited Nov. 13, 2013) (advocating for treatment programs and services for problem gambling).

79. See, for instance, Center for Arizona Policy, "Our Issues," http://www.azpolicy.org/html/ourissues.html (last visited Mar. 25, 2005) (supporting restrictions on Indian gaming based in part on affiliation with Focus on the Family).

80. See California Coalition Against Gambling Expansion, http://ccage.org (last visited Nov. 13, 2013); Granite State Coalition Against Expanded Gambling, http://www.noslots.com (last visited Nov. 13, 2013).

81. Stand Up for California!, "Who We Are," http://standupca.org/about-us (last visited Nov. 13, 2013).

82. Upstate Citizens for Equality, "Sovereignty," http://www.upstate-citizens.org/sovereignty.htm (last visited Nov. 13, 2013).

organizations are entirely opposed to Indian gaming, many resist its expansion and favor more extensive regulation of tribal casinos, revenue sharing with state and local governments, and increased resources to educate the public about the perceived social ills related to gambling. By orchestrating elaborate public-relations campaigns, sponsoring voter initiatives, organizing get-out-the-vote efforts, conducting town-hall meetings, testifying before governing boards, agencies, and commissions, and lobbying policymakers, anti-gaming groups have become a vital political force at the state and local levels.

Consultants, Think Tanks, and Institutes

Research on tribal gaming's social and economic impacts has proliferated with the accelerated growth of the Indian gaming industry.[83] Studies vary in origin and authorship, research design and methodology, intended audience, and, of course, quality. Some studies are commissioned to influence public opinion and policymakers at a point in time, such as when a tribal-state compact is on the horizon, for instance; others purport to employ scientific or scholarly neutrality in service of greater knowledge about legalized gambling generally or tribal gaming specifically. Regardless, such research impacts the policy environment for Indian gaming.

As the National Gambling Impact Study Commission (NGISC) noted in its final report, publicly commissioned or otherwise independently conducted rigorous studies that attempt to assess the impacts of legalized gambling are surprisingly rare.[84] By contrast, analyses of Indian gaming's economic impacts conducted by private consulting firms are relatively common.[85] Many con-

---

83. For an annotated bibliography of many gambling impact studies, see Leigh Gardner, Joseph P. Kalt, and Katherine A. Spilde, *Annotated Bibliography: The Social and Economic Impacts of Tribal and Other Gaming* (Cambridge: Harvard Project on American Indian Economic Development, 2005), http://www.hpaied.org (last visited Nov. 13, 2013).

84. NGISC, *Final Report*, 1-6 to 1-8, 6-14.

85. See, for example, John M. Clapp, et al., *The Economic Impacts of the Foxwoods High Stakes Bingo and Casino on New London County and Surrounding Areas* (Arthur W. Wright and Associates, 1993); Coopers and Lybrand, LLP, *Analysis of the Economic Impact of the Oneida Nation's Presence in Oneida and Madison Counties* (1995); Gerald I. Eyrich, *Economic Impact Analysis: Cabazon Band of Mission Indians* (Constituent Strategies, Inc., n.d.); Stephan A. Hoenack and Gary Renz, *Effects of the Indian-Owned Casinos on Self-Generating Economic Development in Non-Urban Areas of Minnesota* (Plymouth, MN: Stephen A. Hoenack and Associates, 1995); James M. Klas and Matthew S. Robinson, *Economic Benefits of Indian Gaming in the State of Minnesota* (Minneapolis: Marquette Advisors, 1997); James M. Klas and Matthew S. Robinson, *Economic Benefits of Indian Gaming in the State of Oregon* (Minneapolis: Marquette Advisors, 1996).

sultants are retained by states and localities.[86] Some studies are conducted for tribes or under the auspices of tribal gaming associations.[87] A series of prominent annual reports on the status of the Indian gaming industry has been published by an affiliate of an economic consulting firm with support by gaming tribes in the form of confidential information.[88] Research also may be sponsored or conducted by commercial gambling industry associations or corporations.[89] Policy-oriented think tanks have published a number of studies of Indian gaming. The Wisconsin Policy Research Institute, for instance, is a pro-business think tank whose stated mission is to promote governmental accountability. The Institute has commissioned a number of cost-benefit studies of tribal gaming's economic and social impacts on the state of Wisconsin and its residents.[90]

---

86. See, for instance, Lincoln (NE) Human Services Administration, *Socioeconomic Indicators of Legalized Gambling in Lincoln/Lancaster County, Nebraska* (2004); Michael K. Evans, *The Economic Impact of the Indian Gaming Industry in Wisconsin and Potential Impact of Modified Compact Terms* (Boca Raton, FL: Evans, Carroll & Associates, 2002); W.C. Franklin, *Along the Mississippi* (Forum for Applied Research and Public Policy, 1996); Minnesota Planning [Agency], *Minnesota Gambling* (1993) (prepared for Minnesota Department of Administration); Washington State Council on Problem Gambling, *Adult Gambling Prevalence in Washington State* (May 14, 1999) (funded by Washington State Lottery).

87. See, for instance, National Indian Gaming Association, *The Economic Impact of Indian Gaming in 2009* (2010); Jonathan Taylor, *The Economic Impact of Tribal Government Gaming in Arizona* (2012) (prepared for the Arizona Indian Gaming Association); Beacon Economics, *Measuring the Economic Impact of Indian Gaming on California* (2012) (prepared for the California Nations Indian Gaming Association); Robert Whelan & Carsten Jensen, *The Contributions of Indian Gaming to Oregon's Economy in 2011 and 2010* (2012) (prepared for the Oregon Tribal Gaming Alliance); Jonathan Taylor, *Economic & Fiscal Effects of Indian Gaming in Washington 2010* (2012) (prepared for the Washington Indian Gaming Association).

88. See, for example, Alan Meister, *Indian Gaming Industry Report, 2012 Ed.* (Newton, MA: Casino City Press, 2014). Meister's aggregate national gaming revenue estimates are similar to those of the NIGC and NIGA; his widely cited studies, however, take the unprecedented step of attempting to isolate Indian gaming's economic impacts on a state-by-state basis. He relies on a number of data sources, including publicly available information and such confidential sources as tribes, casinos, and gaming associations, and uses a proprietary estimation model as well as other estimates. See id. at 4–6.

89. See, for example, Casino Association of Indiana, *Growing With Indiana: Positive Impact Report* (1998); Jeremy Margolis, *Casinos and Crime: An Analysis of the Evidence* (1997) (prepared for the AGA); Charles Leven, Don Phares, and Claude Louishomme, *The Economic Impact of Gaming in Missouri* (1998) (prepared for business association Civic Progress); Harrah's Entertainment, Inc., *Profile of the American Casino Gambler* (2004).

90. These studies consistently find that Indian casinos cost the state dearly in terms of lost or substituted revenue and social ills such as crime and bankruptcy. Institute affiliates have argued that existing revenue-sharing agreements should be renegotiated so tribes would

A handful of institutes with university affiliations conduct or sponsor research related to tribal gaming. The Institute for the Study of Tribal Gaming Law and Policy, which we co-founded in 2001 as a component of the Northern Plains Indian Law Center at the University of North Dakota School of Law and as the first academic institute dedicated to tribal gaming, serves as an information clearinghouse and conducts scholarly research on Indian gaming with an interdisciplinary focus on intergovernmental relations and the legal, political, social, and economic dimensions of Indian gaming.[91] The University of Nevada, Reno's Institute for the Study of Gambling and Commercial Gaming also was the first academically affiliated program of its kind in the United States. As a platform for academic studies of gambling-related issues that include but do not focus specifically on Indian gaming, the Institute administers grants, publishes scholarly work, and serves as an information clearinghouse.[92] The University of Nevada, Las Vegas Center for Gaming Research is a significant hub for reports, papers, exhibits, and events related to scholarly analysis of gambling and gaming.[93] Affiliates of the Harvard Project on American Indian Economic Development have published a number of prominent studies or sponsored advisory research on the economic impacts of Indian gaming on tribes and surrounding communities.[94]

---

pay their "fair share" to the state. See, for example, William N. Thompson and Robert Schmidt, *Not Exactly "A Fair Share": Native American Casinos and Revenue Sharing in Wisconsin* (Wisconsin Policy Research Institute, 2002); William N. Thompson, Richard Gazel, and Dan Rickman, *Casinos and Crime in Wisconsin: What's the Connection?* (Wisconsin Policy Research Institute, 1996); William N. Thompson, Richard Gazel, and Dan Rickman, *The Economic Impact of Native American Gaming in Wisconsin* (Wisconsin Policy Research Institute, 1995); William N. Thompson, Richard Gazel, and Dan Rickman, *The Social Costs of Gambling in Wisconsin* (Wisconsin Policy Research Institute, 1996), all available at Wisconsin Policy Research Institute, "Gambling," http://www.wpri.org/gambling.htm (last visited Mar. 27, 2005). For other "think tank" studies, see, for example, Paul Davies, *Stacked Deck: Inside the Politics of New York's Dishonest Casino Plan* (Institute for American Values, 2013); Melissa Schettini Kearney, *The Economic Winners and Losers of Legalized Gambling* (Brookings Institution, 2005).

91. See Institute for the Study of Tribal Gaming Law and Policy, http://law.und.edu/npilc/gaming/index.cfm (last visited Nov. 14, 2013).

92. See Institute for the Study of Gambling and Commercial Gaming, http://www.unr.edu/gaming (last visited Nov. 14, 2013). Founding Institute Director and pioneering gambling studies scholar William R. Eadington edited an important early volume on tribal gaming. See William R. Eadington, ed., *Indian Gaming and the Law*, 3d ed. (Reno: Institute for the Study of Gaming and Commercial Gaming, 2004).

93. See Center for Gaming Research, http://gaming.unlv.edu/ (last visited Jan. 31, 2014).

94. See generally Harvard Project on American Indian Economic Development, http://

Indian Gaming and the Ballot

As tribal-state compact negotiations have become highly politicized, especially after *Seminole Tribe*, the political players involved have employed a number of strategies to advance their policy preferences. This is particularly true of tribal governments, which have become increasingly active and influential players in federal, state, and local political arenas.

Lacking formal representation in Congress or state governments, tribes are uniquely positioned in the American political system. Their well-being depends, in many ways, on the goodwill of non-Indian politicians and non-tribal governments to recognize and act on tribal interests. Indian gaming is changing the nature of tribal involvement in state politics.[95] As the political terrain for tribal-state compacting has shifted following *Seminole Tribe*, tribes increasingly have mobilized resources and pursued such sophisticated political strategies as lobbying, making hard and soft campaign contributions, and coalition-building through public relations campaigns in support of or opposition to gaming-related ballot initiatives.[96]

Lobbying and Campaign Contributions

Tribes lobby and contribute to campaigns through efforts and spending of individual tribes and intertribal organizations, such as the National Congress

---

www.hpaied.org (last visited Nov. 14, 2013). Some of these studies were prepared on behalf of various tribal gaming interests. See, for instance, Katherine A. Spilde, Jonathan B. Taylor and Kenneth W. Grant II, *Social and Economic Analysis of Tribal Government Gaming in Oklahoma* (2002) (commissioned by the Oklahoma Indian Gaming Association).

95. See, for instance, Steven Andrew Light, "Indian Gaming and Intergovernmental Relations: The Constraints of Tribal Interest Group Behavior," in Hansen and Skopek, *The New Politics of Indian Gaming*, 135–59; Rand, "Why State Law Matters"; David Wilkins, "An Inquiry Into Indigenous Political Participation: Implications for Tribal Sovereignty," *Kansas Journal of Law and Public Policy* 9 (2000): 733; see also W. Dale Mason, "Tribes and States: A New Era in Intergovernmental Affairs," *Publius* 28 (1998): 111–30.

96. See Richard Witmer and Frederick J. Boehmke, American Indian Political Incorporation: Interest Groups and Public Policy, 1998–2002, unpublished manuscript presented at the Annual Meeting of the Midwest Political Science Association in Chicago, Illinois (Apr. 2004) (describing tribal "interest-group" behavior); Jeffrey Ashley, Tribal Use of Public Relations to Shape Public Policy, unpublished manuscript presented at the Annual Meeting of the Midwest Political Science Association in Chicago, Illinois (Apr. 2004) (discussing how tribes in Arizona successfully publicized a pro-Indian gaming ballot initiative as promoting tribal self-reliance).

of American Indians, NIGA, and regional Indian gaming associations.[97] In the 2007 and 2008 state and national campaign cycles, tribes, particularly in California, were among the largest donors. The Pechanga Band of Luiseño Indians, the Morongo Band of Mission Indians, and the Agua Caliente Band of Cahuilla Indians, along with the organization Tribes for Fair Play, spent a combined total of nearly $130 million on state and national political campaigns. All three tribes had significant gaming interests at stake.[98] While MGM Resorts International, Harrah's Entertainment, and Station Casinos led the top ten casino industry contributors to federal candidates in the 2008 election cycle, six of the remaining top donors were tribes.[99]

One of the challenges for tribes is the perception, still fueled by lingering fallout of the Jack Abramoff lobbying scandal, that tribal political contributions are suspect. Some candidates have refused to accept donations from tribes, notably including U.S. Senator John McCain (D-Ariz.) and, as a gubernatorial candidate in California in 2003, Arianna Huffington called a tribe's donation to her opponent "legalized bribery."[100] More recently, Wisconsin's Republican Governor Scott Walker discouraged a tribe with a proposed off-reservation casino project from contributing to his re-election campaign.[101]

At the same time, numerous other groups also lobby and spend in direct as well as indirect opposition to Indian gaming. From lobbying to campaign contributions to public relations campaigns, commercial and non-tribal gaming interests—as well as community groups and similar associations—are using identical political strategies to sway public opinion and influence policymakers. In pursuit of a legal and regulatory environment that is maximally bene-

---

97. For thorough treatments of tribes' political strategies, focusing on case studies, see generally Hansen and Skopek, *The New Politics of Indian Gaming*; W. Dale Mason, *Indian Gaming: Tribal Sovereignty and American Politics* (Norman, OK: University of Oklahoma Press, 2000).

98. See Rob Capriccioso, "Tribes Among Biggest Campaign Contributors," *Indian Country Today* (Mar. 22, 2011), http://indiancountrytodaymedianetwork.com/2011/03/22/tribes-among-biggest-campaign-contributors-23876 (last visited Nov. 22, 2013).

99. The Viejas Band of Kumeyaay Indians, San Manuel Band of Mission Indians, Pechanga Band of Luiseno Mission Indians, Chickasaw Nation, Morongo Band of Mission Indians, and Mississippi Band of Choctaw Indians, along with the National Thoroughbred Racing Association, complete the top ten contributors. Center for Responsive Politics, "Casinos/Gambling: Top Contributors to Federal Candidates, Parties, and Outside Groups (2008 Election Cycle)," http://www.opensecrets.org/industries/contrib.php?ind=N07&cycle=2008 (last visited Nov. 22, 2013).

100. See Capriccioso, "Tribes Among Biggest Campaign Contributors."

101. Associated Press, "Walker Discourages Campaign Donations From Tribes," (Nov. 11, 2013).

ficial to casino operations, and in an increasingly crowded market for casino patrons, gaming tribes and commercial gambling interests find common cause on some issues and are in competition on others. In New Mexico, for example, following former Republican Governor Gary Johnson's election, both commercial and charitable gaming interests lobbied the state legislature to remove tribes' "unfair advantage" in operating casino-style games, while organizations such as the New Mexico Coalition Against Gambling and the Rocky Mountain Synod Evangelical Lutheran Church in America lobbied against legalized gambling altogether in the state.[102]

Referenda and Initiatives

Facing increased economic competition from tribal casinos, commercial gambling interests, such as horse and dog racetrack owners, have sponsored voter initiatives in Arizona and elsewhere that would expand commercial casino-style gaming or curtail tribal gaming. Tribes have waged extensive public relations campaigns to defeat such initiatives and referenda. They also have fought fire with fire by sponsoring competing initiatives and building broad support coalitions for gaming as a tribal economic development strategy.[103] As frequently is the case, events in California clearly illustrate recent trends.

In 1998, following unsuccessful compact negotiations with Republican Governor Pete Wilson and faced with an unfavorable federal court decision in *Rumsey Indian Rancheria of Wintun Indians v. Wilson*,[104] 40 tribes in California collected some 800,000 signatures to put casino-style gaming to a popular vote. The referendum, known as Proposition 5, guaranteed that any tribe in California eligible to game under IGRA would be allowed to conduct certain types of Class III games. The tribes' "Yes on 5" initiative campaign faced well-funded opposition from a broad range of interests: Wilson, Nevada casinos, organized labor, California's non-tribal gambling industry, and a number of anti-gambling groups.[105] The campaign's official name, "Californians for Indian Self-Reliance," communicated a broad and effective message about tribal self-

---

102. Mason, *Indian Gaming*, 103–10.

103. Ashley, Tribal Use of Public Relations.

104. 64 F.3d 1250 (9th Cir. 1994).

105. Mason, "Tribes, Casinos, and Hardball Politics," 369; Chad M. Gordon, "From Hope to Realization of Dreams: Proposition 5 and California Indian Gaming," in Angela Mullis and David Kamper, eds., *Indian Gaming: Who Wins?* (Los Angeles: UCLA American Indian Studies Center, 2000), 6–7; see also Jeff Cummins, "Lobbying Strategies and Campaign Contributions: The Impact on Indian Gaming in California," in Hansen and Skopek, *The New Politics of Indian Gaming*, 38–56.

sufficiency to the voting public that resonated across the political spectrum.[106] Led by the "Coalition Against Unregulated Gaming," opponents cast tribal casinos as an undesirable industry that caused pollution and deprived non-tribal workers of employment benefits. In response, the tribes focused on exposing Nevada casinos as one of the referendum's primary opponents and highlighting both poor reservation living conditions and the positive socioeconomic inroads made by Indian gaming.[107]

Proposition 5 easily passed, with 63% of the vote. The initiative campaign was the most expensive in U.S. history: together, tribes and their opponents spent over $100 million.[108] Less than a year later, however, the California Supreme Court struck down Proposition 5 on the ground that it violated the state constitution's prohibition against Las Vegas-style casinos.[109] The affected tribes acted quickly and were successful both in negotiating compacts despite the court's decision and in putting Proposition 1A, a proposed state constitutional amendment to allow tribes to conduct casino-style gaming, on the ballot for the next statewide election. After their expensive loss on Proposition 5, the tribes' opponents largely retreated. Proposition 1A passed with an even wider margin in 2000.[110] As Mark Macarro, chair of the Pechanga Band of Luiseno Mission Indians, described the significance of the tribes' successful campaigns,

> For the first time in history, tribes have established what the public policy of a state is, and succeeded in putting a debate forward and having the public side with the tribes in that debate. It seems that tribes no longer have to be relegated to being history's doormats, but can actually engage in public debate and set policy in terms favorable to tribes.[111]

This sentiment was echoed in a more recent context by a lobbyist: "Think about it—the Native Americans who lived in California around the time of the 1849 gold rush were pushed to the brink of genocide. And today, Native Americans

106. Gordon, "From Hope to Realization," 7 ("The notion that voters should help Indians maintain their self-reliance resonated well with liberals, who believe that governments should assist the disadvantaged, and with conservatives, who believe firmly in independence and self-determination.").

107. Mason, "Tribes, Casinos, and Hardball Politics," 369; Gordon, "From Hope to Realization," 7.

108. Id.

109. Hotel Employees and Restaurant Employees Int'l Union v. Davis, 981 P.2d 990 (Cal. 1999).

110. Mason, "Tribes, Casinos, and Hardball Politics," 369; Gordon, "From Hope to Realization," 11.

111. Gordon, "From Hope to Realization," 11.

in that state and throughout the country have become major participants in the political process."[112]

* * *

IGRA established a regulatory scheme for Indian gaming that mandated the negotiation of tribal-state compact agreements with federal oversight. The U.S. Supreme Court's decision in *Seminole Tribe*, which removed tribes' ability to sue states for the failure to negotiate in good faith, created additional political leverage for state policymakers. Over time, a rapidly growing tribal gaming industry has generated considerable attention not only from policymakers, but also from organizations and citizen groups, commercial gaming interests, and associations of gaming tribes. Navigating the post-*Seminole Tribe* political terrain is paramount for many, if not all, tribes with casinos. As the political environment for tribal gaming is complicated by such issues as the spread of revenue-sharing agreements, abrogation of treaty rights, controversies over federal recognition, and tribal land acquisition for off-reservation casinos, tribes are seeking to protect or to advance their interests through the political process.

We turn now to a closer examination of the varied political and legal issues that currently are shaping Indian gaming law and policy.

---

112. Capriccioso, "Tribes Among Biggest Campaign Contributors" (quoting Tom Rodgers, a lobbyist and member of the Blackfeet Tribe).

CHAPTER 6

POLITICAL ISSUES AND POLICY OUTCOMES

Many different officials, agencies, and organizations exercise regulatory authority or otherwise wield influence over Indian gaming law and policy. Although law, in the form of the Indian Gaming Regulatory Act of 1988 (IGRA), federal regulations, and judicial interpretations, is an important force in shaping tribal gaming, so is politics, especially following the U.S. Supreme Court's invalidation of one of IGRA's key enforcement mechanisms in *Seminole Tribe v. Florida*. Both inside and outside IGRA's regulatory framework, policymakers at the federal, state, local, and tribal levels struggle with fashioning and implementing policy on myriad issues related to Indian gaming.

Typically, policymakers engage in a cost-benefit analysis of tribal gaming: do its positive impacts outweigh its negative effects, so that gaming generally should be encouraged within IGRA's existing regulatory scheme, or do the costs outweigh the benefits, such that tribal gaming generally should be discouraged or more stringently regulated? This cost-benefit analysis is complicated by the need to weigh both economic and social impacts, is problematized by politics and ideology, and is made more difficult by a relative dearth of accurate and complete information.[1]

In this chapter, we start by examining the socioeconomic effects of Indian gaming and discuss the importance of full and accurate information to guide policymaking. We then turn to a number of controversial issues in the current public debate over tribal gaming and discuss the roles of law and politics in shaping policy outcomes.

---

1. For a discussion of the concept of an Indian gaming ethic to guide tribal, state, and federal policymaking, see Kathryn R.L. Rand and Steven Andrew Light, "Negotiating a Different Terrain: Morality, Policymaking, and Indian Gaming," in Alan Wolfe and Erik C. Owens, eds., *Gambling: Mapping the American Moral Landscape* (Waco, TX: Baylor University Press, 2009).

SOCIOECONOMIC IMPACTS OF INDIAN GAMING

Economic Impacts

There is no doubt that Indian gaming enterprises impact tribal, local, state, and national economies. The National Indian Gaming Commission (NIGC) reported that the industry generated $26.5 billion in gross revenues in 2009 and 2010, slightly lower than 2008's peak of $26.7 billion after years of steady growth. By 2012, the latest figures available at the time of this writing, tribal gaming revenue appeared to reflect a marginal recovery from the national economic downturn, with a reported record $27.9 billion in gross revenues. The well-respected *Indian Gaming Industry Report*, authored by economist Alan Meister, concluded that Indian gaming was responsible for 679,000 jobs in 2012.[2] But such widely cited figures obscure the complexities of estimating the economic effects of tribal gaming.

Studies of Indian gaming's impacts frequently use cost-benefit analysis to measure whether tribal gaming has net positive or net negative economic impacts on a jurisdiction.[3] This begins with a measure of Indian gaming's direct impacts: the number of jobs created, wages paid to employees, expenditures paid to vendors, and taxes collected, as well as revenue sharing with state and local governments and charitable contributions. Indirect, or ripple, effects of increased business and consumer spending also are estimated, usually through a standardized economic multiplier. This captures the impact of each dollar gen-

---

2. National Indian Gaming Commission (NIGC), *Growth in Indian Gaming Graph 2002–2012*, http://www.nigc.gov/Gaming_Revenue_Reports.aspx (last visited Feb. 4, 2014); see also National Indian Gaming Association (NIGA), *2013 Annual Report*, 31 http://www.indiangaming.org/info/2013_Annual_Report.PDF (last visited Mar. 31, 2014) (estimating 2009 gross revenues from Indian gaming at $26.2 billion); Alan Meister, *Indian Gaming Industry Report, 2014 Ed.* (Newton, MA: Casino City Press, 2014) (estimating 2012 gross revenues at $28.1 billion with a growth rate of two percent over the prior year).

3. Data insufficiencies due to tribes' exemption from public information disclosure requirements, ideological bias, and methodological flaws are among the widely recognized problems with existing studies of the economic impacts of tribal gaming. Critics also assert that many studies weigh incompatible measures of gaming's economic effects against its social costs; such studies also may fail to weigh social benefits against social costs. See Jonathan B. Taylor, Matthew B. Krepps, and Patrick Wang, *The National Evidence on the Socioeconomic Impacts of American Indian Gaming on Non-Indian Communities* (Cambridge, MA: Harvard Project on American Indian Economic Development, Apr. 2000).

erated by tribal gaming as it "ripples" through the local, state, and national economies.

For example, when a tribal casino purchases dinner rolls from a food vendor to stock its all-you-can-eat buffet, the vendor buys the rolls from a supplier, which sources flour from a mill, which obtains wheat from an agri-business, each employing its own workers (who pay payroll and income taxes and also spend their earnings), purchasing its own supplies, and paying its own taxes along the way. Each tribal casino, of course, requires more than dinner rolls to operate. The facility must in the first place be built, complete with access roads, utilities, and other infrastructure; gaming tables, machines, and software must be purchased; on-property hotels and restaurants must be furnished and stocked, and so on. Because typically this infrastructure is sourced from non-tribal businesses—local construction firms, utility companies, national game manufacturers, restaurant suppliers—the indirect effects of tribal casinos are felt most strongly off the reservation.

Thus, tribal gaming's positive economic impacts include job creation and payment of wages, salaries, and benefits; purchases of goods and services; increased income, sales, and property tax revenue; and decreased payment of public entitlements benefits by new job holders both on and off the reservation. At the same time, non-tribal communities and governments may bear significant economic costs of Indian gaming. Potential negative economic costs include law enforcement and fire protection, regulatory expenses, increased traffic and pollution, increased property taxes, and the costs of problem or pathological gambling. Tribal casinos may alter retail spending or employment patterns in ways that take a toll on non-reservation economies, such as an induced substitution effect, in which consumers spend money at tribal casinos that they might otherwise spend elsewhere—that is, off the reservation. Weighing these types of factors, some studies assess whether tribal casinos produce a net positive or net negative impact on a particular economy.[4]

Three national economic impact studies are worth special mention here. The first, conducted by NIGA most recently in 2013, includes in its scope the total positive economic effects of tribal gaming, including anecdotal information about particular tribes. According to NIGA's estimates, tribal government hospitality, restaurant, and entertainment enterprises generated $3.4 billion in total revenue in 2012. Gaming and ancillary businesses generated $6.2 bil-

---

4. See, for example, Katherine A. Spilde, Jonathan B. Taylor, and Kenneth W. Grant II, *Social and Economic Analysis of Tribal Government Gaming in Oklahoma* (Cambridge, MA: Harvard Project on American Indian Economic Development, 2002).

lion in federal taxes and $2.4 billion in state government revenue. In addition, gaming tribes used revenue to build reservation community infrastructure, including schools, hospitals, roads, and water and sewer systems, as well as to fund a variety of government services, such as police and fire protection, education programs, housing, child and elder care, and language, tradition, and cultural preservation initiatives. Tribal governments also invested in economic diversification and made charitable donations.[5]

The second study, Meister's annual *Indian Gaming Industry Report*, provides more detailed economic analysis of tribal gaming than any other regularly published study, including state-by-state figures. The 2014 edition, based on 2012 revenues, found that Indian gaming directly and indirectly resulted in 679,000 jobs, $30 billion in wages, and $7.6 billion in federal, state, and local tax revenue. Tribes also made $1.6 billion in direct payments to federal, state, and local governments. As Meister's study routinely notes, tribal gaming is a highly fragmented industry, with concentrated areas of highly profitable enterprises as well as large pockets of far more modest gaming operations. In 2012, as in prior years, the most lucrative tribal casinos—the top six percent that each generate more than $250 million—accounted for nearly 40% of the industry's total revenue, while the bottom third of tribal gaming operations earned just two percent of total revenue.[6]

Though now significantly more than a decade old, the National Gambling Impact Study Commission's (NGISC) 1999 report on gambling's social and economic impacts remains the most comprehensive government-sponsored attempt to capture the empirical impacts of gambling generally and tribal gaming specifically.[7] At the NGISC's behest, the National Opinion Research Center (NORC) at the University of Chicago used multi-level statistical modeling to systematically examine gaming's socioeconomic effects, comparing both communities with and without a nearby casino as well as the years before and after a casino opened near a sample community. The study found consistent and substantial net benefits and few if any aggregate harms accruing to the

---

5. NIGA, 2013 Annual Report, 28–35.

6. Meister, *Indian Gaming Industry Report, 2014 Ed.*, 3–4, 89. Meister's report routinely includes detailed information about his data and methodology as well.

7. National Gambling Impact Study Commission (NGISC), *Final Report* (1999), http//: govinfo.library.unt.edu/ngisc/reports/finrpt.html (last visited Mar. 26, 2005). The NGISC decried the lack of "impartial, objective research" on legalized gambling, calling for further research by various federal agencies. Id. at 6–14.

communities near which casinos had located.[8] Using the NORC study's data, researchers affiliated with the Harvard Project on American Indian Economic Development found that because communities near tribal casinos tend to be underdeveloped and impoverished, they experience greater socioeconomic gains once casinos are introduced than do comparable communities near non-tribal casinos.[9]

There also are numerous state and regional studies of tribal gaming's economic impacts, often commissioned by state Indian gaming associations. Recent examples include statewide economic impacts of tribal governments and businesses in Oklahoma, conducted by Oklahoma City University's Economic Research & Policy Institute; the annual economic and fiscal impacts of the tribal casino gaming industry in Oregon since 2003, commissioned by the Oregon Tribal Gaming Alliance; and statewide social and economic impacts of Indian gaming in Arizona, commissioned by the Arizona Indian Gaming Association.[10]

Few studies, however, focus on the economic benefits of Indian gaming to tribes, which are most pronounced for reservation-based tribes facing high poverty and unemployment rates. The NORC study, for example, did not include any tribal communities in its sample. Statewide studies rarely isolate effects on tribal communities, focusing instead on impacts affecting the state's residents as a whole. Critics suggest this oversight is important. One of IGRA's primary goals is to encourage tribal economic development and self-sufficiency, and therefore assessing whether Indian gaming is accomplishing this goal requires attention to gaming's economic impacts on tribes.

---

8. Among other economic benefits were a 12% drop in unemployment, a 13% decline in income from income maintenance programs, and a 17% decrease in income from unemployment insurance programs. Dean Gerstein et al., *Gambling Impact and Behavior Study: Report to the National Gambling Impact Study Commission* (Chicago: National Opinion Research Center (NORC), Apr. 1, 1999), 70–71 (hereinafter NORC Report).

9. Taylor, Krepps, and Wang, *National Evidence*, 1. We discuss the study's findings concerning Indian gaming's social impacts below.

10. Steven C. Agee, *The Statewide Impacts of Oklahoma Tribes* (Oklahoma City University Economic Research & Policy Institute, 2012) (estimating the "total contribution of all tribal activities to the state" and finding that the 38 tribes in Oklahoma directly and indirectly created over 87,000 jobs and generated $2.5 billion in state income and $10.8 billion in state production of goods and services); Robert Whelan and Carsten Jensen, *The Contributions of Indian Gaming to Oregon's Economy in 2011 and 2010* (Portland: ECONorthwest, 2012) (estimating the in-state economic impacts of the nine tribal casinos in Oregon as $1.5 billion in output, 13,153 jobs, and $506.9 million in wages and benefits); Jonathan B. Taylor, *The Economic Impact of Tribal Government Gaming in Arizona* (Sarasota, FL: Taylor Policy Group, 2012) (estimating that Indian gaming in Arizona is responsible for over 22,000 jobs and nearly $1 billion in economic impacts).

American Indians, particularly those living on reservations, face extraordinarily high poverty and unemployment rates. When IGRA was enacted, 60% of those on South Dakota's Pine Ridge Reservation lived in poverty, and nearly 90% were unemployed.[11] Against this and similar baselines, Indian gaming may lead to marked economic improvements for many tribes. Tribal gaming revenue generates direct impacts—sales, wages, jobs, and taxes— that are virtually unassailable net positives for tribal communities. The ripple effects induced by gaming revenue further multiply its benefits to tribes. Tribal governments also use gaming revenue to fund basic community infrastructure and to provide essential public services to tribal members, improving reservation quality of life with both quantifiable and qualifiable benefits. As tribes use gaming revenue to leverage diversified economic development, tribal enterprises generate additional revenue, jobs, and other benefits.

By contrast, the economic "costs" of Indian gaming to tribes mostly take the form of lessened economic benefits—a "but-for" effect. The preexisting underdeveloped condition of many reservation economies minimizes positive multiplier effects, as most vendors from which tribes purchase goods and services are located off-reservation. Reservation communities typically lack the physical, technological, legal, and regulatory infrastructure necessary to support a business development environment.[12] Further, revenue sharing with state and local governments directly siphons off gaming revenue. And where tribes have chosen to make per capita payments, which benefit individual tribal members, tribal government revenue decreases.

Social Impacts

Like Indian gaming's economic impacts, its social effects may be positive or negative and accrue to tribal and non-tribal communities alike. The three most frequently cited and studied social impacts of Indian gaming are problem and pathological gambling, crime, and reservation quality of life.

---

11. See U.S. Census Bureau, *Social and Economic Characteristics, American Indians and Native Alaska Areas* (1990), https://www.census.gov/geo/reference/pdfs/GARM/Ch5GARM.pdf (last visited Apr. 1, 2014).

12. See, e.g., Donald Laverdure, Deputy Assistant Secretary, Office of Assistant Secretary-Indian Affairs, Statement Before the U.S. Senate Committee on Indian Affairs (Jan. 28, 2010), http://www.indian.senate.gov/sites/default/files/upload/files/DonaldLaverduretestimony.pdf (addressing "chronic joblessness" on many reservations).

The social costs of problem and pathological gambling are far-reaching. Pathological gamblers often exhibit destructive and desperate behavior, including debt accumulation, criminal activity, substance abuse, domestic abuse, and suicidal ideation.[13] The rates of household debt and unemployment and public entitlements benefits are also higher for problem and pathological gamblers than for non-gamblers or low-risk gamblers.[14] The NORC study found higher rates of mental health treatment, manic and depressive episodes, and alcohol and drug dependency among problem and pathological gamblers. Problem and pathological gamblers also have higher rates of arrest and conviction, domestic partner abuse, and divorce.[15] Spouses and children of pathological or problem gamblers are more likely to experience emotional problems and addictions of their own.[16]

---

13. The American Psychiatric Association has classified pathological gambling as an impulse control disorder and uses ten criteria to identify pathological gambling; pathological gamblers meet at least five criteria, while problem gamblers meet fewer than five criteria. NGISC, *Final Report*, 4-1. In its 1999 report, the NGISC cited estimates that in 1998 between 1.2 and 1.5% of the adult population in the U.S. (or approximately 3 million people) were pathological gamblers at least at some point during their lives, while another 1.5 to 3.9% of adults (or between 3 and 7.8 million people) were problem gamblers. Id. at 4-1.

Many studies seeking to measure the impacts of problem and pathological gambling use small samples within the treatment population (that is, among those people seeking treatment for problem or pathological gambling) and often lack statistical controls. Thus, although there seems to be little doubt that pathological gamblers experience negative social impacts, some researchers urge caution in interpreting existing studies. See National Research Council, *Pathological Gambling: A Critical Review* (Apr. 1, 1999), 5-2.

14. NGISC, *Final Report*, 7-21. Fifteen percent of pathological gamblers received unemployment benefits in the prior year, compared to less than five percent of non-gamblers; a larger percentage of problem and pathological gamblers received welfare benefits than other categories of gamblers; and the average household debt of a pathological gambler was higher than for any other category of gambler. Id.

15. NORC Report, 29–31. More than half of pathological gamblers reported that they have had an emotionally harmful family argument about gambling. NGISC, *Final Report*, 7-21; Henry R. Lesieur, "Costs and Treatment of Pathological Gambling," in James H. Frey, ed., *Gambling: Socioeconomic Impacts and Public Policy* (New York: Sage, 1998), 155–56; NORC Report, 59–60.

16. See "Problem Gambling and Intimate Partner Violence," *The Wager* 8 (Feb. 12, 2003). Nearly one-quarter of women reporting they were the victims of intimate partner violence stated that their abusers were problem gamblers. The study found that women with intimate partners who were problem gamblers were ten times more likely to suffer violence at the hands of their partner. Id.; see also National Research Council, *Pathological Gambling*, 5-2 (summarizing studies of the social costs of problem and pathological gambling).

Although the economic and personal costs incurred by the individual prob-lem or pathological gambler can be devastating, the costs to society are consid-erable as well.[17] Taking into account the greater prevalence of divorce, poor physical and mental health, unemployment and lessened productivity, bank-ruptcy, and entanglement with the criminal justice system among problem and pathological gamblers, as well as the costs of treating problem gambling, the NORC study estimated that each pathological gambler costs society $10,550 over his or her lifetime, while each problem gambler costs society just under half that amount.[18] Multiplying the estimated individual costs to society of problem and pathological gamblers by the estimated prevalence of problem and pathological gambling in the general population, the NORC study calculated that society at the end of the twentieth century incurred costs of about $4 billion each year.[19]

There is no doubt that problem and pathological gambling has negative so-cial impacts; however, some researchers have questioned whether the spread of legalized gambling, including the recent proliferation of tribal gaming fa-cilities, significantly increases problem and pathological gambling. Common wisdom suggests that with increased opportunities to gamble comes increased problem gambling, but some argue that the prevalence of problem gambling has remained relatively constant in the face of widely expanded legalized gam-bling. Rather than more problem gamblers, these researchers have suggested, increased gambling opportunities create only more low-risk gamblers.[20]

---

17. NGISC, *Final Report*, 4-14; see also Lesieur, "Costs and Treatment of Pathological Gambling," 155–56.

18. NORC Report, 52–53. A problem gambler costs society $5,130 over the course of his or her lifetime. Id.

19. Id. at 53. Several studies of state-by-state impacts employ a similar approach. For example, in a 1995 study of the economic impacts of Indian gaming in Wisconsin, re-searchers used three levels of estimation of the economic costs of "compulsive" or "problem" gamblers: for the "low estimate," a cost of $6,500 for each problem gambler; for the "medium range," a cost of $13,000; and for the "high range," a cost of $18,500. Multiplied by ap-proximately 25,000 (based on the assumption that tribal casinos in Wisconsin have led 0.7% of the state's adult population, or about 25,000 people, to become problem gamblers), the study estimated that Indian gaming caused social costs ranging from the "low" estimate of $160 million to the "high" estimate of $450 million each year. See William N. Thompson, Ricardo Gazel, and Dan Rickman, *The Economic Impact of Native American Gaming in Wis-consin* (Wisconsin Policy Research Institute, 1995).

20. See Spilde, Taylor, and Grant, *Tribal Government Gaming in Oklahoma*, 48. "[I]n light of the large extent to which gambling has been legalized in America over the past few decades, the failure to find an obvious pattern of increasing prevalence of pathological gam-bling should raise serious doubts about just how likely the disorder is to be triggered by in-creasing opportunities to gamble." Id. at 47 (citing Public Sector Gaming Study Commission,

Casinos commonly are blamed for increases in street crime, such as pros-titution, illegal drugs, violent crime, and theft, as well as white-collar and or-ganized crime.[21] Many studies, however, report mixed results on the links between gambling and crime.[22] Some researchers have cited a lack of evidence supporting significant increases in street or organized crime as legalized gam-bling has expanded.[23] Others have suggested that casinos are no different than many large tourist attractions, such as concert venues or sports arenas, in at-tracting crime; indeed, after controlling for the influx of tourists, crime rates may remain stable or even decrease.[24] Some studies have found that casinos, particularly in areas with high unemployment rates, have had the effect of re-ducing poverty-related crimes.[25]

The most recent comprehensive national study, NORC's analysis of social and economic changes in 100 communities between 1980 and 1997, measured the effects of "casino proximity" on criminal activity, concluding that the pres-ence of a casino in or near a community did not significantly increase crime.[26]

Gambling Policy and the Role of the State: An Assessment of America's Gambling Industry and the Rights and Responsibilities of State Governments (Tallahassee, FL: Florida Institute of Government, Florida State University, Mar. 2000)).

21. See John Warren Kindt, "Increased Crime and Legalizing Gambling Operations: The Impact on the Socio-Economics of Business and Government," *Criminal Law Bulletin* 43 (1994): 538–55. Relying both on studies linking problem and pathological gambling to crime and on studies linking casinos to crime, one researcher unequivocally concluded that "casino gambling causes significant increases in crime." Earl L. Grinols, "Casino Gambling Causes Crime," *Policy Forum* (University of Illinois Institute of Government and Public Af-fairs) 13 (2000), 3 (discussing his own research concluding that in 1996, "casinos accounted for 10.3% of the observed violent crime and 7.7% of the observed property crime in casino counties").

22. See William N. Thompson, Ricardo Gazel, and Dan Rickman, *Casinos and Crime in Wisconsin* (Wisconsin Policy Research Institute, 1996), 2–6 (describing inconsistent re-sults of empirical studies of crime and legalized gambling).

23. See William J. Miller and Martin D. Schwartz, "Casino Gambling and Street Crime," in Frey, *Gambling: Socioeconomic Impacts and Public Policy*, 126 ("[O]nly rarely is any evi-dence offered to support the claim that casino gambling increases street crime.").

24. NGISC, *Final Report*, 7-13; Miller and Schwartz, "Casino Gambling and Street Crime," 126 ("Simply, any event that brings together large numbers of people in one spot offers the potential to increase both the crime level and the infrastructure costs to the local taxpayers.").

25. Taylor, Krepps, and Wang, *National Evidence*, 26–28.

26. To the contrary, it appeared that crime rates were reduced, "but not in an over-whelming way." NORC Report, 71. The NORC study cautioned, however, that "[t]his is not to say that there is no casino-related crime or the like; rather, these effects are either small enough as not to be noticeable in the general wash of the statistics, or whatever problems

Using the same data, Harvard researchers determined that the introduction of a tribal casino to a previously economically depressed locale may reduce rather than increase crime.[27] The NGISC found existing research on the issue inconclusive.[28] Nevertheless, the perceived connection between casinos and crime has a powerful influence on public opinion and policymaking.

Has Indian gaming improved reservation quality of life? Some contend that it has exacerbated differences between tribes and their non-Indian neighbors and has fueled tribal political unrest, causing membership disputes, political in-fighting, and controversies over the legitimacy of tribal governments.[29] A casino-based economy is regarded by some tribal members as inconsistent with traditional tribal values. The Navajo Nation, for example, famously chose not to pursue gaming for a lengthy period of time, based in part on traditional Navajo beliefs.[30] In 2006, the Nation created the Navajo Nation Gaming Enterprise (NNGE), a tribally owned business entity, and since has opened four gaming operations. The NNGE mission is to build "a Navajo gaming economy" through the development and operation of as many as a half-dozen casi-

---

that are created along these lines when a casino is built may be countered by other effects." Id. at 70.

27. Taylor, Krepps, and Wang, *National Evidence*, 26–27. As did the NORC study, Taylor, Krepps, and Wang cautioned that further research is required to fully test this hypothesis.

28. NGISC, *Final Report*, 7-12.

29. See generally Kathryn R.L. Rand and Steven A. Light, "Virtue or Vice? How IGRA Shapes the Politics of Native American Gaming, Sovereignty, and Identity," *Virginia Journal of Social Policy and the Law* 4 (1997): 419–24 (discussing intratribal disputes related to gaming); James May, "California: To Be Indian, or Not To Be," *Indian Country Today*, Aug. 9, 2000; Michelle DeArmond, "Man Sues to Gain Admission to Inland Tribe," *Press-Enterprise* (Riverside, CA), Jan. 15, 2004 (discussing membership dispute among the Pechanga Band of Luiseno Mission Indians in southern California); Louis Sahagun, "Gaming Tribe Seeks to Expel Tenth of its Own," *Los Angeles Times*, Feb. 1, 2004 (discussing membership dispute among Redding Rancheria). In Iowa, the NIGC closed the Meskwaki Tribe's casino for over six months in 2003 after finding that a formally unrecognized tribal council was controlling the casino's profits. After the casino re-opened, tribal members associated with the rival government faction were barred from the casino. See Mark Siebert, "Casino Reopening Begins Tribe's Healing," *Des Moines Register*, Jan. 1, 2004; Mark Siebert, "Welcome Mat Is Out at Meskwaki Casino," *Des Moines Register*, Dec. 31, 2003; William Petroski, "Casino Closure Troubles Midwest's Indian Leaders," *Des Moines Register*, June 6, 2003.

30. See Washington Matthews, "Noqoìlpi, the Gambler: A Navajo Myth," *Journal of American Folklore* 2 (1889): 89–94; Roberta John, "No Gambling on Navajo Myths," *Navajo Times*, Aug. 14, 1997 (on the conflict between gambling and traditional Navajo spirituality); Brett Pulley, "Tribes Weighing Tradition vs. Casino Growth," *New York Times*, Mar. 16, 1999, A1.

nos.[31] At the same time, some predict that the current boom in legalized gambling will be short-lived and that tribal economies dependent on casino revenues will collapse.[32]

Moreover, although Indian gaming's economic benefits to tribal governments and reservation economies are difficult to dispute, some argue that economic impacts do not adequately translate into social benefits. American Indians face disproportionately high rates of infant mortality, suicide, substance abuse, obesity, and mental health problems. They have significantly higher incidences of death from illnesses such as diabetes, tuberculosis, and alcoholism, and are more likely to be victims of violent crime than are members of any other racial group in the nation.[33]

In a 2005 study of tribal gaming's socioeconomic effects, Harvard researchers found substantial reductions between 1990 and 2000 in the poverty and unemployment rates for American Indians living on reservations. Per capita income growth outstripped that of the non-Indian population. Although the researchers concluded that "rapid" economic development was occurring on reser-

---

31. The first Navajo casino, Fire Rock Navajo Casino near Gallup, New Mexico, opened in 2008, followed by the Flowing Water Navajo Casino near Shiprock, New Mexico in 2010, the Northern Edge Navajo Casino near Farmington, New Mexico in 2012, and Twin Arrows Navajo Casino Resort near Flagstaff, Arizona in 2013. As of this writing, a fifth, Pinta Road Casino & Travel Center, was in the planning stage. NNGE's goals include job creation, development of a private sector to provide goods and services to the Navajo casinos and related businesses, and revenue generation for the Navajo Nation government. By fall 2012, the NNGE reported the creation of 700 jobs and $5 million in profits. See, e.g., Jenny Kane, "Navajo Nation Gaming Enterprise CEO Resigns," *Daily Times* (Farmington, NM), Oct. 27, 2012.

32. See, for example, "Seminole Casino Plan Inspires Hope and Fear," *New York Times*, Dec. 29, 2003 (describing tribal members' concerns that plans for the Seminole Hard Rock Hotel and Casino carry too great a financial risk). For the most part, these concerns do not seem to be borne out by the data. As noted above, Indian gaming as a whole appears to have weathered the recent national economic recession. See Meister, *Indian Gaming Industry Report, 2014 Ed.*, 3–5 (predicting modest growth for the industry). Nevertheless, the economic downturn impacted the supposedly "recession-proof" legalized gambling industry, including tribal gaming. The most prominent—and surprising—example was the Mashantucket Pequot Tribe's Foxwoods Resort Casino, which restructured a $2.3 billion debt, raising several legal issues (discussed in Chapter 7).

33. Center for Disease Control and Prevention Office of Minority Health and Health Equity, "American Indian & Alaska Native Populations," http://www.cdc.gov/minorityhealth/populations/REMP/aian.html (last visited Mar. 31, 2014); U.S. Commission on Civil Rights, *A Quiet Crisis: Federal Funding and Unmet Needs in Indian Country* (Washington, DC, July 2003), 34–35; Lawrence A. Greenfield and Steven K. Smith, *American Indians and Crime* (Washington, DC: U.S. Department of Justice, 1999).

vations throughout the United States, improvements in quality of life indicators for gaming tribes generally outpaced those for non-gaming tribes. Yet poverty, unemployment, overcrowding and housing deficits, and low median incomes still plague both gaming and non-gaming tribes.[34] According to U.S. Census data, 27% of all American Indians lived in poverty in 2011, a greater proportion than any other group, and nearly double the national average.[35]

Although gaming is not the cause of pernicious socioeconomic conditions on many reservations, perhaps the most prominent criticism of Indian gaming is its failure to lift all Native Americans out of poverty. Critics have cited the wide divergence between extraordinarily lucrative tribal casinos, such as the Mashantucket Pequots' Foxwoods Resort Casino in Connecticut, and tribal casinos in the Midwest or Great Plains states that may be barely breaking even or operating at a loss. Indian gaming, some charge, is doing too little for some tribes and too much for others.[36] Conversely, the contrast of "too little" government subsidies and "too much" of gaming profits generates concern about the corrupting influence of wealth on reservations.[37]

The social benefits of Indian gaming stem from strengthened tribal self-governance, self-sufficiency, and self-determination—in other words, from the varied dimensions of tribal sovereignty. Tribes use gaming revenue to fund a wide range of services, programs, and projects that improve reservation qual-

---

34. See generally Jonathan B. Taylor and Joseph Kalt, Cabazon, *the Indian Gaming Regulatory Act, and the Socioeconomic Consequences of American Indian Governmental Gaming* (Cambridge, MA: Harvard Project on American Indian Economic Development, 2005). A 2000 Associated Press analysis of federal unemployment, poverty, and public assistance records showed that although tribal gaming operations experienced varied success, the unemployment rates on many reservations remained far above the national average. David Pace, "Casino Revenue Does Little to Improve Lives of Many Indians, Study Shows," *Milwaukee Journal Sentinel*, Sept. 1, 2000, 8A.

35. The poverty rate for American Indians exceeds 30% in nine states, including Arizona, Maine, Minnesota, Montana, Nebraska, New Mexico, North Dakota, South Dakota, and Utah. U.S. Census, *Poverty Rates for Selected Detailed Race and Hispanic Groups by State and Place: 2007–2011* (Feb. 2013), http://www.census.gov/prod/2013pubs/acsbr11-17.pdf (last visited Mar. 31, 2014).

36. See Donald L. Barlett and James B. Steele, "Wheel of Misfortune," *Time* (Dec. 16, 2002), 47–49; Michael Rezendes, "Few Tribes Share in Casino Windfall," *Boston Globe*, Dec. 11, 2000, A1. For a critique of this charge, see Kathryn R.L. Rand, "There Are No Pequots on the Plains: Assessing the Success of Indian Gaming," *Chapman Law Review* 5 (2002): 48–49, 55–59.

37. See Bill Lueders, "Buffaloed: Casino Cowboys Take Indians for a Ride," *Progressive* (Aug. 1, 1994) ("It's killing our people. They never had money in their lives and they don't know what to do.") (quoting Clyde Bellecourt, a founding member of the American Indian Movement).

ity of life. A number of success stories illustrate tribal gaming's positive social impacts.

The Chickasaw Nation in Oklahoma employs over 10,000 people in 60 businesses in the state, leveraging gaming revenue to diversify the tribe's economic interests to include banking, healthcare, and other professional services. Gaming revenue has helped the tribe to open a transitional living facility for at-risk adolescents, a diabetes treatment center, senior centers, and a softball field, to name just a few of the tribe's projects.[38] In Minnesota, the Shakopee Mdewakanton Sioux Community reported in 2012 that it had made a total of $262 million in charitable donations and more than $523 million in loans to other tribes for economic development projects.[39] The Tohono O'odham Nation in southern Arizona has constructed a new community college and nursing home, and uses gaming revenue to fund health care, fire protection, and youth recreation centers, while in 2009 the Salt River Pima-Maricopa Indian Community opened a medical complex serving tribal members as well as the surrounding community.[40] In California, the Viejas Band of Kumeyaay Indians uses gaming revenue to pay for law enforcement, road maintenance, and waste removal.[41]

Tribes also have used casino profits to build museums and heritage centers celebrating and preserving their histories, instituted Native language classes in their schools, and infused indigenous values and traditions into public services and institutions ranging from clinics to courts.[42] Summarized NIGA Chair Ernest L. Stevens, Jr., "Indian gaming has served to build strong tribal governments, and promote tribal economic self-sufficiency. Tribes have a long

---

38. See Steven C. Agee, *Estimating the Oklahoma Economic Impact of the Chickasaw Nation* (Oklahoma City University Economic Research & Policy Institute, May 2012); Chickasaw Nation, http://www.chickasaw.net/ (last visited July 23, 2013).

39. Shakopee Mdewakanton Sioux Community, *2012 Donation Report* (2012), http://www.shakopeedakota.org/pdf/donationRpt2012.pdf (last visited Mar. 31, 2014).

40. Indian Gaming: Oversight Hearing on the Indian Gaming Regulatory Act Before the Senate Committee on Indian Affairs (July 25, 2001) (statement of David LaSarte), https://bulk.resource.org/gpo.gov/hearings/107s/74522.txt (last visited Mar. 31, 2014); Taylor, *Economic Impact of Tribal Government Gaming in Arizona*.

41. NGISC, *Final Report*, 6-15 (quoting Anthony R. Pico, Chairman of the Viejas Band of Kumeyaay Indians). "It means fewer people on welfare and ultimately more people paying taxes," said Jacob Coin, the executive director of the California Nations Indian Gaming Association, of increasing tribal employment in the state. Lou Hirsh and Jim Sams, "Tribal Employment Is Growing," *Desert Sun* (Palm Springs, CA), June 2, 2004 (reporting that tribes in California employ more than 44,000 people).

42. Maria Napoli, "Native Wellness for the New Millennium: The Impact of Gaming," *Journal of Sociology and Social Welfare* 29 (2002): 17–34; see also Rand, "There Are No Pequots"; NIGA, *Economic Impact of Indian Gaming*.

way to go because too many of our people continue to live with disease and poverty, but Indian gaming offers hope for the future."[43]

DEVELOPING ISSUES

Against the complex and complicated backdrop of IGRA after *Seminole Tribe*, a broad range of political actors considers the appropriate weight to be given Indian gaming's perceived socioeconomic costs and benefits within the context of specific issues, many of which are related to tribal-state compacting. The terms of political debate on these issues have ramifications beyond local jurisdictions; indeed, what happens in Connecticut may well affect tribal gaming in California and Colorado. As hot-button issues for political contestation across the country, these policy debates arise and develop on a near-daily basis. They both illustrate the role of law and politics in shaping Indian gaming and portend future tribal gaming law and policy.

Under IGRA's terms, tribal-state compact provisions, and thus negotiations, may include (1) the application of the state's and the tribe's criminal and civil laws and regulations "that are directly related to, and necessary for, the licensing and regulation" of Class III games, (2) allocation of criminal and civil jurisdiction between the state and the tribe "necessary for the enforcement of such laws and regulations," (3) payments to the state to cover the state's costs of regulating the tribe's Class III games, (4) tribal taxation of Class III gaming, limited to amounts comparable to the state's taxation of similar activities, (5) remedies for breach of contract, (6) operating and facility maintenance standards, including licensing, and (7) "any other subjects that are directly related to the operation of gaming activities."[44]

A typical compact, then, might include such provisions as a list of permissible Class III games, hardware and software requirements for slot machines and other electronic gaming machines, tribal and state licensing of casino employees and vendors, application of state liquor or food safety laws, minimum age requirements for casino employees and patrons, application of state or federal standards for commercial facilities and workplace safety, tribal participation in state workers compensation programs, and specific remedies and procedures for resolving disputes over the compact's terms. IGRA allows states to negotiate tribal reimbursement for state regulatory costs associated with Indian gaming. States also may negotiate tribal payments to offset the costs of law

---

43. Indian Gaming: Oversight Hearing (statement of Ernest L. Stevens, Jr.).
44. 25 U.S.C. §2710(d)(3)(C).

enforcement, noise, pollution, or traffic abatement, environmental impacts, infrastructural improvements, such as utility, sewer, or road construction, and problem and pathological gambling education and treatment programs.[45]

The politics of Indian gaming are direct outcomes of the law and policy that govern it. The increasing complexities of tribal-state compacting reflect the complicated post-*Seminole Tribe* political environment. Beyond the specific types of provisions authorized by IGRA, states have negotiated other policy issues, some arguably outside IGRA's catch-all of "any other subjects that are directly related to the operation of gaming activities," such as revenue sharing and tribal treaty rights.[46] IGRA's prerequisites for tribal gaming—that it must be conducted by an "Indian tribe" on "Indian lands"—have instigated controversy over the federal government's tribal recognition process and tribes' acquisition of new lands.

Revenue Sharing

IGRA explicitly prohibits state taxation of tribal casinos as a condition of signing a tribal-state compact.[47] As interpreted by the Secretary of the Interior, however, tribes can make payments to states in return for additional benefits beyond the right to operate Class III gaming. Sometimes called "exclusivity payments," such provisions typically require tribes to pay a percentage of casino revenues in return for the exclusive right to operate casino-style gaming in a state that allows charitable gambling but not commercial casinos.[48] As long as

---

45. See, for example, North Dakota Attorney General, *Gaming Compacts*, http://www.ag.nd.gov/Gaming/GACompacts/GACompacts.htm (last visited Apr. 1, 2014); California Gambling Control Commission, *Ratified Tribal-State Gaming Compacts (New and Amended)*, http://www.cgcc.ca.gov/?pageID=compacts (last visited Apr. 1, 2014).

46. 25 U.S.C. § 2710(d)(3)(C)(vii).

47. IGRA states:
    … nothing in this section shall be interpreted as conferring upon a State or any of its political subdivisions authority to impose any tax, fee, charge, or other assessment upon an Indian tribe or upon any other person or entity authorized by an Indian tribe to engage in a Class III activity.
Id. § 2710(d)(4).

48. See generally Steven Andrew Light, Kathryn R.L. Rand, and Alan P. Meister, "Spreading the Wealth: Indian Gaming and Revenue-Sharing Agreements," *North Dakota Law Review* 80 (2004): 657–79; Eric S. Lent, Note, "Are States Beating the House? The Validity of Tribal-State Revenue Sharing Under the Indian Gaming Regulatory Act," *Georgetown Law Journal* 91 (2003): 451; Gatsby Contreras, Note, "Exclusivity Agreements in Tribal-State Compacts: Mutual Benefit Revenue-Sharing or Illegal State Taxation?," *Journal of Gender, Race and Justice* 5 (2002): 487. In *Sault Ste. Marie Tribe of Chippewa Indians v. Engler*, the Sixth Circuit Court of Appeals addressed the issue of a state's abrogation of promised exclusiv-

the payments provide what the Interior Department has labeled "a valuable economic benefit," such as "substantial exclusivity" in the market, they presumably will not run afoul of IGRA's prohibition on state taxation, charges, or other assessments against tribes.[49] Through exclusivity and other valuable concessions, states have been able to make revenue sharing a pivotal point in compact negotiations in the "surest—perhaps only—way" that states legally may require tribes to make payments to the state beyond reimbursement for the state's regulatory costs.[50] The Mashantucket Pequots in Connecticut were the first tribe to sign on to a revenue-sharing provision, agreeing in 1992 to pay 25% of gross slot machine revenues to the state.[51]

Revenue-sharing agreements with state and local governments include percentage payments, fixed compact payments, fees and taxes, contributions to community funds, and redistribution to non-gaming tribes. Most payments are based on a percentage of gaming revenue. Some tribes, like the Pequots and Mohegans in Connecticut, pay a fixed percentage directly to the state. Other tribes, such as those in California, New Mexico, New York, and Wisconsin, make payments based on a sliding percentage scale. Tribes in Arizona, Louisiana, Michigan, and Washington have signed agreements with local governments to fund public services, schools, or programs seeking to lessen the effects of problem and pathological gambling.[52] California's Revenue Sharing Trust Fund uniquely requires "tribe-to-tribe" revenue sharing. Using the fees generated by "licenses" to operate more than a minimum number of slot machines, each non-gaming tribe in California is paid up to $1.1 million each year.[53]

---

ity, and held that under such circumstances, a tribe would not be required to continue to make payments to the state according to the terms of the revenue-sharing agreement. 271 F.3d 235 (6th Cir. 2001).

49. Statement of Aurene M. Martin, Acting Assistant Secretary for Indian Affairs, Before the U.S. Senate Committee on Indian Affairs (July 9, 2003), 2.

50. Kelly B. Kramer, "Current Issues in Indian Gaming: Casino Lands and Gaming Compacts," *Gaming Law Review* 7 (2003): 333.

51. NGISC, *Final Report*, 6-21. Under the terms of the agreement, the tribe could consent to abrogate exclusivity, as it did to allow the Mohegans to build the Mohegan Sun Casino. Id.

52. Meister, *Indian Gaming Industry Report, 2014 Ed.*, 90–95; John Stearns, "Tribes Work to Stem Gambling Addictions," *Arizona Republic*, June 19, 2004.

53. Ashley Grant, "Tribal Casino Compacts Go Under Microscope," *Grand Forks Herald* (ND), Feb. 15, 2004, 4; Louis Sahagun, "State Point Man for Gaming Tribes Is Bold Leader," *Los Angeles Times*, Jan. 18, 2004, A1. Some lauded the agreement as a way to spread the wealth of the Indian gaming industry more equitably among all tribes. Others see the provision as an infringement of tribal sovereignty. See John McCarthy, "Indian Gaming

In the last decade, revenue-sharing agreements have become the political linchpin for tribal-state compacts, and states are reaping the benefits of tribal gaming's success. In 2012, the two Connecticut gaming tribes paid the state about $318 million, California tribes provided approximately $395 million, and Oklahoma tribes paid roughly $128 million. In Florida, the Seminole Tribe alone paid the state about $180 million.[54]

Although revenue sharing has played out largely in the political arena after *Seminole Tribe*, a few such agreements also have been subject to litigation.[55] Because California has consented to suit under IGRA, the federal courts in California set some of the few legal precedents governing revenue sharing. In 2003, the Ninth Circuit decided *In re Indian Gaming Related Cases*, which concerned the revenue sharing provisions in the compacts negotiated under Democratic Governor Gray Davis. The Ninth Circuit adopted the Interior Secretary's general approach and upheld the revenue sharing provisions in light of the meaningful concessions on the part of the state as well as the provisions' consistency with IGRA's goals.[56]

During California's 2004 recall campaign, Republican gubernatorial candidate Arnold Schwarzenegger promised that he would require tribal casinos to pay their "fair share," or 25% of gambling revenue—an estimated $1.25 billion annually, to the state. After his election, Schwarzenegger set about renegotiating the compacts. To meet the standard set by the Interior Secretary and the Ninth Circuit in *Indian Gaming Related Cases*, the state offered to increase the number of slot machines allowed in exchange for a larger share of tribal gaming revenue. Schwarzenegger successfully negotiated a set of new compacts that required each tribe, in exchange for unlimited slot machines, to make an initial payment to the state of $1 billion, and additional annual payments estimated to range between $150 million and $275 million, including payments to the state's general fund. Schwarzenegger continued to negotiate new or amended compacts with additional tribes in 2006, including the Rincon Band of Luiseno Mission Indians, that generally sought increased revenue sharing in exchange for higher limits on slot machines.

_____

Under Fire," *Indian Gaming* (May 2004), 14 (describing California's efforts to negotiate revenue-sharing agreements as "extorting Indian tribes").

54. Meister, *Indian Gaming Industry Report, 2014 Ed.*, 95.

55. See, for example, Panzer v. Doyle, 680 N.W.2d 666 (Wis. 2004) (invalidating negotiated compacts, which included revenue-sharing provision, on state constitutional law grounds); Sault Ste. Marie Tribe of Chippewa Indians v. Engler, 271 F.3d 235 (6th Cir. 2001) (addressing whether state had abrogated tribal exclusivity thus voiding compact's revenue--sharing provision).

56. In re Gaming Related Cases, 331 F.3d 1094 (9th Cir. 2003).

In 2007, the Rincon Band filed suit in federal court alleging that Schwarzenegger's revenue-sharing demands were in bad faith. Under its 1999 compact, the tribe operated 1,600 slot machines. The tribe sought to increase its slot limit to 2,500 machines, and in return the state sought 15% of the net win on each of the additional 900 machines as well as an additional annual flat-fee payment—in all, the state's revenue sharing demand amounted to nearly $38 million each year, to be paid into the state's general fund. The state's own expert, the highly respected gambling studies scholar and economist William R. Eadington, estimated that the additional slot machines would increase the tribe's annual profits by $39 million, but after paying the state's revenue-sharing demands the tribe's net would drop to $1.7 million. "This substantial fee, 37 times greater than what Rincon receives, is unreasonable," concluded the district court. Further, the fact that the fee would be paid into the state's treasury made it "difficult to regard the State's proposed plan as anything more than a tax when it functions as a tax."[57]

The Ninth Circuit agreed, clarifying that once a tribe proffers evidence of bad faith—here, the demand for what amounts to a tax—the burden shifts to the state to demonstrate good faith.[58] "[W]hen the 'nature of the fees' is general fund revenue sharing—a bald demand for payment of a tax—the State faces a very difficult task to rebut the evidence of bad faith necessarily arising from that demand."[59] The court was skeptical of the value of the concessions offered by the state, distinguishing *Indian Gaming Related Cases* on the value of the exclusivity afforded the tribes under the earlier compacts. Here, too, the court was persuaded by the financial analysis of the 37-to-1 ratio of the state's financial benefit over the tribe's: "the relative value of the demand versus the concession here strongly suggests the State was improperly using its authority over compact negotiations to impose, rather than negotiate for, a fee."[60] The court's decision was influenced by IGRA's legislative history as well as the history of federal Indian policy:

---

57. Rincon Band of Luiseno Mission Indians v. Schwarzenegger, No. 04CV1151, 2008 WL 6136699 (S.D. Cal. Apr. 29, 2008).

58. IGRA provides that the court "shall consider any demand by the State for direct taxation of the Indian tribe ... as evidence that the State has not negotiated in good faith." 25 U.S.C. § 2710(d)(7)(B)(iii). As construed by the Ninth Circuit, the state can counter with evidence that the revenue will be used for "the public interest, public safety, criminality, financial integrity, and adverse economic impacts on existing gaming activities." Rincon Band of Luiseno Mission Indians v. Schwarzenegger, 602 F.3d 1019, 1032 (9th Cir. 2010), *cert. denied*, 131 S. Ct. 3055 (2011) (quoting 25 U.S.C. § 2710(d)(7)(B)(iii)).

59. Rincon Band, 602 F.3d at 1032.

60. Id. at 1042.

[W]e are mindful that many states, and especially California, are currently writhing in the financial maw created by the clash of certain mandatory state expenditures at a time when state revenues have plummeted from historic levels. However, we are also keenly aware of our nation's too-frequent breach of its trust obligations to Native Americans when some of its politically and economically powerful citizens and states have lusted after what little the Native Americans have possessed. In developing IGRA, Congress anticipated that states might abuse their authority over compact negotiations to force tribes to accept burdens on their sovereignty in order to obtain gaming opportunities. That is why the good faith requirement exists, and why IGRA condemns state taxation demands.[61]

The court concluded, "The State's demand for 10–15% of Rincon's net win, to be paid into the State's general fund, is simply an impermissible demand for the payment of a tax by the tribe. None of the State's arguments suffices to rebut the inference of bad faith such an improper demand creates."[62]

Tribal Treaty Rights

Though far less common than revenue sharing, state demands for tribes to relinquish centuries-old treaty rights have met with significant tribal resistance and public controversy. Some have argued that state demands regarding treaty rights are both unfair and illegal, while others assert that tribal treaty rights are legitimate points of negotiation. Because states can avoid judicial determination of the legality of their negotiation strategies by asserting state sovereign immunity, in practice *Seminole Tribe* created opportunities for states to leverage political clout over tribes in an almost no-holds-barred form of negotiation.

In Wisconsin, for example, Republican Governor Tommy Thompson insisted in the late-1990s that the abrogation of tribes' hunting and fishing treaty rights as well as state taxation of reservation cigarette and gasoline sales were

---

61. Id. (citations omitted).

62. Id. In 2013, in the wake of the litigation, the Rincon Band successfully negotiated a compact with Democratic Governor Jerry Brown. See "Rincon Band Becomes First California Tribe to Renegotiate Tribal-State Gaming Compact with Federal Courts," *Indian Country Today*, Feb. 13, 2013, http://indiancountrytodaymedianetwork.com/2013/02/13/rincon-band-becomes-first-california-tribe-renegotiate-tribal-state-gaming-compact (last visited Apr. 7, 2014).

fair game to include in the renegotiation of existing gaming compacts.[63] "The governor views these discussions as laying out the parameters of a partnership between the state and tribes," explained Thompson's chief of staff at the time. "It is not in any way unreasonable for the governor to expect them to show flexibility on some non-gaming issues if they are going to continue to benefit from the monopoly they enjoy on gaming enterprises."[64] Although the tribes were successful in deflecting Thompson's demands on treaty right relinquishment, the state's position resonated with the public and policymakers. Thompson was "quietly cheered" by other governors looking for strategies to curb Indian gaming.[65] Tribal leaders in the state saw Thompson's leveraging of treaty rights against gaming as evidencing the need for federal constraints on state compact negotiations.[66]

As it appears that few states have followed Thompson's treaty-rights tactic, it may represent the ceiling of state hardball compact negotiation strategies. But some organizations and policymakers have called for just as extreme measures in the context of Indian gaming, including the outright abolishment of tribal sovereignty.[67] It is plain that for some, nothing is off the tribal-state negotiation table.

---

63. Kathryn R.L. Rand and Steven A. Light, "Do 'Fish and Chips' Mix? The Politics of Indian Gaming in Wisconsin," *Gaming Law Review* 2 (1998): 129–42.

64. Amy Rinard, "State's Delaying Talks, Tribes Say; No Meeting With Governor 'Until Progress Is Made' in Negotiations," *Milwaukee Journal Sentinel*, Aug. 1, 1997.

65. Timothy Egan, "Backlash Growing as Indians Make Stand for Sovereignty," *New York Times*, Mar. 9, 1998; Rand and Light, "Fish and Chips," 137.

66. See, for example, Gaiashkibos, Chair of the Lac Courte Oreilles Band of Lake Superior Chippewa Indians, Statement Before the U.S. Senate Committee on Indian Affairs (May 12, 1998); see also Rand and Light, "Fish and Chips," 137–39.

67. See, for example, Cate Montana, "New Washington State GOP Resolution Fails to Impress Tribes," *Indian Country Today*, July 26, 2000, http://www.indiancountry.com/content.cfm?id=737 (last visited Apr. 11, 2005) (describing Washington State Republican Party June 2000 resolution calling for termination of "non-republican" forms of government, including tribes, as well as party's subsequent apology); One Nation United, "Who We Are," http://www.onenationok.com (last visited Apr. 11, 2005) (describing the organization as representing "thousands of working Americans who feel misguided federal policy is driving Americans apart by fueling divisiveness between tribal governments and their neighbors" and seeking "to restore basic fairness in the marketplace by leveling the playing field between tribally-owned enterprises and the rest of the nation's business community"); Upstate Citizens for Equality, "Sovereignty," http://www.upstate-citizens.org/sovereignty.htm (last visited Apr. 11, 2005) ("The fundamental issue is sovereignty. UCE adamantly opposes the establishment of an independent, sovereign Cayuga Indian nation within New York State.").

Federal Tribal Acknowledgment

Before *Cabazon* and IGRA, the federal recognition process was fairly arcane and relatively uncontroversial. With the tremendous growth in Indian gaming, the acknowledgment process is perceived by many as the gateway to casino gambling. As a result, the process often is hotly contested by interested individuals, community organizations, non-tribal governments, and competing gaming tribes, and occasionally is bankrolled by outside investors and non-tribal gaming interests.[68]

The Bureau of Indian Affairs' (BIA) recognition in 2004 of the Schaghticoke Tribal Nation in Connecticut—and its subsequent and unprecedented reversal—generated significant controversy. The Nation would have been Connecticut's third federally recognized tribe, joining the Mashantucket Pequots and the Mohegans, both with hugely successful casinos. The Schaghticokes' recognition efforts and plans to partner with the city of Bridgeport on a casino were bankrolled by Subway Restaurants founder Frederick A. DeLuca. Vocal critics, ranging from citizen groups such as the Connecticut Alliance Against Casino Expansion to state and federal officials including Connecticut Attorney General Rick Blumenthal, decried DeLuca's and the tribe's efforts, calling for a moratorium on federal tribal recognition, federal funding for local efforts to block acknowledgment, and revision of the state's recognition process (the Schaghticokes have long been recognized as a tribe under Connecticut law).[69] A 2004 Interior Department internal investigation found no impropriety in the BIA's acknowledgment decision and no evidence that the Schaghticokes

---

68. As of 2011, 272 tribal groups were seeking recognition from the federal government's Office of Federal Acknowledgment. Gale Courey Toensing, "Federal Acknowledgment: Can the BIA's Acknowledgment Process Be Fixed?" *Indian Country Today*, http:// indiancountrytodaymedianetwork.com/2012/08/08/federal-recognition-can-bias-acknowledgment-process-be-fixed-127942 (last visited Apr. 1, 2014). The number of tribal groups in the queue held steady over the course of nearly a decade. See Iver Peterson, "Would-Be Tribes Entice Investors," *New York Times*, Mar. 29, 2004.

69. See William Yardley, "A Split Tribe, Casino Plans and One Little Indian Boy in the Middle," *New York Times*, Feb. 15, 2004, 29; Stacey Stowe, "Fourth Tribe Is Recognized in Connecticut, Casino Feared," *New York Times*, Jan. 30, 2004, B1; Rick Green, "Tribe's Backer Wants Bridgeport Casino," *Hartford Courant*, Feb. 13, 2004, A1. Connecticut leaders were successful in instigating a congressional investigation of the Schaghticokes' federal recognition. Said Eastern Pequot Tribal Chair Marcia Jones Flowers, "Political influence is at work here, but it is not being exercised by our tribe. Rather, incredible influence is being brought to bear by a small group of people whose real goal is to stop Indian gaming in Connecticut." Rick Green, "Pressure on Schaghticokes," *Hartford Courant*, May 6, 2004, B1.

had "directly or indirectly influenced" BIA officials. Nevertheless, some state and federal officials continued to express dissatisfaction and frustration. In 2005, after an 18-month-long orchestrated opposition campaign by local, state, and federal officials in Connecticut, the BIA reversed its decision. The Schaghti-cokes appealed, claiming the reversal was a result of unlawful political influence and a violation of due process. The federal district court rejected the claim and the Schaghticokes appeared to have exhausted their legal options in 2010, when the U.S. Supreme Court declined to hear the case.[70]

A 2001 federal General Accounting Office investigative report on the BIA's allegedly improper recognition of a Massachusetts tribe concluded that

> the end result [of such cases] could be that the resolution of tribal recognition cases will have less to do with the attributes and qualities of a group as an independent political entity deserving of a government-to-government relationship with the United States and more to do with the resources that petitioners and third parties can marshal to develop a successful political and legal strategy.[71]

The BIA has rejected assertions of bias or impropriety in its role in tribal recognition, citing the standardized and deliberative nature of the formal administrative acknowledgment process.[72]

Regardless, the process is incremental, at best. Since 1978, when Congress authorized the BIA to recognize tribes through an administrative process, it has approved just 17 applications and denied 34, including recent rejections of the Golden Hill Paugussett in Connecticut and the Nipmuc Nation in Massachusetts, both of which had expressed interest in tribal gaming.[73] Since 2009, the BIA has granted acknowledgment to just one tribe and denied recognition to five. The tribe that was acknowledged, the Shinnecock Indian Nation in New York, had formally petitioned in 1978. It was recognized 32 years later, in

---

70. See Schaghticoke Tribal Nation v. Kempthorne, 587 F.Supp.2d 389 (D. Conn. 2008), *aff'd*, 587 F.3d 132 (2nd Cir. 2009), *cert. denied*, Schaghticoke Tribal Nation v. Salazar, 131 S. Ct. 127 (2010), *rehearing denied*, 131 S. Ct. 698 (2010); U.S. Department of the Interior, "The Department of the Interior Issued Reconsidered Final Determination to Decline Federal Acknowledgement of the Schaghticoke Tribal Nation," Press Release, Oct. 12, 2005, http://www.doi.gov/news/05_News_Releases/051012a.htm (last visited Oct. 24, 2005).

71. Peterson, "Would-Be Tribes Entice Investors."

72. Id.

73. Office of Federal Acknowledgement, Status Summary of Acknowledgement Cases (Nov. 12, 2013), http://www.bia.gov/WhoWeAre/AS-IA/OFA/index.htm (last visited Apr. 1, 2014).

2010. Overall, 272 tribal groups as of 2011 were actively seeking recognition from the Office of Federal Acknowledgment.[74]

Tribes assert that the federal recognition process is being unfairly politicized by opponents of Indian gaming, penalizing Native American groups whose petitions for acknowledgment are driven not by the lure of casino riches but by the redress of historical wrongs, preservation or resurrection of tribal culture and traditions, and the much-needed federal support for tribal members that comes with formal recognition. In 2013, Assistant Secretary for Indian Affairs Kevin Washburn announced the Interior Department's intent to revise the administrative recognition process.[75]

Regardless of the outcomes for specific American Indian groups seeking federal acknowledgment, there is little doubt that Indian gaming has dramatically colored the politics of tribal recognition.

Tribal Land Acquisition and Off-Reservation Gaming

Casinos located near population centers are more likely to experience financial success than are those in geographically isolated and underpopulated areas. Many tribal reservations fall in the latter category. An increasing number of tribes have explored the possibility of acquiring land for the purpose of opening a casino, with varying degrees of political support.

As we discuss in Chapter 3, IGRA generally prohibits gaming on newly acquired trust lands, but also provides a number of exceptions to its general rule.[76] Most notably, gaming will be permitted on newly acquired lands if the Interior Secretary determines, and the state's governor concurs, that gaming would be in the best interest of the tribe and its members and would not be detrimental to the surrounding community.[77] Gaming on newly acquired lands

---

74. Toensing, "Federal Acknowledgment."

75. Office of the Assistant Secretary-Indian Affairs, "Washburn Announces Consideration of Revisions to Federal Acknowledgement Regulations," Press Release, June 21, 2013, http://www.bia.gov/News/index.htm (last visited July 24, 2013). In January 2014, the BIA issued proposed findings in favor of federal acknowledgement for the Pamunkey Indian Tribe of Virginia and against recognition of the Meherrin Indian Tribe of North Carolina. Office of the Assistant Secretary-Indian Affairs, "Washburn Issues Proposed Findings for Two Federal Acknowledgment Petitioners," Press Release, Jan. 17, 2014, http://www.bia.gov/cs/groups/public/documents/text/idc1-024786.pdf (last visited Apr. 8, 2014).

76. 25 U.S.C. §2719.

77. Id. §2719(b)(1)(A). IGRA's other exceptions may apply, depending on the particular circumstances of a tribe's acquisition of land. For example, newly acquired trust lands within or contiguous to a tribe's existing reservation are exempt from the general prohibi-

under this exception typically is referred to as off-reservation gaming to distinguish it from other exceptions involving reservation lands.

Because of the gubernatorial concurrence requirement as well as the mandated consultation with local officials, off-reservation gaming necessarily involves political negotiation, often resulting in give-and-take between the tribe and the state. The specifics are tailored to the particular political environment. In 2004, for example, California's Republican Governor Arnold Schwarzenegger announced an agreement with the Lytton Band of Pomo Indians authorizing the construction of the largest urban casino in the United States. Located near Oakland on a major commuter artery, the San Pablo Casino would generate an estimated $150 million per year in revenue payments to the state. In the face of vociferous political opposition, the governor backed out and declared a prohibition on any urban tribal casinos.[78]

Less than a decade later, two new off-reservation casinos were in the final stages of state approval. In 2010, the federal government approved two off-reservation applications in California, for the North Fork Rancheria of Mono Indians and the Enterprise Rancheria of the Estom Yumeka Maidu. Both were approved by Democratic Governor Jerry Brown. As of this writing, the North Fork casino had achieved final approval by the state legislature, prompting calls to reform state policy on off-reservation gaming and generating legal challenge under California's constitution, while the Enterprise project was awaiting legislative approval.[79]

In the mid-2000s, Colorado's Republican Governor Bill Owens rejected a billion-dollar-offer from the Cheyenne and Arapaho Indians for a 500-acre parcel near Denver and the state's blessing in pursuit of building one of the

---

tion, and for a tribe without a reservation, lands within its last recognized reservation in the state in which the tribe presently is located similarly are exempt, as are lands acquired through settlement of a land claim. Id. §§ 2719(a), 2719(b)(1)(B)(i). None of these situations, though, is subject to the specified secretarial and gubernatorial approval in section 2719(b)(1)(A). For any exception, the requirements of "Indian lands" also must be met. Id. § 2703(4). As we note in Chapter 3, determinations of existing or past reservation boundaries and the exercise of tribal governmental authority over lands are fact-intensive inquiries. See, e.g., Kansas v. United States, 249 F.3d 1213 (10th Cir. 2001).

78. Dean E. Murphy, "California Deal Authorizes Huge Casino Near Oakland," *New York Times*, Aug. 20, 2004. The proposed off-reservation casino generated significant political controversy in Congress. See generally Oversight Hearing on S. 113 Before the U.S. Senate Committee on Indian Affairs (Apr. 5, 2005), http://indian.senate.gov/mainpage.htm (last visited Aug. 28, 2005).

79. See Marc Benjamin, "Legislators Want New Policy After North Fork Casino Approval," *Fresno Bee*, July 7, 2013; Anthony York, "New Tribal Casino Gets Rare Approval," *L.A. Times*, June 29, 2013.

world's largest casino developments.[80] Oregon's Democratic Governor Ted Ku-longoski in spring 2005 approved a tribal casino in the scenic Columbia River Gorge, some 40 miles east of Portland. The Confederated Tribes of Warm Springs in return pledged to share a significant percentage of the 500,000-square foot casino's revenue with the state. After Kulongoski was defeated by Democrat John Kitzhaber in the 2010 gubernatorial election, the tribe's casino project stalled in the face of Kitzhaber's opposition.[81]

Following the lead of Minnesota's Republican Governor Tim Pawlenty's un-realized efforts in the mid-2000s to partner with three impoverished tribes in the state's rural northwest in a proposed tribal-state venture near the Twin Cities of Minneapolis and St. Paul,[82] Democratic Massachusetts Governor Deval Patrick recently negotiated a compact with the Mashpee Wampanoag Tribe to allow the recently acknowledged and currently landless tribe to open a casino. The state's plans, stemming from its legalization of casino gambling to stop the flood of gaming dollars to neighboring states, alternate between a state-licensed casino on non-tribal land to a tribal casino governed by IGRA and conditioned on the tribe's successful land-into-trust application.[83]

Despite the proliferation and diversity of proposed off-reservation casino ventures, IGRA's legal restrictions in conjunction with the variables of state and local politics make it extremely difficult for tribes to acquire off-reservation

---

80. See Dave Curtin, "Tribes Won't Pursue Pueblo Casino," *Denver Post*, Oct. 4, 2005; Fox Butterfield, "Indians' Wish List: Big-City Sites for Casinos," *New York Times*, Apr. 8, 2005.

81. See Kathie Durbin, "Tribe Plans Temporary Casino," *Columbian* (Vancouver, WA), Feb. 11, 2011; Brad Cain, "Tribal Casino Off Tribal Land Gets OK in Ore.," *Seattle Times*, Apr. 6, 2005, http://seattletimes.com/html/localnews/2002232636_casino06m.html (last visited Apr. 11, 2014).

82. In return for the state's support of the joint venture, the Leech Lake, White Earth, and Red Lake Chippewa Bands would have paid an initial $200 million licensing fee to the state, financed an estimated $575 million bond issue, and paid the state approximately $160 million per year. The tribes would have received up to $180 million annually over the first five years of the casino's operation. In the face of political opposition, the tribal-state casino, however, did not materialize. See Pat Doyle, "Backers of Metro Casino Give New Financial Details," *Minneapolis Star-Tribune*, Mar. 30, 2005.

83. At the time of this writing, the tribe's land-into-trust application had not been ap-proved, nor had the compact (which was renegotiated by the governor after the first com-pact was disapproved by the Interior Secretary). See, e.g., Gerry Tuoti, "Clock Ticking on Mashpees' Land-in-Trust Bid," *Taunton Daily Gazette*, July 14, 2013, http://www.taunton gazette.com/x1806124691/Clock-ticking-on-Mashpees-land-in-trust-bid (last visited Apr. 1, 2014); George Brennan, "Road to Taunton Casino Meets State, Federal Speed Bumps," *Cape Cod Times*, July 8, 2013, http://www.southcoasttoday.com/apps/pbcs.dll/article?AID=/ 20130708/NEWS/307080307 (last visited Apr. 1, 2014).

land for the express purpose of casino development.[84] For decades, only three tribes operated off-reservation casinos: the Forest County Potawatomi in Wisconsin, the Kalispel Tribe, located in Washington State, and the Keweenaw Bay Indian Community in Michigan.[85] In 2010, Obama administration Interior Secretary Ken Salazar issued a memorandum directing the BIA to develop clear and sound policy governing land-into-trust applications for the purpose of gaming.[86] At that time, the Secretary had approved only five applications under the "best interests" or "two-part determination" provision and 36 applications under the reservation and "equal footing" exceptions. The new approach to land-into-trust opened the floodgates—in a relative sense.

In 2011, Assistant Secretary for Indian Affairs Larry Echo Hawk approved the two California applications by the North Fork Rancheria and the Enterprise Rancheria noted above. Two more applications in Oklahoma, one for 127 acres for gaming purposes in 2012 for the Tonkawa Tribe and one for 21 acres for a casino in 2013 for the Kaw Nation, were approved by Echo Hawk's successor, Kevin Washburn.[87]

While the issue of tribal land acquisition for the purpose of opening a casino most likely will remain in the spotlight in a number of communities, the vast majority of tribal efforts to seek community and state support for off-reservation casino developments fade long before they reach the stage of Interior Secretary and gubernatorial approval mandated by IGRA. Nevertheless, federal policymakers continue to consider whether to amend IGRA to curb the possibility that off-reservation casinos would proliferate.

* * *

---

84. See generally Steven A. Light and Kathryn R.L. Rand, "Are All Bets Off? Off-Reservation Indian Gaming in Wisconsin," *Gaming Law Review* 5 (2001): 351–63; Heidi McNeil Staudenmaier, "Off-Reservation Native American Gaming: An Examination of the Legal and Political Hurdles," *Nevada Law Journal* 4 (2004): 301–18.

85. Kramer, "Current Issues," 330. The Potawatomi Tribe's efforts were successful under IGRA's exceptions for obtaining a governor's concurrence. In 1992, federal officials ruled the tribe possessed trust ownership of the land on which its Greater Milwaukee bingo hall was built prior to IGRA's enactment. Richard P. Jones, "Tribes Push Casinos on Many Fronts," *Milwaukee Journal Sentinel*, Sept. 18, 2000.

86. Memorandum from Secretary of Interior Ken Salazar to Assistant Secretary-Indian Affairs Larry Echo Hawk, "Decisions on Indian Gaming Applications," June 18, 2010, http://www.bia.gov/WhoWeAre/AS-IA/OIG/index.htm (last visited July 31, 2013).

87. See Office of the Assistant Secretary-Indian Affairs, "Washburn Issues Secretarial Determination on Gaming Application for Kaw Nation of Oklahoma," Press Release, May 24, 2013, http://www.bia.gov/News/index.htm (last visited July 31, 2013).

As our discussion of the debates surrounding IGRA's socioeconomic impacts and developing issues shows, politics and its close handmaiden, ideology, continue to drive Indian gaming policy across the United States. Within IGRA's framework and against the increasingly complicated background of tribal-state compacting, how will tribes, states, and the federal government continue to negotiate and implement Indian gaming law and policy? We turn now to some speculative observations on the future of tribal gaming.

CHAPTER 7

CONCLUSION: THE FUTURE OF INDIAN GAMING

The emergence and spectacular growth of the Indian gaming industry, and the dynamic nature of the law, politics, and policy that shape it, give rise to many questions whose answers will determine its future trajectory, including these:

- Will federal law and state public policy remain generally amenable to Indian gaming as a means of tribal economic development?
- Will tribes continue to use gaming to leverage reservation economic development and to strengthen tribal governments and tribal sovereignty?
- Will legalized gambling prove to be a stable economic base for tribal and state governments alike?
- How will market maturation, along with the aftermath of the national economic recession, affect the industry?
- Will the continuing development of federal Indian law—particularly U.S. Supreme Court decisions—support or hinder tribes' exercise of sovereignty and the federal government's fulfillment of its trust responsibility?
- Will states continue to seek compacting concessions from tribes, and will tribes continue to make them? Will the federal courts or the Interior Secretary adopt clear and enforceable legal limitations on revenue sharing?
- What disruptive innovations will be the biggest game-changers in casino financing and design, gaming technology and architecture, or intertribal and interstate partnerships?
- Will online and mobile gaming be legalized, and if so, how will it affect bricks-and-mortar casinos? Will legalization treat tribes as governments or as commercial operators?

The future of Indian gaming is tethered to a number of political, legal, and economic developments that can either stabilize or disrupt the industry. In particular, tribes and states find themselves at odds over how best to promote win-win outcomes through tribal gaming.

THE FUTURE OF LEGALIZED GAMBLING

As the National Gambling Impact Study Commission concluded in 1999, "the United States has been transformed from a nation in which legalized gambling was a limited and a relatively rare phenomenon into one in which such activity is common and growing."[1] Today, some form of gaming is legal in 48 states and the District of Columbia. Between 1993 and 2007, annual revenue generated by the entire legalized gambling industry steadily increased from about $35 billion to an estimated $125 billion.[2] But some industry observers warned that the growth in gaming was just the latest in legalized gambling's "classic 'boom and bust' cycles."[3] The recession's impact on the legalized gambling sector, including the bankruptcy filings of a few Atlantic City and Las Vegas casinos, seemed to give credence to a looming bust.[4] Others point to the industry's overall bounce-back after the national fiscal crisis as proof that legalized gambling remains a safe bet.[5]

Yet states increasingly are dependent on gambling revenues to fill coffers and avoid politically unpopular strategies such as raising income or property taxes. States are becoming more reliant on gambling to fund essential services, such as public education, medical care for the poor, and infrastructure and road maintenance. In fiscal year 2010, eight states collected more than $1 bil-

---

1. National Gambling Impact Study Commission, *Final Report* (1999), 1-1, http://gov info.library.unt.edu/ngisc/index.html (last visited Apr. 6, 2005).

2. American Gaming Association, "Gaming Revenue: 10-Year Trends," http://www.amer-icangaming.org/Industry/factsheets/statistics_detail.cfv?id=8 (last visited Apr. 13, 2005); Coleman Bazelon, Kevin Neels, and Pallavi Seth, *Beyond the Casino Floor: Economic Impacts of the Commercial Casino Industry* (Brattle Group, Feb. 2012), available at http://www.americangaming.org/sites/default/files/uploads/docs/final_final_brattle_study_2-3-12.pdf (last visited Apr. 3, 2014).

3. See, for example, John Warren Kindt, "The Business-Economic Impacts of Licensed Casino Gambling in West Virginia: Short-Term Gain but Long-Term Pain," http://www.pbs.org/wgbh/pages/frontline/shows/gamble/procon/kindt.html (last visited Apr. 13, 2005).

4. See, for example, Patrick Fitzgerald and Peg Brickly, "Atlantic Club Casino Hotel Files for Bankruptcy," *Wall Street Journal*, Nov. 7, 2013, http://online.wsj.com/news/articles/SB10001424052702304672404579182310842731866 (last visited Apr. 9, 2014); Howard Stutz, "Station Casinos Back on Track Post-bankruptcy CFO Says," *Las Vegas Review-Journal*, Mar. 19, 2013, http://www.reviewjournal.com/business/casinos-gaming/station-casinos-back-track-post-bankruptcy-cfo-says (last visited Apr. 9, 2014).

5. See, for example, I. Nelson Rose, "Gambling and the Law: Of Course It Was a Depression" (2010), http://www.gamblingandthelaw.com/index.php/articles/283-of-course-it-was-a-depression (last visited Dec. 12, 2013). For a scholarly analysis of the correlation between business cycles and legalized gambling, see Csilla Horvath and Richard Paap, "The Effect of Recessions on Gambling Expenditures," *Journal of Gambling Studies* 28 (2012): 703–17.

lion a year in gaming-related revenue from lotteries, casinos, racinos, and pari-mutuels, and ten more states exceeded $500 million.[6]

With state revenue shortfalls, many localities looked to tribal casinos as spurs for job creation and economic development. After all, in 2012 tribal gaming generated nearly 680,000 jobs and $7.6 billion in federal, state, and local tax revenue. Tribal-state compacts increasingly contain revenue-sharing provisions in which tribes make payments directly into community funds for public education or other local services, accounting for $1.6 billion in direct payments to federal, state, and local governments in 2012.[7] Some local and state officials, including Democratic Massachusetts Governor Deval Patrick, are courting tribal partners for innovative approaches to the expansion of legalized gambling, such as tribal casino licenses under state law, off-reservation casinos, and other ventures with commercial gaming interests.[8]

At the same time, movement toward widespread legalization of Internet gaming may change states' willingness to invest in Indian gaming. As of this writing, three states had authorized online gambling (Nevada, New Jersey, and Delaware) while Congress continued to consider federal authorization. With Americans already betting some $4 billion online already, New Jersey's Republican Governor Chris Christie hoped to collect $180 million in state taxes on legalized Internet gaming in 2013, though subsequent estimates were much lower.[9]

Federal legalization of online gaming appears to be the only realistic avenue for a regulatory policy in line with IGRA's goals and grounded in tribal sovereignty. State legalization appears likely to treat tribes no differently than commercial gaming operators, with a goal of state taxation and regulation of all legalized online gaming. We have advocated for an "Indian Gaming Ethic" to guide federal, state, and tribal policymaking in the area of legalized gambling.

---

6. Lucy Dadayan and Robert B. Ward, "Back in the Black," Nelson A. Rockefeller Institute of Government (June 23, 2011), available at http://www.rockinst.org/pdf/government_finance/2011-06-23-Back_in_the_Black.pdf (last visited Apr. 3, 2014).

7. Alan Meister, *Indian Gaming Industry Report, 2014 Ed.* (Newton, MA: Casino City Press, 2014), 3–4, 89.

8. See generally "Casino Gambling in Massachusetts," *Boston Globe*, at http://www.bostonglobe.com/metro/specials/casinos (last visited Apr. 3, 2014).

9. Pamela M. Prah, "Tribes, States Eye Multibillion-Dollar Online Gambling," *USA Today*, Dec. 11, 2013, http://www.usatoday.com/story/news/nation/2013/12/11/indian-tribes-states-eye-online-gambling/3986473/ (last visited Apr. 3, 2014); Caroline Winter, "Why New Jersey Fell Far Short of Online Gambling Expectations," *Bloomberg Business Week*, Apr. 1, 2014, http://www.businessweek.com/articles/2014-04-01/why-new-jersey-fell-far-short-of-online-gambling-expectations (reporting that New Jersey lowered estimates of revenue collection by as much as $150 million).

This Ethic incorporates three ideals: protection of, respect for, and responsible exercise of tribal sovereignty; promotion of tribal economic development, self-sufficiency, and strong tribal governments; and a general understanding of Indian gaming as a means to serve tribes, tribal members, and tribal values while contributing positively to the community.

Legalization of Internet or mobile gaming raises a number of concerns, including a possible fundamental disruption of the political compromise that gave rise to the current Indian gaming industry. In the context of online gaming, therefore, the Indian Gaming Ethic encourages Congress, states, and tribes to consider these issues as intrinsic to the policymaking process: the impact of online gaming on tribes' gaming operations, particularly for tribes that continue to experience high levels of poverty and unemployment; the impact of regulations on tribal sovereignty; equitable and respectful means of settling intergovernmental disputes; job creation through online gaming; government accessibility and accountability for negative socioeconomic impacts caused by online gaming; and ethical and responsible expansion of legalized gambling.[10]

It appears that legalized gambling in all its forms—tribal casinos, commercial casinos, state lotteries, charitable gambling, and pari-mutuel wagering—has become fully integrated into national, tribal, state, and local economies, and that widespread legalization of Internet gaming is just around the corner.

TRIBAL ECONOMIC DIVERSIFICATION

In large part with the experience and expertise gained and revenue earned from tribal gaming enterprises, many tribes have looked to other economic development strategies to diversify and stabilize reservation economies, especially as Indian gaming has become more dependent on the political demands of state and local policymakers and as online gaming may threaten the future of bricks-and-mortar casinos. More and more, tribes are pursuing long-term, multi-million-dollar investments in business ventures ranging from light manufacturing to banking. "There is a sense of urgency in Indian country to diversify tribal economies, which is why we're seeing tribal leaders invest in all forms of enterprises, from airline assembly plants to minimarts to shopping centers,"

---

10. Kathryn R.L. Rand and Steven Andrew Light, "Indian Gaming on the Internet: How the Indian Gaming Ethic Should Guide Tribes' Assessment of the Online Gaming Market," *Gaming Law Review & Economics* 15 (2011): 681–91.

said California Nations Indian Gaming Association spokesperson David Pallermo.[11]

Many tribes have focused economic diversification efforts in the hospitality sector, complementing gaming operations. Tribes continue to open hotels, golf courses, gas stations, RV parks—even, at long last, chain restaurants.[12] The Mississippi Band of Choctaw Indians, often lauded as a leader in tribal economic diversification, operates a range of business ventures along with its gaming enterprises, including tech and industrial parks, and defense manufacturing, commercial printing, and professional staffing businesses. All told, the tribe employs some 6,000 full-time workers, making it one of the ten largest employers in the state.[13] Even tribes with only modestly successful gaming enterprises are able to use gaming revenue to invest in other businesses. In North Dakota, for example, the Turtle Mountain Band of Chippewa has operated a metal fabrication manufacturing company, as well as data services and information technology enterprises, and has contracted with federal agencies including the U.S. Department of Defense.[14]

Dozens of tribes across the country are pursuing similar diversification strategies.[15] For example, the Fond du Lac Band of Lake Superior Chippewa in Wisconsin employs 1,400 workers in insurance, construction, logging, and other ventures, while the Coeur d'Alene Tribe in Idaho operates businesses in agriculture, manufacturing, and web services.[16] Perhaps the biggest tribal commercial deal in recent years was the Seminole Tribe of Florida's $965 million purchase of the Hard Rock brand, including cafes, hotels, and casinos, in 2007.[17]

---

11. Gillian Flaccus, "Seeing Need to Diversify, Tribes Looking Beyond Casinos," *Detroit News*, Mar. 29, 2003, http://www.detnews.com/2003/business/0303/30/business-122000.htm (last visited Apr. 10, 2005).

12. See Wyandotte Nation, "Wyandotte Nation Opens New SONIC in Seneca," Press Release, Nov. 18, 2013 (describing the combination pipe and ribbon-cutting ceremony to mark the opening of the drive-through restaurant).

13. Mississippi Band of Choctaw Indians, "Businesses," http://www.choctaw.org/businesses/index.html (last visited Dec. 16, 2013).

14. See Chippewa Tribal Industries, http://www.chippewatribal-ind.com/ (last visited Apr. 3, 2014).

15. See Valerie Red-Horse and Derril Jordan, "Tribal Economic Diversification: Expanding Beyond Gaming," *Casino Enterprise Management*, Oct. 2011, http://www.casino enterprisemanagement.com/articles/october-2011/tribal-economic-diversification-expanding-beyond-gaming (last visited Dec. 16, 2013).

16. See Mark Fogarty, "The Growing Economic Might of Indian Country," *Indian Country Today*, Mar. 15, 2013, http://indiancountrytodaymedianetwork.com/2013/03/15/growing-economic-might-indian-country-148196 (last visited Dec. 16, 2013).

17. See Matt Krantz, "Seminole Tribe of Florida Buys Hard Rock Cafes, Hotels, Casinos," *USA Today*, Dec. 7, 2006, http://usatoday30.usatoday.com/money/industries/food/

Although tribes plainly will seek to stabilize and grow reservation economies as well as strengthen tribal governments and tribal sovereignty through diverse economic ventures, it appears that the continued relative profitability of tribal gaming enterprises will keep Indian gaming a staple of many tribal economies for the foreseeable future.

Tribes as Governments and Gaming Operators

Legal and political issues also arise from tribes' dual status as both governments and gaming operators. Once the Great Recession hit tribal casinos, questions arose about federal bankruptcy laws' applicability to tribes, leading some experts to advocate for tribes to enact tribal bankruptcy codes. As sovereign nations, most legal experts opined that tribes are unable to file for bankruptcy protection under federal law, while tribes' sovereign status also prevented creditors from seizing the assets of a defaulting tribe.[18]

The most pressing questions were inspired by the surprising (but apparently temporary) turn of fortune of the Mashantucket Pequots' highly profitable Foxwoods Resort Casino, which appeared to be on the brink of bankruptcy in 2009. A few years earlier, the tribe had entered into a landmark licensing deal with then-MGM Mirage to open the MGM Grand at Foxwoods, with 800 hotel rooms, 1,400 slot machines and a 4,000-seat theater. After laying off 700 workers in the wake of a 13% decline in profits in 2008, the tribe faced the due date for a $700 million line of credit. Angering creditors, then-tribal chair Michael Thomas promised to continue to honor per capita payments to tribal members

---

2006-12-07-seminoles-hardrock_x.htm (last visited Dec. 16, 2013). The deal is thought to be the largest involving an American Indian tribe. Id.

18. See, e.g., Amanda L. Cartwright, "Can Native American-Owned Casinos File for Chapter 11?", *American Bankruptcy Institute Journal*, Oct. 2012; Alexander Hogan, "Protecting Native American Communities by Preserving Sovereign Immunity and Determining the Place of Tribal Businesses in the Federal Bankruptcy Code," *Columbia Human Rights Law Review* 43 (2012): 569; Corina Rocha Pendali, "When the Chips Are Down: Do Indian Tribes with Insolvent Gaming Operations Have the Ability to File for Bankruptcy Under the Federal Bankruptcy Code?", *UNLV Gaming Law Journal* 2 (2011): 255; Anthony S. Broadman, "Indian Self-Governance and Bankruptcy: The Case for Tribal Law," *Casino Enterprise Management*, Feb. 1, 2011, http://www.casinoenterprisemanagement.com/articles/february-2011/indian-self-governance-and-bankruptcy-case-tribal-law (last visited Apr. 5, 2014).

despite the Tribe's escalating debt, leading to his ouster by the tribal council. "[W]e opened the doors at the MGM Grand, and five months later, Lehman crashes and the world falls apart," said Rodney Butler, who was elected chair in 2009. In 2013, the tribe successfully negotiated an agreement with more than 100 creditors, including Bank of America and Wells Fargo, to restructure about $2.3 billion of debt. Shortly thereafter, the tribe and MGM Resorts International announced the dissolution of their licensing agreement, and the MGM Grand was rebranded as the Fox Tower.[19]

As tribes are more widely perceived as sophisticated business owners, federal laws meant to protect tribes are subject to challenge. In *Wells Fargo Bank v. Lake of the Torches Economic Development Corporation*, the federal court voided a tribe's $50 million bond debt, a controversial and significant development in the unmapped area of tribal finance and federal law. The Lac du Flambeau Chippewa Tribe in Wisconsin, through its Lake of the Torches Economic Development Corporation, in 2008 had entered into a deal—a trust indenture—with Wells Fargo Bank to refinance and expand the tribe's Grand Soleil casino project in Natchez, Mississippi. The Grand Soleil project, in the works since 2005, had hit hard times and as a result, the tribe was unable to make the promised bond payments due under the trust indenture. The bond was secured by the tribe's revenue at its Lake of the Torches Resort Casino in Vilas County, Wisconsin. Wells Fargo sued the tribe for breach of the deal and asked the court to put the tribe's casino in receivership. The tribe argued that the trust indenture was, in fact, a management contract under IGRA, as evidenced by such provisions as Wells Fargo's right to hire and fire key personnel, including the casino manager. Because the deal had not been submitted to and approved by the NIGC as a management contract, the tribe's argument continued, it was void. The federal district court agreed and dismissed Wells Fargo's suit: "The bonds are void merely because they are collateral to an unapproved management contract." The U.S. Court of Appeals for the Seventh Circuit upheld the decision, similarly concluding that the indenture

19. Michael Sokolove, "Foxwoods Is Fighting for Its Life," *New York Times Magazine*, Mar. 14, 2012, http://www.nytimes.com/2012/03/18/magazine/mike-sokolove-foxwood-casinos.html?pagewanted=all&_r=0 (last visited Apr. 5, 2014); Emily Glazer, "Casino Owner Reaches Debt Deal," *Wall Street Journal*, June 30, 2013, http://online.wsj.com/news/articles/SB10001424127887323368920457857410404761046 8 (last visited Apr. 5, 2014). Tribal Chair Thomas later faced federal criminal charges. "Former Mashantucket Pequot Chairman, Current Treasurer Plead Not Guilty to Stealing $800,000," *Indian Country Today*, Jan. 8, 2013, http://indiancountrytodaymedianetwork.com/2013/01/08/former-mashantucket-pequot-chairman-current-treasurer-plead-not-guilty-stealing-800000 (last visited Apr. 5, 2014).

constitutes a management contract under IGRA and that, as a condition of its validity, it should have been submitted to the Chairman of
the NIGC for approval prior to its implementation. The parties' failure to secure such approval renders the Indenture void in its entirety
and thus invalidates the Corporation's waiver of sovereign immunity.[20]

Some commentators predicted that the ruling would discourage investors from
doing business with tribes, especially at the height of the economic recession
when uncertainty loomed large, as there is very little legal precedent for what
happens when a tribal casino goes bankrupt or a tribe defaults on a loan. While
the court's decision was controversial, it provided some guidance in this area.
Yet it is extremely difficult to prove a negative—that is, to determine whether
Wells Fargo Bank had any additional impact on tribal-commercial ventures.

In 2007, in *San Manuel Indian Bingo & Casino v. NLRB*, the federal appeals
court upheld the National Labor Relations Board (NLRB) ruling that the National Labor Relations Act applies to tribal enterprises. The NLRB's 2004 ruling reversed its earlier position that tribal businesses were exempt from the
Act, along with the federal government, states, and political subdivisions. The
agency instead concluded that because tribes were not expressly included in
the statutory exemption provision, "Congress purposely chose not to exclude
Indian tribes from the Act's jurisdiction." The U.S. Court of Appeals for the
D.C. Circuit agreed, holding that the Act is a statute of general application and
therefore applies to tribal commercial enterprises.[21] The NLRB's position opened
the door to labor unions' organizing tribal casino employees. In 2011, the Interior Department's Deputy Solicitor for Indian Affairs urged the NLRB to return to its original position exempting tribes from the Act, and a legislative

---

20. Wells Fargo Bank v. Lake of the Torches Econ. Dev. Corp., 677 F. Supp.2d 1056
(W.D. Wis. 2010), *aff'd*, 658 F.3d 684 (7th Cir. 2011). While the NIGC's treatment of collateral agreements (IGRA employs an "anti-loophole" definition of "management contract"
as including all collateral agreements) has been somewhat controversial, it is meant to prevent lenders and tribes from avoiding the management contract requirements by simply
putting prohibited provisions in side deals.

21. San Manuel Band Indian Bingo & Casino v. NLRB, 341 N.L.R.B. 1055 (2004), *aff'd*,
745 F.3d 1306 (D.C. Cir. 2007). See also, for example, Derek Ghan, "Federal Labor Law
and the Mashantucket Pequots: Union Organizing at Foxwoods Casino," *American Indian
Law Review* 37 (2012): 515; Vicki Limas, "The Tuscarorganization of the Tribal Workforce,"
Michigan State Law Review 2008: 467; Bryan H. Wildenthal, "Federal Labor Law, Indian
Sovereignty, and the Canons of Construction," *Oregon Law Review* 86 (2007): 413; Anna Wer-
muth, "Union's Gamble Pays Off: In *San Manuel Indian Bingo & Casino*, the NLRB Breaks
the Nation's Promise and Reverses Decades-Old Precedent to Assert Jurisdiction Over Tribal
Enterprises on Indian Reservations," *The Labor Lawyer* 21 (2005): 81.

"fix" was introduced in Congress.[22] Though neither effort was successful, at the time of this writing, additional challenges to the NLRB's assertion of jurisdiction over tribal enterprises were expected to be decided in the Tenth and Sixth Circuits.[23]

Law Reform to "Fix" Indian Gaming

In the first decade of the twenty-first century, those who felt Indian gaming was "broken" focused on law reform to fix perceived problems related to the rapid expansion of tribal gaming. This included federal efforts to curtail the so-called practice of "reservation shopping" by tribes seeking to open off-reservation casinos on land near metropolitan areas and transportation arteries, to give states, localities, or other tribes greater say in the process of approving new gaming operations, and to ban tribes from seeking casinos across state lines.[24] Many tribal and industry representatives were concerned that if Congress took up the issue of off-reservation gaming, it would open up IGRA to amendment to address other perceived problems with Indian gaming, such as the alleged hijacking of federal tribal acknowledgment by the lure of gaming profits, or to acquiesce to the growing sense that states are entitled to a cut of tribal gaming profits through revenue-sharing agreements. The possibility of a congressional free-for-all to "fix" Indian gaming had tribal and industry association leaders extremely concerned. "We see no need to open up the act," stated J. Kurt Luger, Executive Director of the Great Plains Indian Gaming Association.[25]

---

22. Letter from Patrice H. Kunesh, Deputy Solicitor for Indian Affairs, to Lafe Solomon, Acting General Counsel, NLRB, Dec. 7, 2011, available at http://turtletalk.files.wordpress.com/2011/12/nlrb-12-7-11.pdf (last visited Apr. 5, 2014); Tribal Labor Sovereignty Act, H.R. 2335, 112th Cong. (2011).

23. In 2013, the NLRB issued three decisions—involving the Chickasaw Nation's WinStar World Casino in Oklahoma, the Little River Band's Little River Casino Resort, and the Saginaw Chippewa Indian Tribe's Soaring Eagle Casino and Resort, both in Michigan—relying on *San Manuel Indian Bingo & Casino* to assert jurisdiction over the tribes. Chickasaw Nation, 359 N.R.L.B. 163 (2013); Little River Band of Ottawa Indians, 359 N.R.L.B. 54 (2013); Soaring Eagle Casino & Resort, 359 N.L.R.B. 92 (2013).

24. Fox Butterfield, "Indians' Wish List: Big-City Sites for Casinos," *New York Times*, Apr. 8, 2005. In 2005 and 2008, we testified before the U.S. Senate Indian Affairs Committee concerning the regulation of Indian gaming and other issues. See Kathryn R.L. Rand and Steven Andrew Light, Statement Before the U.S. Senate Committee on Indian Affairs (Apr. 27, 2005); Kathryn R.L. Rand and Steven Andrew Light, Statement Before the U.S. Senate Committee on Indian Affairs (Apr. 17, 2008).

25. Jodi Rave, "Western Governors Consider Changes to Indian Gaming Law," *Missou-*

More recently, legislative reform efforts have focused on a "*Carcieri* fix" to allow the U.S. Interior Secretary to take land into trust for tribes acknowledged after 1934, as well as multiple pushes to legalize Internet gaming, while curtailing off-reservation gaming also continues to be a significant political lightning rod that connects the two. In late 2013, Sen. Dianne Feinstein (D-Calif.), a staunch opponent of the expansion of Indian gaming, told the Senate Indian Affairs Committee that "any *Carcieri* fix must address concerns about tribal gaming," including federal recognition of additional tribes, "out of state" tribal casinos, and the Department of the Interior's authority over trust lands and gaming.[26] Tribes called for a "clean" fix focused solely on the power to take land into trust, as opposed to legislation that would amend IGRA or constrain tribal gaming.[27]

Political Influence

Because IGRA makes casino-style gaming contingent upon the successful negotiation of tribal-state compacts, tribes increasingly are participating as insiders in the American political process. Yet garnering political support for casino-style tribal gaming requires a considerable investment and outlay of political and financial capital. Tribes see expenditures on lobbying, campaign contributions, ballot initiatives, and public relations as the means to make their voices heard in the crowded federal, state, and local political arenas— and as the vehicle both to preserve and to advance their interests.[28] Neverthe-

lian (Mont.), Mar. 30, 2005, http://missoulian.com/news/state-and-regional/western-governors-consider-changes-to-indian-gaming-law/article_94f6ed67-7d5b-57e0-98ad-29b 30fff627e.html (last visited Dec. 16, 2013). Luger argued for enforcement of IGRA's existing provisions for taking land into trust rather than a possible amendment to deter off-reservation gaming. Id.

26. See Gale Courey Toensing, "Feinstein Insists *Carcieri* Fix Address Her Opposition to Tribal Gaming," *Indian Country Today*, Dec. 2, 2013, http://indiancountrytodaymedianetwork.com/2013/12/02/feinstein-carcieri-fix-must-address-concerns-about-tribal-gaming-152514 (last visited Dec. 16, 2013). In 2013, Sen. Feinstein introduced legislation intended to make it more difficult for land to be taken into trust for gaming purposes. Tribal Gaming Eligibility Act, S. 477, 113th Cong. (2013).

27. See Rob Capriccioso, "So Close! How the Senate Almost Passed a Clean *Carcieri* Fix," *Indian Country Today*, Sept. 19, 2013, http://indiancountrytodaymedianetwork.com/2013/09/19/how-clean-carcieri-fix-almost-passed-senate-151346 (last visited Dec. 16, 2013) (describing the failure in the 112th Congress to pass legislation addressing the Court's *Carcieri* decision).

28. See Kenneth N. Hansen and Tracy A. Skopek, eds., *The New Politics of Indian Gaming* (Reno: University of Nevada Press, 2011); Glenn F. Bunting and Dan Morain, "Tribes

less, tribes' efforts remain constrained by their status inside and outside the American political system.

Tribes continue to frame Indian gaming as a vehicle through which to further tribal self-governance and economic self-sufficiency, and more recently as the foundation for tribal-state partnerships to support both tribal and local economies. The former argument pulls less weight today, while the latter has met with general success in influencing voters and policymakers. However, if tribes are perceived as using gaming revenue to manipulate the electoral process or influence public policy for tribal gain, the non-Indian public's reaction is downright chilly, at best.[29] Tribes also have become wary of tapping into public distaste for the appearance that any "special interest" is "buying" political influence or votes. For opponents, "one slur tactic has been to tie Indian donations directly to gaming—as if every dollar every tribe spends on contributions is meant to promote the endless proliferation of slot machines."[30]

It should go without saying that tribes are not the only ones attempting to influence public policy outcomes through lobbying and political expenditures.[31] The recent visibility of Indian gaming, however, and the fact that tribal governments' political spending has increased rather dramatically in recent years have led many observers to pay particular attention to tribal activities in these areas. Much of this attention has been critical.[32] Commenting on tribal government donations of more than $1 million to President Obama's 2012 re-election campaign, National Congress of American Indians executive director

---

Take a Wait-and-See Recall Stance," *Los Angeles Times*, Aug. 17, 2003, B1 ("The tribes were invisible until they started writing checks. There is no better illustration of the power of money in politics.") (quoting Jim Knox of California Common Cause).

29. See Jeffrey Ashley, Tribal Use of Public Relations to Shape Public Policy, unpublished manuscript presented at the Annual Meeting of the Midwest Political Science Association in Chicago, Illinois (Apr. 2004) (discussing how tribes in Arizona successfully publicized a pro-Indian gaming ballot initiative as promoting tribal self-reliance); Chad M. Gordon, "From Hope to Realization of Dreams: Proposition 5 and California Indian Gaming," in Angela Mullis and David Kamper, eds., *Indian Gaming: Who Wins?* (Los Angeles: UCLA American Indian Studies Center, 2000), 7–8.

30. Rob Capriccioso, "Tribes Among Biggest Campaign Contributors," *Indian Country Today*, Mar. 22, 2011, http://indiancountrytodaymedianetwork.com/2011/03/22/tribes-among-biggest-campaign-contributors-23876 (last visited Apr. 3, 2014).

31. See id.; Jerry Reynolds, "Lobbying Money Raises Hard Questions" [Editorial], *Indian Country Today*, Apr. 16, 2004 (arguing that all large political contributions and lobbying efforts—not just tribes'—call into question the integrity of the American political system).

32. See, for example, Donald L. Barlett and James B. Steele, "Playing the Political Slots," *Time*, Dec. 16, 2002.

Jacqueline Pata said, "We don't get everything we want, but we are actually able to participate in the dialogue." Countered prominent tribal gaming opponent Cheryl Schmit, "Tribal casinos make a lot of money and make major contributions. Our voice is not heard in this process."[33]

It seems a safe bet that proposed amendments to IGRA and other legislation impacting Indian gaming will continue to be introduced and debated in Congress, while states and localities adjust their own laws and policies to address issues raised by tribal gaming. American Indian tribes undoubtedly will continue to seek to influence policy outcomes at federal, state, and local levels, exerting political influence where they can. At the same time, of course, other organizations similarly will attempt to shape policy, as well.

* * *

As we have seen throughout the second edition of this book, the law and policy of Indian gaming is complex and complicated, fraught with intricacies and pitfalls. Because of its foundation in tribal sovereignty and federal Indian law, tribal gaming law and policy is grounded in both historical and contemporary events and concepts that understandably may be unfamiliar to practitioners, policymakers, and the public, despite the proliferation of tribal casinos across the U.S. and accompanying media attention. Moreover, even a complete conversance with IGRA is insufficient to comprehend the wide range of political strategies and actors that may influence policy outcomes.

Indian gaming has changed dramatically since those first bingo halls were opened in Florida and California some three decades ago. One could scarcely have imagined the fundamental changes that have occurred in the 26 years since IGRA was enacted. Because of their critically important roles in determining where tribal gaming will head in its next three decades, practitioners and policymakers alike must be cognizant of that history, the underlying legal and regulatory framework, and current jurisprudential and political realities in navigating the ever-changing terrain of this complex field. The future of Indian gaming depends on it.

---

33. Fredreka Schouten, "Tribal Donations Increase to President Obama's Campaign," *USA Today*, May 15, 2012, http://usatoday30.usatoday.com/news/washington/story/2012-05-14/tribal-giving-increases-to-obama-campaign/54962446/1 (last visited Apr. 3, 2014).

APPENDIX A

Researching Indian Gaming

Policymakers and practitioners, students and scholars alike must be thorough as well as creative in researching topics related to Indian gaming so as to obtain the most accurate, complete, and up-to-date information available. It is important to view all accounts, whether journalistic, anecdotal, or academic, with a careful and critical eye to methodology, framing, and findings. Complicating matters, because of the inherent role of politics in determining the law and policy of Indian gaming, a myriad of issues related to tribal gaming across the United States develop and evolve on a day-to-day basis. Although we have yet to find an exclusive source for "one-stop shopping," there is a relative wealth of information on tribal gaming if one knows where to look, and how to start.

Academic Institutes and Information Clearinghouses

Several institutes and information clearinghouses are affiliated with universities and conduct and publish scholarly research as well as distribute information on gambling generally or Indian gaming specifically. We start with our own institute, which we co-founded and co-direct, and which focuses on Indian gaming, as does our blog, *Indian Gaming Now*.

Institute for the Study of Tribal Gaming Law and Policy
https://law.und.edu/npilc/gaming/index.cfm
> The first and only academic institute dedicated exclusively to Indian gaming. A component of the University of North Dakota School of Law's Northern Plains Indian Law Center, the Institute's mission is to provide information and assistance related to Indian gaming to all interested governments and organizations, assist tribes in pursuing economic development and strengthening tribal governments, and conduct scholarly and practical research to advance the state of knowledge about tribal gaming. The co-directors, Rand and Light, are a law professor and a political scientist,

and therefore adopt an interdisciplinary perspective on Indian gaming, incorporating law, political science, and public administration.

Indian Gaming Now
http://indiangamingnow.com/
  Rand and Light blog on all things Indian gaming and related issues.

* * *

Alberta Gambling Research Institute
http://www.abgamblinginstitute.ualberta.ca/
  A consortium among the University of Alberta, University of Calgary, and the University of Lethbridge, the Institute's primary purpose is to support and promote research into gambling, including aboriginal or First Nations gaming operations, in the Canadian province of Alberta.

Center for Gaming Research at the University of Nevada, Las Vegas
http://gaming.unlv.edu/
  Provides an extensive database of links to resources on gaming ranging from advocacy groups to information on problem and pathological gambling, as well as a robust collection of podcasts. Home of the UNLV Gaming Press.

Center for Gambling Studies at Rutgers University
http://socialwork.rutgers.edu/centersandprograms/centerforgamblingstudies.aspx
  With a focus on problem gambling and housed in social work, the Center conducts research and provides training and intervention programs.

Gambling and the Law
http://www.gamblingandthelaw.com/
  Includes analysis of the gaming industry by a leading expert in gambling law at Whittier Law School. Provides a diverse list of links to gaming-related Internet sites.

Harvard Project on American Indian Economic Development
http://hpaied.org/
  An excellent resource for general research on tribal governance, social and economic conditions on reservations, and tribal economic development initiatives. Affiliates have conducted several rigorous studies on the social and economic effects of tribal gaming. The Project's web site also links to an annotated bibliography of gambling impact studies.

International Gaming Institute at the University of Nevada, Las Vegas
http://www.unlv.edu/igi

> An academic and continuing education program as well as a scholarly resource, the Institute publishes the *UNLV Gaming Research and Review Journal.*

Institute for the Study of Gambling and Commercial Gaming at the University of Nevada, Reno
http://www.unr.edu/gaming

> Pioneering in its emphasis on encouraging and publishing scholarly research on gambling and the gaming industry. The Institute sponsors an international conference featuring scholarship on gambling. The Institute's web site has links to various electronic publications and general sources for gaming news, as well as books published under its imprint.

Library Gaming Collection at the University of Nevada, Las Vegas
http://library.nevada.edu/speccol/gaming/

> A comprehensive online clearinghouse for gambling-related information, including links to corporate archives and financial reports, fiction and popular books about gambling, links to scholarly monographs and periodicals, oral histories, and photographs.

JOURNALS

As of this book's first edition nearly a decade ago, very few academic journals were devoted to publishing scholarly research on gambling. Today there are many more, most either law reviews or peer-reviewed journals with an interdisciplinary emphasis. None has an exclusive focus on Indian gaming. A number of the journals listed below periodically publish articles on tribal gaming or related topics, and several of the law reviews have published a symposium issue on Indian gaming. We start with arguably the premier journal in this area, at least for law practitioners, and certainly in terms of routinely publishing on Indian gaming.

Gaming Law Review and Economics: Regulation, Compliance, and Policy
http://www.liebertpub.com/overview/gaming-law-review-and-economics-regulation-compliance-and-policy/16/

> Focuses on peer-reviewed articles as well as case summaries by legal scholars and practitioners. Publishes with some frequency articles on Indian gaming, including the occasional symposium issue.

American Indian Culture and Research Journal
http://aisc.metapress.com/content/120819
> The premier interdisciplinary journal on American Indian studies. Affiliated with the UCLA American Indian Studies Center, the journal publishes research related to tribal culture, traditions, and practices, tribal sovereignty, policy issues, and American Indian literature.

American Indian Law Journal
http://www.law.seattleu.edu/academics/journals/ailj
> Affiliated with Seattle University School of Law, this student-edited online journal publishes articles on Indian law, including in the areas of tax, property, contracts, gaming, and environmental law.

American Indian Law Review
http://www.law.ou.edu/content/american-indian-law-review-2
> Affiliated with the University of Oklahoma School of Law, this student-edited journal publishes research on federal Indian law and related topics.

Journal of Gambling Business and Economics
http://www.ubplj.org/index.php/jgbe/index
> An international peer-reviewed journal focused on academic research as well as content relevant to commercial industry.

Journal of Gambling Issues
http://www.camh.net/egambling/
> A Canadian online journal that publishes peer-reviewed research on the prevalence and treatment of problem and pathological gambling.

UNLV Gaming Law Journal
http://law.unlv.edu/unlv-gaming-law-journal.html
> A student-edited law journal at the William S. Boyd School of Law, published in conjunction with the International Masters of Gaming Law.

Society for the Study of Gambling Newsletter
http://www.societystudygambling.co.uk/about-the-society/
> Provides updates on research about gambling.

UNLV Gaming Research and Review Journal
http://www.unlv.edu/hotel/gaming-research-review-journal
> Publishes interdisciplinary peer-reviewed research especially on subjects related to the commercial gaming industry, including casino operations, gaming law and regulation, management, technology, community relations, and responsible gaming.

Trade Publications

Casino City Press
http://www.casinocitypress.com/
> Reports, directories, and other publications on the gaming industry generally and the tribal gaming industry specifically. Publishes the well-respected annual *Indian Gaming Industry Report.*

Casino Enterprise Management Magazine
http://www.casinoenterprisemanagement.com
> Monthly trade publication that regularly addresses issues directly related to tribal casinos.

Casino Journal
http://www.casinojournal.com/publications/3
> Commercial trade publication.

Casino Lawyer
http://www.gaminglawmasters.com/magazines/
> Magazine published twice annually by the International Masters of Gaming Law, with articles of global reach, including regular features related to Indian gaming.

Gambling Compliance
http://www.gamblingcompliance.com/
> Daily online news, analysis, and "independent business intelligence" pertaining to the global gambling industry.

Indian Gaming Magazine
http://www.indiangaming.com/home/
> American Indian Gaming Industry trade publication.

Responsible Gaming Quarterly
http://www.ncrg.org/resources/rgq
> Published jointly by the American Gaming Association and the National Center for Responsible Gambling. Highlights industry efforts to prevent or combat problem and pathological gambling.

The WAGER and *BASIS*
http://www.basisonline.org/
> The Worldwide Addiction Gambling Education Report (*The WAGER*) and Brief Addiction Science Information Source (*BASIS*) are published by the

Cambridge Health Alliance, a center for the study of addictive behavior
and an affiliate of Harvard Medical School.

NEWS AND CURRENT EVENTS

Indian Country Today
http://www.indiancountry.com/
   Links to articles on a host of issues, including Indian gaming.

indianz.com
http://www.indianz.com
   Provides links to news occurring in Indian country, including regular coverage of Indian gaming.

NativeWeb
http://www.nativeweb.org/
   An online clearinghouse for Native American and global indigenous news
   sources.

Pechanga.net
http://www.pechanga.net/
   Well-reputed media clearinghouse, updated daily and jam-packed with
   articles on Indian gaming and other topics from media sources across the
   United States.

BOOKS

In the last decade, the growing fascination with gambling writ large, as well
as the increasing number of law schools that now offer gambling law in the
curriculum, have prompted authors to take up topics related to gambling history, law, and addiction. Accompanying inclusion of federal Indian law, policy, and history in more law and graduate programs has expanded the market
for casebooks, case studies of particular tribes, and historical overviews.

   A still-small but significant number of scholarly books explore Indian gaming from varying perspectives.[1] On tribal gaming, we start, naturally enough,

---

1. Indian gaming—or more specifically, as framed by the controversial story of Mashantucket Pequots and their successful Foxwoods Resort and Casino in Connecticut—also has
been the subject of several book-length journalistic accounts. See Jeff Benedict, *Without
Reservation: The Making of America's Most Powerful Indian Tribe and Foxwoods, the World's*

with our own work, including two additional books we co-authored, and three recent edited volumes to which we contributed chapters.

Steven Andrew Light and Kathryn R.L. Rand, *Indian Gaming and Tribal Sovereignty: The Casino Compromise* (Lawrence, KS: University Press of Kansas, 2005)

> A comprehensive scholarly account, grounded in tribal sovereignty, of the legal and political compromises that have shaped Indian gaming. Includes a discussion of how popular culture influences policymaking, extensive analysis of socioeconomic impacts, and suggestions for various policy reforms intended to balance competing imperatives among tribes and states while creating win-win outcomes and respecting tribal sovereignty.

Kathryn R.L. Rand and Steven Andrew Light, *Indian Gaming Law: Cases and Materials* (Durham, NC: Carolina Academic Press, 2008) (with accompanying *Instructor's Manual*)

> Comprehensive interdisciplinary casebook with foundation in tribal history and sovereignty that includes excerpts from case law, statutes, and regulations as well as from books, journal articles, and testimony by key authorities in the field. Includes case studies of individual tribes, group and individual exercises to promote understanding, web links to capture dynamic developments in Indian gaming, and supplementary background resources.

David G. Schwartz and Pauliina Raento, eds., *Gambling, Space, and Time: Shifting Boundaries and Cultures* (Reno: University of Nevada Press, 2012)

> Multidisciplinary volume of essays loosely tethered by a sociocultural framework of boundaries that divide and organize gambling spaces as well as cultures and perceptions of gambling. Rand and Light contribute a chapter on Indian gaming in North Dakota.

Kenneth N. Hanson and Tracy A. Skopek, eds., The New Politics of Indian Gaming: The Rise of Reservation Interest Groups (Reno: University of Nevada Press, 2011)

> A collection of essays focusing on intergovernmental relations that argues that tribes are behaving like—or, in effect, are—interest groups seeking

---

Largest Casino (New York: HarperCollins, 2000); Kim Isaac Eisler, *Revenge of the Pequots: How a Small Native American Tribe Created the World's Most Profitable Casino* (New York: Simon & Schuster, 2001); Brett D. Fromson, *Hitting the Jackpot: The Inside Story of the Richest Indian Tribe in History* (New York: Atlantic Monthly Press, 2003). These exposé-style best-sellers have been critiqued for their sensationalized and often inaccurate attempts to cast doubt on the Pequots' authenticity and the legitimacy of the tribe's financial success. See Kathryn R.L. Rand, "There Are No Pequots on the Plains: Assessing the Success of Indian Gaming," *Chapman Law Review* 5 (2002): 47–86.

to influence the political and governmental process in their favor. Light contributes a chapter focusing on tribal political behavior in the form of campaign donations in Minnesota; Rand's chapter documents how tribes in Wisconsin use the courts to shape state law and policy.

Alan Wolfe and Erik C. Owens, eds., *Gambling: Mapping the American Moral Landscape* (Waco, TX: Baylor University Press, 2009)
> Stemming from a conference sponsored by the Boisi Center for Religion and American Public Life at Boston College, this edited volume collects essays reflecting on the morality of gambling from scholars in a wide range of disciplines, including Hispanic studies, economics, sociology, criminology, history, political science, law, strategic management, psychiatry, and theology. Rand and Light contribute a chapter on the distinct attributes of morality and policymaking in the context of Indian gaming.

* * *

Thomas Barker and Marjie Britz, *Jokers Wild: Legalized Gambling in the Twenty-first Century* (Westport, CT: Praeger, 2000)
> A history of legalized gambling in the U.S., from colonial times through the end of the twentieth century, including a chapter on Indian gaming.

Yale D. Belanger, ed., *First Nations Gaming in Canada* (Winnipeg, MB: University of Manitoba Press, 2011)
> A multidisciplinary examination of Aboriginal gaming in Canada.

Anthony N. Cabot and Keith C. Miller, *The Law of Gambling and Regulated Gaming: Cases and Materials* (Durham, NC: Carolina Academic Press, 2011)
> A casebook designed for classroom use with a strong emphasis on regulatory models. Includes a section on Indian gaming.

William C. Canby, Jr., 5th ed., *American Indian Law in a Nutshell* (St. Paul, MN: West Group, 2011)
> A concise summary of the major points of federal Indian law.

Jessica R. Cattelano, High Stakes: Florida Seminole Gaming and Sovereignty (Durham, NC: Duke University Press, 2008)
> First-person ethnographic account of the history of the Seminole Tribe in Florida, which first opened a bingo hall in 1979 and after a lengthy, turbulent journey of political, legal, and economic jockeying with the state, today has a billion-dollar casino business that includes control of the Hard Rock brand.

Eve Darian-Smith, *New Capitalists: Law, Politics, and Identity Surrounding Casino Gaming on Native American Land* (Belmont, CA: Wadsworth, 2004)
A basic overview of tribal gaming focusing on colonization, Western stereotyping, and a case study of one tribe's experience with casino-style gaming.

William R. Eadington, ed., *Indian Gaming and the Law*, 3rd ed. (Reno: Institute for the Study of Gambling and Commercial Gaming, 2004)
Edited by a giant in the field, the pathbreaking Director of the Institute for the Study of Gambling and Commercial Gaming at the University of Nevada-Reno. Contains commentary by key players on how and why IGRA was enacted.

John M. Findlay, *People of Chance: Gambling in American Society from Jamestown to Las Vegas* (New York: Oxford University Press, 1986)
Sociohistorical account of the spread of legalized gambling across the United States.

Kathryn Gabriel, *Gambler Way: Indian Gaming in Mythology, History, and Archaeology* (Boulder, CO: Johnson Books, 1996)
Traces the history of traditional tribal gaming.

Ambrose I. Lane, *Return of the Buffalo* (Westport, CT: Bergin & Garvey, 1995)
Details the history of the Cabazon Band of Mission Indians and the tribe's relationship to the landmark 1987 U.S. Supreme Court case.

John Lyman Mason and Michael Nelson, *Governing Gambling* (New York: Century Foundation, 2001)
Political scientists provide an overview of the influence of politics on gambling policy at the federal, state, and tribal levels.

W. Dale Mason, *Indian Gaming: Tribal Sovereignty and American Politics* (Norman, OK: University of Oklahoma Press, 2000)
Political scientist's account of the politics of Indian gaming, particularly in New Mexico and Oklahoma. Remains a standard in the field.

Edward A. Morse and Ernest P. Gross, *Governing Fortune: Casino Gambling in America* (Ann Arbor, MI: University of Michigan Press, 2007)
A public-policy focused account of casino-style gaming, including a chapter on Indian gaming.

Angela Mullis and David Kamper, eds., *Indian Gaming: Who Wins?* (Los Angeles: UCLA American Indian Studies Center, 2000)
Contains chapters on such topics as influential court decisions, California politics, economic development, and tribal perspectives on Indian gaming.

Paul Pasquaretta, *Gambling and Survival in Native North America* (Tucson: University of Arizona Press, 2003)

> Anthropologist provides scholarly account of gambling metaphors in colonial and literary contexts with a focus on the historical struggles of the Mashantucket Pequots.

Steven L. Pevar, *The Rights of Indians and Tribes*, 4th ed. (New York: Oxford, 2012)

> A standard in the field that addresses such topics as tribal sovereignty, treaties, the federal trust responsibility, and the regulation of non-Indians on reservations, as well as federal law including the Indian Civil Rights Act, the Indian Child Welfare Act, and IGRA.

Gerda Reith, *The Age of Chance: Gambling and Western Culture* (London: Routledge, 1999)

> Sociolegal account of the cultural and social implications of gambling across cultures.

Ralph A. Rossum, *The Supreme Court and Tribal Gaming:* California v. Cabazon Band of Mission Indians (Lawrence, KS: University Press of Kansas, 2011)

> Describes the origins, arguments, and effects of the landmark 1987 U.S. Supreme Court decision that prompted Congress to enact IGRA.

David G. Schwartz, *Roll the Bones: The History of Gambling, Casino Edition* (Las Vegas, NV: Winchester, 2013)

> Coordinator of the Gaming Studies Research Center at the University of Nevada, Las Vegas tells the global story of gambling and focuses on the rise of commercial casinos.

David G. Schwartz, *Suburban Xanadu: The Casino Resort on the Las Vegas Strip and Beyond* (New York: Routledge, 2003)

> An entertaining read that traces the evolution of the casino resort.

Anton Treuer, *Everything You Wanted to Know About Indians But Were Afraid to Ask* (Minneapolis: Borealis Books, 2012)

> Non-scholarly book with roughly 120 questions and answers, ranging from the broad to the specific, designed to assist the non-Indian layperson in understanding some of the basics about American Indians.

Kevin Washburn, *Gambling and Gambling Law: Cases and Materials* (New York, NY: Aspen, 2011)

> A casebook designed for classroom use.

David E. Wilkins and Heidi Kiiwetinepinesiik Stark, *American Indian Politics and the American Political System*, 3rd ed. (Lanham, MD: Rowman & Littlefield, 2010)

> A comprehensive and highly readable overview of tribal governance and tribes' historical and contemporary relationship to the American political system authored originally by a noted political scientist and Indian studies scholar. An excellent starting point for understanding tribal sovereignty, federal Indian policy, and intergovernmental relations from an indigenous perspective.

ASSOCIATIONS AND ORGANIZATIONS

A diverse group of associations and organizations provide information about Indian gaming or other forms of legalized gambling. We focus here on some of the more prominent groups that maintain an informative online presence.

National Indian Gaming Association (NIGA)
http://www.indiangaming.org/

> An umbrella organization of more than 180 tribes and other associate members that functions as a political lobbying group and an educational resource on issues related to Indian gaming, economic development, and tribal sovereignty. NIGA sponsors regular reports on tribal gaming's economic impacts, and maintains an online clearinghouse of resources including studies, books, and testimonies before regulatory commissions or in legislative hearings. Many of these resources are available for downloading; others may be ordered for a fee. NIGA's online library also includes a database of studies on Indian gaming's social and economic impacts on local, state, and tribal jurisdictions.

A number of regional Indian gaming associations maintain useful web sites:

Arizona Indian Gaming Association
http://www.azindiangaming.org

California Nations Indian Gaming Association
http://www.cniga.com

Great Plains Indian Gaming Association
http://www.gpiga.com

Minnesota Indian Gaming Association
http://www.mnindiangamingassoc.com/

Oklahoma Indian Gaming Association
http://www.okindiangaming.org

American Gaming Association (AGA)
http://www.americangaming.org/
As the most prominent commercial gaming trade association, the AGA
lobbies policymakers on such legal and regulatory matters as federal taxation, Internet gambling, and travel and tourism, and seeks to inform the
public as well as industry insiders. It publishes a well-regarded annual report on the state of the industry and maintains links to a number of studies on problem and pathological gambling that, not surprisingly, tend to
favor industry views.

International Masters of Gaming Law
http://www.gaminglawmasters.com/
A global association of attorneys, regulators, executives, and academic
affiliates who share expertise in gaming law. The organization exchanges
professional information and expertise through its members' practice in
the field as well as through annual conferences and publications, including its own magazines, such as *Casino Lawyer*, and symposia published in law journals. A number of members have expertise in Indian
gaming, work in the industry or for tribes, and practice as well as publish accordingly.

National Center for Responsible Gaming
http://www.ncrg.org/
With industry contributions, funds scientific research on pathological and
youth gambling. Promotes public awareness and seeks prevention, diag-
nostic, intervention and treatment strategies. With the American Gaming Association, publishes *Responsible Gaming Quarterly*.

National Congress of American Indians (NCAI)
http://www.ncai.org/
As the major national association of tribal governments, NCAI monitors
federal policy and coordinates efforts to inform federal decisions that affect tribal government interests. At http://www.ncai.org/policy-issues/
economic-development-commerce/gaming, NCAI articulates its pro-
gaming stance and provides its resolutions on particular issues, such as
tribal access to Internet gaming markets.

National Council on Problem Gambling
http://www.ncpgambling.org
> The Council advocates for research, education, treatment, and prevention programs, holds an annual national conference, and maintains an extensive web site on issues related to problem and pathological gambling.

Native American Rights Fund (NARF)
http://www.narf.org
> NARF provides legal representation and technical assistance to Indian tribes, organizations, and individuals on issues such as federal recognition, treaty rights, sovereignty, Indian lands, and voting rights. The site provides updates on pending cases as well as links to documents from recent and pending cases, including briefs. NARF maintains the National Indian Law Library, with links to tribal ordinances and constitutions as well as other resources.

Government Resources

With its complex regulatory scheme involving tribal, state, and federal agencies, laws, and regulations, one might expect a wealth of easily accessible public information on the law and public policy governing tribal gaming. In fact, the availability of information related to Indian gaming varies dramatically across and within tribal, state, and the federal government.

Tribes

Tribes are not subject to public information disclosure requirements due to their recognized inherent sovereignty, and typically limit the type and amount of data about Indian gaming that they make publicly available. A history of maltreatment by states and the federal government, as well as concerns regarding how data about the relative success of Indian gaming may be used by federal or state policymakers, disinclines many tribes to disclose information about casino revenues or management practices.

Most gaming tribes maintain a web site to market their casino facilities (the National Indian Gaming Commission maintains a list of tribes currently operating gaming facilities along with contact information for each, at http://www.nigc.gov/Reading_Room/List_and_Location_of_Tribal_Gaming_Operations.aspx, and there are a number of ad-supported web sites that provide links to tribal casino web pages). Some tribal governments have web sites that include information about tribal history, tribal gaming commissions, and how the tribe uses gaming revenue. Several sites provide information about tribal governments, while the National Conference of State Legislatures, at http://www.ncsl.org/research/state-tribal-institute/list-of-federal-and-state-recognized-tribes.aspx, lists federally acknowledged tribes by state.

States

Given state open records laws, one might assume that the text of the tribal-state gaming compacts that govern how casino-style gaming is regulated would be easily accessible, as would be information about how state gaming commissions and other state agencies promulgate regulations and enforce relevant state and federal law. At times, however, information related to Indian gaming is less readily available than one might think. Each state with a gaming commission does have a web page, however, and those with tribal gaming often make their tribal-state compacts available on those pages. Another excellent resource is USAgov.gov, which has a page on state gaming commissions, searchable at http://www.usa.gov/.

State laws governing gambling are relatively easy to find. One can access each state government's web site through USAgov.gov (http://www.usa.gov/Agencies/State-and-Territories.shtml). NIGA also maintains a list of state gambling laws and regulations on its web site.

Federal

National Indian Gaming Commission (NIGC)
http://www.nigc.gov

Through IGRA, Congress empowered the NIGC to regulate tribal gaming and enforce IGRA's provisions. Along with information on the Commission itself, the NIGC web site is the most reliable online resource, providing links to federal regulations, annual reports on tribal gaming revenue by region, and specialized resources including game classification opinions, judicial decisions, management contracts, approved tribal gaming ordinances, compliance reports, and enforcement actions. The web site also explains how to make Freedom of Information Act requests.

Bureau of Indian Affairs (BIA)
http://www.bia.gov/

The BIA is generally responsible for providing services to some 1.9 million American Indians or Alaska Natives both directly and indirectly through grants, contracts, and compacts, and for administering and managing 55 million acres of federal trust lands and 57 million acres of subsurface mineral estates. It also administers the procedures for tribal federal acknowledgement.

Department of the Interior
http://www.doi.gov/index.html
> The Secretary of the Interior has a number of responsibilities related to Indian gaming, including approving or mediating tribal-state compacts, approving tribal per capita payment plans, and approving gaming on newly acquired trust land.

Department of Justice Office of Tribal Justice
http://www.justice.gov/otj/
> Coordinates internal divisions working on issues related to tribes within the Justice Department as well as the Department's interactions with tribes, federal agencies, Congress, state and local governments, professional associations, and public interest groups.

Financial Crimes Enforcement Network (FinCEN)
http://www.fincen/gov/
> FinCEN investigates crimes related to the federal Bank Secrecy Act, which imposes certain recordkeeping and reporting requirements on casinos, including tribal casinos.

U.S. Senate Committee on Indian Affairs
http://www.indian.senate.gov/
> Regularly holds legislative and oversight hearings on issues related to tribes and Indian Country. The Committee's web site provides streaming audio coverage of these activities as well as information on pending legislation, briefings, and past hearings or other Committee actions.

Statutes, Regulations, and Court Cases

For easy reference, in Appendix B we reprint the text of the Indian Gaming Regulatory Act of 1988 (25 U.S.C. §§ 2701–21) and in Appendix C we provide a reference chart of federal regulations related to tribal gaming. A number of sources, such as Gambling Law US (http://www.gambling-law-us.com/State-Laws/) provide the text or summaries of applicable federal gambling laws, federal regulations, and most basic state gambling laws. The NIGC maintains a list of the regulations it has promulgated, including the minimum internal control standards (MICS) that govern how tribes regulate casino-style gaming operations (http://www.nigc.gov).

Throughout this book we reference dozens of cases in which IGRA's provisions or other issues related to Indian gaming have been litigated in state or federal court. Of particular note, we treat in depth two foundational cases for tribal gaming: *California v. Cabazon Band of Mission Indians*, 480 U.S. 202 (1987), in which the U.S. Supreme Court held that states could not regulate tribal gaming that does not violate state public policy, and *Seminole Tribe v. United States*, 517 U.S. 44 (1996), in which the Supreme Court held that Congress did not have the power to authorize tribal lawsuits against states to enforce IGRA's good-faith negotiation requirement. Many tribal courts issue written opinions that may include decisions on Indian gaming and related issues; practitioners therefore are well advised not to overlook tribal case law.

General resources for accessing judicial opinions and topics related to federal Indian law or tribal law include:

Cornell University's Legal Information Institute
http://www.law.cornell.edu/wex/american_indian_law

Findlaw for Legal Professionals
http://corporate.findlaw.com/law-library/indigenous-peoples-law/

Law Library of Congress (American Indian Constitutions and Legal Materials)
http://www.loc.gov/law/help/american-indian-consts/index.php

National Indian Law Library of the Native American Rights Fund
http://www.narf.org/nill/

New England School of Law
http://libraryguides.nesl.edu/native_american_law

REPORTS

The NIGC, NIGA, and the Harvard Project on American Indian Economic Development all maintain links on their web sites to annual or other reports detailing tribal gaming's social and economic impacts. In addition to the reports and studies generated by the NIGC, NIGA, and the Harvard Project, two others deserve mention.

National Gambling Impact Study Commission Final Report
http://govinfo.library.unt.edu/ngisc/reports/fullrpt.html
> Charged by Congress with producing a comprehensive study of the legal and factual impacts of gambling, the National Gambling Impact Study Commission released its final report in 1999. The report includes analy-

sis of a comprehensive study by the National Opinion Research Center at the University of Chicago on gambling's social and economic impacts on individuals and communities. One chapter of the final report specifically addresses Indian gaming, as do the Commission's closing recommendations.

Alan Meister, *Indian Gaming Industry Report, 2014 Ed.* (Newton, MA: Casino City Press, 2014)

Conducted by an economist with the assistance of information provided by tribal governments and other sources, this annual report has become an industry benchmark. Estimating tribal gaming's economic impacts at the state as well as national level, the report also details the impacts of tribal-state revenue-sharing agreements.

* * *

We close with a simple, albeit easily overlooked, suggestion. Many online media outlets or news aggregators will allow one to create a customized "news alert" service free of charge. Simply select "Indian gaming" as key words and provide a valid e-mail address to the media source. Google News, Yahoo News, and similar search engines will perform Internet searches with the advantages of automation and economy of scale. The services will cull news stories containing the key words from media sources spanning the Internet and push it directly to the subscriber. Given the efficiency of these online resources in providing daily updates on events occurring throughout the United States, we would be remiss if we failed to mention this basic yet highly effective media research tool as a means to stay abreast of the vast and rapidly developing law and policy of Indian gaming.

The Indian Gaming Regulatory Act of 1988

Public Law No. 100-497, 102 Stat. 2467
(October 17, 1988)
Codified at 25 U.S.C. §§ 2701–2721

§ 2101. Findings

The Congress finds that—

(1) numerous Indian tribes have become engaged in or have licensed gaming activities on Indian lands as a means of generating tribal governmental revenue;

(2) Federal courts have held that section 81 of this title requires Secretarial review of management contracts dealing with Indian gaming, but does not provide standards for approval of such contracts;

(3) existing Federal law does not provide clear standards or regulations for the conduct of gaming on Indian lands;

(4) a principal goal of Federal Indian policy is to promote tribal economic development, tribal self-sufficiency, and strong tribal government; and

(5) Indian tribes have the exclusive right to regulate gaming activity on Indian lands if the gaming activity is not specifically prohibited by Federal law and is conducted within a State which does not, as a matter of criminal law and public policy, prohibit such gaming activity.

§ 2702. Declaration of policy

The purpose of this chapter is—

(1) to provide a statutory basis for the operation of gaming by Indian tribes as a means of promoting tribal economic development, self-sufficiency, and strong tribal governments;

(2) to provide a statutory basis for the regulation of gaming by an Indian tribe adequate to shield it from organized crime and other corrupting influences, to ensure that the Indian tribe is the primary beneficiary of the gaming operation, and to assure that gaming is conducted fairly and honestly by both the operator and players; and

(3) to declare that the establishment of independent Federal regulatory authority for gaming on Indian lands, the establishment of Federal standards for gaming on Indian lands, and the establishment of a National Indian Gaming Commission are necessary to meet congressional concerns regarding gaming and to protect such gaming as a means of generating tribal revenue.

§ 2703. Definitions

For purposes of this chapter—

(1) The term "Attorney General" means the Attorney General of the United States.

(2) The term "Chairman" means the Chairman of the National Indian Gaming Commission.

(3) The term "Commission" means the National Indian Gaming Commission established pursuant to section 2704 of this title.

(4) The term "Indian lands" means—

(A) all lands within the limits of any Indian reservation; and

(B) any lands title to which is either held in trust by the United States for the benefit of any Indian tribe or individual or held by any Indian tribe or individual subject to restriction by the United States against alienation and over which an Indian tribe exercises governmental power.

(5) The term "Indian tribe" means any Indian tribe, band, nation, or other organized group or community of Indians which—

(A) is recognized as eligible by the Secretary for the special programs and services provided by the United States to Indians because of their status as Indians, and

(B) is recognized as possessing powers of self-government.

(6) The term "class I gaming" means social games solely for prizes of minimal value or traditional forms of Indian gaming engaged in by individuals as a part of, or in connection with, tribal ceremonies or celebrations.

(7) (A) The term "class II gaming" means—

    (i) the game of chance commonly known as bingo (whether or not electronic, computer, or other technologic aids are used in connection therewith)—

        (I) which is played for prizes, including monetary prizes, with cards bearing numbers or other designations,

        (II) in which the holder of the card covers such numbers or designations when objects, similarly numbered or designated, are drawn or electronically determined, and

        (III) in which the game is won by the first person covering a previously designated arrangement of numbers or designations on such cards, including (if played in the same location) pull-tabs, lotto, punch boards, tip jars, instant bingo, and other games similar to bingo, and

    (ii) card games that—

        (I) are explicitly authorized by the laws of the State, or

        (II) are not explicitly prohibited by the laws of the State and are played at any location in the State, but only if such card games are played in conformity with those laws and regulations (if any) of the State regarding hours or periods of operation of such card games or limitations on wagers or pot sizes in such card games.

(B) The term "class II gaming" does not include—

    (i) any banking card games, including baccarat, chemin de fer, or blackjack (21), or

    (ii) electronic or electromechanical facsimiles of any game of chance or slot machines of any kind.

(C) Notwithstanding any other provision of this paragraph, the term "class II gaming" includes those card games played in the State of Michigan, the State of North Dakota, the State of South Dakota, or the State of Washington, that were actually operated in such State by an Indian tribe on or before May 1, 1988, but only to the extent of the nature and scope of the card games that were actually operated by an Indian tribe in such State on or before such date, as determined by the Chairman.

(D) Notwithstanding any other provision of this paragraph, the term "class II gaming" includes, during the 1-year period beginning on October 17, 1988, any gaming described in subparagraph (B)(ii) that was legally operated on Indian lands on or before May 1, 1988, if the Indian tribe having jurisdiction over the lands on which such gaming was operated requests the State, by no later than the date that is 30 days after October 17, 1988, to negotiate a Tribal-State compact under section 2710(d)(3) of this title.

(E) Notwithstanding any other provision of this paragraph, the term "class II gaming" includes, during the 1-year period beginning on December 17, 1991, any gaming described in subparagraph (B)(ii) that was legally operated on Indian lands in the State of Wisconsin on or before May 1, 1988, if the Indian tribe having jurisdiction over the lands on which such gaming was operated requested the State, by no later than November 16, 1988, to negotiate a Tribal-State compact under section 2710(d)(3) of this title.

(F) If, during the 1-year period described in subparagraph (E), there is a final judicial determination that the gaming described in subparagraph (E) is not legal as a matter of State law, then such gaming on such Indian land shall cease to operate on the date next following the date of such judicial decision.

(8) The term "class III gaming" means all forms of gaming that are not class I gaming or class II gaming.

(9) The term "net revenues" means gross revenues of an Indian gaming activity less amounts paid out as, or paid for, prizes and total operating expenses, excluding management fees.

(10) The term "Secretary" means the Secretary of the Interior.

§ 2704. National Indian Gaming Commission

(a) Establishment

There is established within the Department of the Interior a Commission to be known as the National Indian Gaming Commission.

(b) Composition; investigation; term of office; removal

(1) The Commission shall be composed of three full-time members who shall be appointed as follows:

(A) a Chairman, who shall be appointed by the President with the advice and consent of the Senate; and

(B) two associate members who shall be appointed by the Secretary of the Interior.

(2) (A) The Attorney General shall conduct a background investigation on any person considered for appointment to the Commission.

(B) The Secretary shall publish in the Federal Register the name and other information the Secretary deems pertinent regarding a nominee for membership on the Commission and shall allow a period of not less than thirty days for receipt of public comment.

(3) Not more than two members of the Commission shall be of the same political party. At least two members of the Commission shall be enrolled members of any Indian tribe.

(4) (A) Except as provided in subparagraph (B), the term of office of the members of the Commission shall be three years.

(B) Of the initial members of the Commission

(i) two members, including the Chairman, shall have a term of office of three years; and

(ii) one member shall have a term of office of one year.

(5) No individual shall be eligible for any appointment to, or to continue service on, the Commission, who—

(A) has been convicted of a felony or gaming offense;

(B) has any financial interest in, or management responsibility for, any gaming activity; or

(C) has a financial interest in, or management responsibility for, any management contract approved pursuant to section 2711 of this title.

(6) A Commissioner may only be removed from office before the expiration of the term of office of the member by the President (or, in the case of associate member, by the Secretary) for neglect of duty, or malfeasance in office, or for other good cause shown.

(c) Vacancies

Vacancies occurring on the Commission shall be filled in the same manner as the original appointment. A member may serve after the expiration of his term of office until his successor has been appointed, unless the member has been removed for cause under subsection (b)(6) of this section.

(d) Quorum

Two members of the Commission, at least one of which is the Chairman or Vice Chairman, shall constitute a quorum.

(e) Vice Chairman

The Commission shall select, by majority vote, one of the members of the Commission to serve as Vice Chairman. The Vice Chairman shall serve as Chairman during meetings of the Commission in the absence of the Chairman.

(f) Meetings

The Commission shall meet at the call of the Chairman or a majority of its members, but shall meet at least once every 4 months.

(g) Compensation

(1) The Chairman of the Commission shall be paid at a rate equal to that of level IV of the Executive Schedule under section 5315 of title 5.

(2) The associate members of the Commission shall each be paid at a rate equal to that of level V of the Executive Schedule under section 5316 of title 5.

(3) All members of the Commission shall be reimbursed in accordance with title 5 for travel, subsistence, and other necessary expenses incurred by them in the performance of their duties.

§ 2705. Powers of Chairman

(a) The Chairman, on behalf of the Commission, shall have power, subject to an appeal to the Commission, to—

(1) issue orders of temporary closure of gaming activities as provided in section 2713 (b) of this title;

(2) levy and collect civil fines as provided in section 2713 (a) of this title;

(3) approve tribal ordinances or resolutions regulating class II gaming and class III gaming as provided in section 2710 of this title; and

(4) approve management contracts for class II gaming and class III gaming as provided in sections 2710 (d)(9) and 2711 of this title.

(b) The Chairman shall have such other powers as may be delegated by the Commission.

§ 2706. Powers of Commission

(a) Budget approval; civil fines; fees; subpoenas; permanent orders

The Commission shall have the power, not subject to delegation—

(1) upon the recommendation of the Chairman, to approve the annual budget of the Commission as provided in section 2717 of this title;

(2) to adopt regulations for the assessment and collection of civil fines as provided in section 2713 (a) of this title;

(3) by an affirmative vote of not less than 2 members, to establish the rate of fees as provided in section 2717 of this title;

(4) by an affirmative vote of not less than 2 members, to authorize the Chairman to issue subpoenas as provided in section 2715 of this title; and

(5) by an affirmative vote of not less than 2 members and after a full hearing, to make permanent a temporary order of the Chairman closing a gaming activity as provided in section 2713(b)(2) of this title.

(b) Monitoring; inspection of premises; investigations; access to records; mail; contracts; hearings; oaths; regulations

The Commission—

(1) shall monitor class II gaming conducted on Indian lands on a continuing basis;

(2) shall inspect and examine all premises located on Indian lands on which class II gaming is conducted;

(3) shall conduct or cause to be conducted such background investigations as may be necessary;

(4) may demand access to and inspect, examine, photocopy, and audit all papers, books, and records respecting gross revenues of class II gaming conducted on Indian lands and any other matters necessary to carry out the duties of the Commission under this chapter;

(5) may use the United States mail in the same manner and under the same conditions as any department or agency of the United States;

(6) may procure supplies, services, and property by contract in accordance with applicable Federal laws and regulations;

(7) may enter into contracts with Federal, State, tribal and private entities for activities necessary to the discharge of the duties of the Commission and, to the extent feasible, contract the enforcement of the Commission's regulations with the Indian tribes;

(8) may hold such hearings, sit and act at such times and places, take such testimony, and receive such evidence as the Commission deems appropriate;

(9) may administer oaths or affirmations to witnesses appearing before the Commission; and

(10) shall promulgate such regulations and guidelines as it deems appropriate to implement the provisions of this chapter.

(c) Report

The Commission shall submit a report with minority views, if any, to the Congress on December 31, 1989, and every two years thereafter. The report shall include information on—

(1) whether the associate commissioners should continue as full or part-time officials;

(2) funding, including income and expenses, of the Commission;

(3) recommendations for amendments to the chapter; and

(4) any other matter considered appropriate by the Commission.

§ 2707. Commission staffing

(a) General Counsel

The Chairman shall appoint a General Counsel to the Commission who shall be paid at the annual rate of basic pay payable for GS-18 of the General Schedule under section 5332 of title 5.

(b) Staff

The Chairman shall appoint and supervise other staff of the Commission without regard to the provisions of title 5 governing appointments in the competitive service. Such staff shall be paid without regard to the provisions of chapter 51 and subchapter III of chapter 53 of such title relating to classification and General Schedule pay rates, except that no individual so appointed may receive pay in excess of the annual rate of basic pay payable for GS-17 of the General Schedule under section 5332 of that title.

(c) Temporary services

The Chairman may procure temporary and intermittent services under section 3109 (b) of title 5, but at rates for individuals not to exceed the daily equivalent of the maximum annual rate of basic pay payable for GS-18 of the General Schedule.

(d) Federal agency personnel

Upon the request of the Chairman, the head of any Federal agency is authorized to detail any of the personnel of such agency to the Commission to assist the Commission in carrying out its duties under this chapter, unless otherwise prohibited by law.

(e) Administrative support services

The Secretary or Administrator of General Services shall provide to the Commission on a reimbursable basis such administrative support services as the Commission may request.

§2708. Commission—access to information

The Commission may secure from any department or agency of the United States information necessary to enable it to carry out this chapter. Upon the request of the Chairman, the head of such department or agency shall furnish such information to the Commission, unless otherwise prohibited by law.

§2709. Interim authority to regulate gaming

Notwithstanding any other provision of this chapter, the Secretary shall continue to exercise those authorities vested in the Secretary on the day before October 17, 1988, relating to supervision of Indian gaming until such time as the Commission is organized and prescribes regulations. The Secretary shall provide staff and support assistance to facilitate an orderly transition to regulation of Indian gaming by the Commission.

§2710. Tribal gaming ordinances

(a) Exclusive jurisdiction over class I and class II gaming activity

(1) Class I gaming on Indian lands is within the exclusive jurisdiction of the Indian tribes and shall not be subject to the provisions of this chapter.

(2) Any class II gaming on Indian lands shall continue to be within the jurisdiction of the Indian tribes, but shall be subject to the provisions of this chapter.

(b) Regulation of class II gaming activity; net revenue allocation; audits; contracts

(1) An Indian tribe may engage in, or license and regulate, class II gaming on Indian lands within such tribe's jurisdiction, if—

(A) such Indian gaming is located within a State that permits such gaming for any purpose by any person, organization or entity (and such gaming is not otherwise specifically prohibited on Indian lands by Federal law), and

(B) the governing body of the Indian tribe adopts an ordinance or resolution which is approved by the Chairman.

A separate license issued by the Indian tribe shall be required for each place, facility, or location on Indian lands at which class II gaming is conducted.

(2) The Chairman shall approve any tribal ordinance or resolution concerning the conduct, or regulation of class II gaming on the Indian lands within the tribe's jurisdiction if such ordinance or resolution provides that—

(A) except as provided in paragraph (4), the Indian tribe will have the sole proprietary interest and responsibility for the conduct of any gaming activity;

(B) net revenues from any tribal gaming are not to be used for purposes other than—

(i) to fund tribal government operations or programs;

(ii) to provide for the general welfare of the Indian tribe and its members;

(iii) to promote tribal economic development;

(iv) to donate to charitable organizations; or

(v) to help fund operations of local government agencies;

(C) annual outside audits of the gaming, which may be encompassed within existing independent tribal audit systems, will be provided by the Indian tribe to the Commission;

(D) all contracts for supplies, services, or concessions for a contract amount in excess of $25,000 annually (except contracts for professional legal or accounting services) relating to such gaming shall be subject to such independent audits;

(E) the construction and maintenance of the gaming facility, and the operation of that gaming is conducted in a manner which adequately protects the environment and the public health and safety; and

(F) there is an adequate system which—

(i) ensures that background investigations are conducted on the primary management officials and key employees of the gaming enterprise and that oversight of such officials and their management is conducted on an ongoing basis; and

(ii) includes—

(I) tribal licenses for primary management officials and key employees of the gaming enterprise with prompt notification to the Commission of the issuance of such licenses;

(II) a standard whereby any person whose prior activities, criminal record, if any, or reputation, habits and associations pose a threat to the public interest or to the effective regulation of gaming, or create or enhance the dangers of unsuitable, unfair, or illegal practices and methods and activities in the conduct of gaming shall not be eligible for employment; and

(III) notification by the Indian tribe to the Commission of the results of such background check before the issuance of any of such licenses.

(3) Net revenues from any class II gaming activities conducted or licensed by any Indian tribe may be used to make per capita payments to members of the Indian tribe only if—

(A) the Indian tribe has prepared a plan to allocate revenues to uses authorized by paragraph (2)(B);

(B) the plan is approved by the Secretary as adequate, particularly with respect to uses described in clause (i) or (iii) of paragraph (2)(B);

(C) the interests of minors and other legally incompetent persons who are entitled to receive any of the per capita payments are protected and preserved and the per capita payments are disbursed to the parents or legal guardian of such minors or legal incompetents in such amounts as may be necessary for the health, education, or welfare, of the minor or other legally incompetent person under a plan approved by the Secretary and the governing body of the Indian tribe; and

(D) the per capita payments are subject to Federal taxation and tribes notify members of such tax liability when payments are made.

(4) (A) A tribal ordinance or resolution may provide for the licensing or regulation of class II gaming activities owned by any person or entity other than the Indian tribe and conducted on Indian lands, only if the tribal licensing requirements include the requirements described in the subclauses of subparagraph (B)(i) and are at least as restrictive as those established by State law governing similar gaming within the jurisdiction of the State within which such Indian lands are located. No person or entity, other than the Indian tribe, shall be eligible to receive a tribal license to own a class II gaming activity conducted on Indian lands within the jurisdiction of the Indian tribe if such person or entity would not be eligible to receive a State license to conduct the same activity within the jurisdiction of the State.

(B) (i) The provisions of subparagraph (A) of this paragraph and the provisions of subparagraphs (A) and (B) of paragraph (2) shall not bar the continued operation of an individually owned class II gaming operation that was operating on September 1, 1986, if—

>(I) such gaming operation is licensed and regulated by an Indian tribe pursuant to an ordinance reviewed and approved by the Commission in accordance with section 2712 of this title,

>(II) income to the Indian tribe from such gaming is used only for the purposes described in paragraph (2)(B) of this subsection,

>(III) not less than 60 percent of the net revenues is income to the Indian tribe, and

>(IV) the owner of such gaming operation pays an appropriate assessment to the National Indian Gaming Commission under section 2717(a)(1) of this title for regulation of such gaming.

(ii) The exemption from the application of this subsection provided under this subparagraph may not be transferred to any person or entity and shall remain in effect only so long as the gaming activity remains within the same nature and scope as operated on October 17, 1988.

(iii) Within sixty days of October 17, 1988, the Secretary shall prepare a list of each individually owned gaming operation to which clause (i) applies and shall publish such list in the Federal Register.

(c) Issuance of gaming license; certificate of self-regulation

(1) The Commission may consult with appropriate law enforcement officials concerning gaming licenses issued by an Indian tribe and shall have thirty days to notify the Indian tribe of any objections to issuance of such license.

(2) If, after the issuance of a gaming license by an Indian tribe, reliable information is received from the Commission indicating that a primary management official or key employee does not meet the standard established under subsection (b)(2)(F)(ii)(II) of this section, the Indian tribe shall suspend such license and, after notice and hearing, may revoke such license.

(3) Any Indian tribe which operates a class II gaming activity and which—

(A) has continuously conducted such activity for a period of not less than three years, including at least one year after October 17, 1988; and

(B) has otherwise complied with the provisions of this section may petition the Commission for a certificate of self-regulation.

(4) The Commission shall issue a certificate of self-regulation if it determines from available information, and after a hearing if requested by the tribe, that the tribe has—

    (A) conducted its gaming activity in a manner which—

        (i) has resulted in an effective and honest accounting of all revenues;

        (ii) has resulted in a reputation for safe, fair, and honest operation of the activity; and

        (iii) has been generally free of evidence of criminal or dishonest activity;

    (B) adopted and is implementing adequate systems for—

        (i) accounting for all revenues from the activity;

        (ii) investigation, licensing, and monitoring of all employees of the gaming activity; and

        (iii) investigation, enforcement and prosecution of violations of its gaming ordinance and regulations; and

    (C) conducted the operation on a fiscally and economically sound basis.

(5) During any year in which a tribe has a certificate for self-regulation—

    (A) the tribe shall not be subject to the provisions of paragraphs (1), (2), (3), and (4) of section 2706 (b) of this title;

    (B) the tribe shall continue to submit an annual independent audit as required by subsection (b)(2)(C) of this section and shall submit to the Commission a complete resume on all employees hired and licensed by the tribe subsequent to the issuance of a certificate of self-regulation; and

    (C) the Commission may not assess a fee on such activity pursuant to section 2717 of this title in excess of one quarter of 1 per centum of the gross revenue.

(6) The Commission may, for just cause and after an opportunity for a hearing, remove a certificate of self-regulation by majority vote of its members.

(d) Class III gaming activities; authorization; revocation; Tribal-State compact

(1) Class III gaming activities shall be lawful on Indian lands only if such activities are—

    (A) authorized by an ordinance or resolution that—

        (i) is adopted by the governing body of the Indian tribe having jurisdiction over such lands,

(ii) meets the requirements of subsection (b) of this section, and

(iii) is approved by the Chairman,

(B) located in a State that permits such gaming for any purpose by any person, organization, or entity, and

(C) conducted in conformance with a Tribal-State compact entered into by the Indian tribe and the State under paragraph (3) that is in effect.

(2) (A) If any Indian tribe proposes to engage in, or to authorize any person or entity to engage in, a class III gaming activity on Indian lands of the Indian tribe, the governing body of the Indian tribe shall adopt and submit to the Chairman an ordinance or resolution that meets the requirements of subsection (b) of this section.

(B) The Chairman shall approve any ordinance or resolution described in subparagraph (A), unless the Chairman specifically determines that—

(i) the ordinance or resolution was not adopted in compliance with the governing documents of the Indian tribe, or

(ii) the tribal governing body was significantly and unduly influenced in the adoption of such ordinance or resolution by any person identified in section 2711 (e)(1)(D) of this title.

Upon the approval of such an ordinance or resolution, the Chairman shall publish in the Federal Register such ordinance or resolution and the order of approval.

(C) Effective with the publication under subparagraph (B) of an ordinance or resolution adopted by the governing body of an Indian tribe that has been approved by the Chairman under subparagraph (B), class III gaming activity on the Indian lands of the Indian tribe shall be fully subject to the terms and conditions of the Tribal-State compact entered into under paragraph (3) by the Indian tribe that is in effect.

(D) (i) The governing body of an Indian tribe, in its sole discretion and without the approval of the Chairman, may adopt an ordinance or resolution revoking any prior ordinance or resolution that authorized class III gaming on the Indian lands of the Indian tribe. Such revocation shall render class III gaming illegal on the Indian lands of such Indian tribe.

(ii) The Indian tribe shall submit any revocation ordinance or resolution described in clause (i) to the Chairman. The Chairman shall publish such ordinance or resolution in the Federal Register and the revocation provided by such ordinance or resolution shall take effect on the date of such publication.

(iii) Notwithstanding any other provision of this subsection—

(I) any person or entity operating a class III gaming activity pursuant to this paragraph on the date on which an ordinance or resolution described in clause (i) that revokes authorization for such class III gaming activity is published in the Federal Register may, during the 1-year period beginning on the date on which such revocation ordinance or resolution is published under clause (ii), continue to operate such activity in conformance with the Tribal-State compact entered into under paragraph (3) that is in effect, and

(II) any civil action that arises before, and any crime that is committed before, the close of such 1-year period shall not be affected by such revocation ordinance or resolution.

(3) (A) Any Indian tribe having jurisdiction over the Indian lands upon which a class III gaming activity is being conducted, or is to be conducted, shall request the State in which such lands are located to enter into negotiations for the purpose of entering into a Tribal-State compact governing the conduct of gaming activities. Upon receiving such a request, the State shall negotiate with the Indian tribe in good faith to enter into such a compact.

(B) Any State and any Indian tribe may enter into a Tribal-State compact governing gaming activities on the Indian lands of the Indian tribe, but such compact shall take effect only when notice of approval by the Secretary of such compact has been published by the Secretary in the Federal Register.

(C) Any Tribal-State compact negotiated under subparagraph (A) may include provisions relating to—

(i) the application of the criminal and civil laws and regulations of the Indian tribe or the State that are directly related to, and necessary for, the licensing and regulation of such activity;

(ii) the allocation of criminal and civil jurisdiction between the State and the Indian tribe necessary for the enforcement of such laws and regulations;

(iii) the assessment by the State of such activities in such amounts as are necessary to defray the costs of regulating such activity;

(iv) taxation by the Indian tribe of such activity in amounts comparable to amounts assessed by the State for comparable activities;

(v) remedies for breach of contract;

(vi) standards for the operation of such activity and maintenance of the gaming facility, including licensing; and

(vii) any other subjects that are directly related to the operation of gaming activities.

(4) Except for any assessments that may be agreed to under paragraph (3)(C)(iii) of this subsection, nothing in this section shall be interpreted as conferring upon a State or any of its political subdivisions authority to impose any tax, fee, charge, or other assessment upon an Indian tribe or upon any other person or entity authorized by an Indian tribe to engage in a class III activity. No State may refuse to enter into the negotiations described in paragraph (3)(A) based upon the lack of authority in such State, or its political subdivisions, to impose such a tax, fee, charge, or other assessment.

(5) Nothing in this subsection shall impair the right of an Indian tribe to regulate class III gaming on its Indian lands concurrently with the State, except to the extent that such regulation is inconsistent with, or less stringent than, the State laws and regulations made applicable by any Tribal-State compact entered into by the Indian tribe under paragraph (3) that is in effect.

(6) The provisions of section 1175 of title 15 shall not apply to any gaming conducted under a Tribal-State compact that—

(A) is entered into under paragraph (3) by a State in which gambling devices are legal, and

(B) is in effect.

(7) (A) The United States district courts shall have jurisdiction over—

(i) any cause of action initiated by an Indian tribe arising from the failure of a State to enter into negotiations with the Indian tribe for the purpose of entering into a Tribal-State compact under paragraph (3) or to conduct such negotiations in good faith,

(ii) any cause of action initiated by a State or Indian tribe to enjoin a class III gaming activity located on Indian lands and conducted in violation of any Tribal-State compact entered into under paragraph (3) that is in effect, and

(iii) any cause of action initiated by the Secretary to enforce the procedures prescribed under subparagraph (B)(vii).

(B) (i) An Indian tribe may initiate a cause of action described in subparagraph (A)(i) only after the close of the 180-day period beginning on the date on which the Indian tribe requested the State to enter into negotiations under paragraph (3)(A).

(ii) In any action described in subparagraph (A)(i), upon the introduction of evidence by an Indian tribe that—

(I) a Tribal-State compact has not been entered into under paragraph (3), and

(II) the State did not respond to the request of the Indian tribe to negotiate such a compact or did not respond to such request in good faith,

the burden of proof shall be upon the State to prove that the State has negotiated with the Indian tribe in good faith to conclude a Tribal-State compact governing the conduct of gaming activities.

(iii) If, in any action described in subparagraph (A)(i), the court finds that the State has failed to negotiate in good faith with the Indian tribe to conclude a Tribal-State compact governing the conduct of gaming activities, the court shall order the State and the Indian Tribe to conclude such a compact within a 60-day period. In determining in such an action whether a State has negotiated in good faith, the court—

(I) may take into account the public interest, public safety, criminality, financial integrity, and adverse economic impacts on existing gaming activities, and

(II) shall consider any demand by the State for direct taxation of the Indian tribe or of any Indian lands as evidence that the State has not negotiated in good faith.

(iv) If a State and an Indian tribe fail to conclude a Tribal-State compact governing the conduct of gaming activities on the Indian lands subject to the jurisdiction of such Indian tribe within the 60-day period provided in the order of a court issued under clause (iii), the Indian tribe and the State shall each submit to a mediator appointed by the court a proposed compact that represents their last best offer for a compact. The mediator shall select from the two proposed compacts the one which best comports with the terms of this chapter and any other applicable Federal law and with the findings and order of the court.

(v) The mediator appointed by the court under clause (iv) shall submit to the State and the Indian tribe the compact selected by the mediator under clause (iv).

(vi) If a State consents to a proposed compact during the 60-day period beginning on the date on which the proposed compact is submitted by the mediator to the State under clause (v), the proposed compact shall be treated as a Tribal-State compact entered into under paragraph (3).

(vii) If the State does not consent during the 60-day period described in clause (vi) to a proposed compact submitted by a mediator under clause (v), the mediator shall notify the Secretary and the Secretary shall prescribe, in consultation with the Indian tribe, procedures—

(I) which are consistent with the proposed compact selected by the mediator under clause (iv), the provisions of this chapter, and the relevant provisions of the laws of the State, and

(II) under which class III gaming may be conducted on the Indian lands over which the Indian tribe has jurisdiction.

(8) (A) The Secretary is authorized to approve any Tribal-State compact entered into between an Indian tribe and a State governing gaming on Indian lands of such Indian tribe.

(B) The Secretary may disapprove a compact described in subparagraph (A) only if such compact violates—

(i) any provision of this chapter,

(ii) any other provision of Federal law that does not relate to jurisdiction over gaming on Indian lands, or

(iii) the trust obligations of the United States to Indians.

(C) If the Secretary does not approve or disapprove a compact described in subparagraph (A) before the date that is 45 days after the date on which the compact is submitted to the Secretary for approval, the compact shall be considered to have been approved by the Secretary, but only to the extent the compact is consistent with the provisions of this chapter.

(D) The Secretary shall publish in the Federal Register notice of any Tribal-State compact that is approved, or considered to have been approved, under this paragraph.

(9) An Indian tribe may enter into a management contract for the operation of a class III gaming activity if such contract has been submitted to, and approved by, the Chairman. The Chairman's review and approval of

such contract shall be governed by the provisions of subsections (b), (c), (d), (f), (g), and (h) of section 2711 of this title.

(e) Approval of ordinances

For purposes of this section, by not later than the date that is 90 days after the date on which any tribal gaming ordinance or resolution is submitted to the Chairman, the Chairman shall approve such ordinance or resolution if it meets the requirements of this section. Any such ordinance or resolution not acted upon at the end of that 90-day period shall be considered to have been approved by the Chairman, but only to the extent such ordinance or resolution is consistent with the provisions of this chapter.

§ 2711. Management contracts

(a) Class II gaming activity; information on operators

(1) Subject to the approval of the Chairman, an Indian tribe may enter into a management contract for the operation and management of a class II gaming activity that the Indian tribe may engage in under section 2710(b)(1) of this title, but, before approving such contract, the Chairman shall require and obtain the following information:

(A) the name, address, and other additional pertinent background information on each person or entity (including individuals comprising such entity) having a direct financial interest in, or management responsibility for, such contract, and, in the case of a corporation, those individuals who serve on the board of directors of such corporation and each of its stockholders who hold (directly or indirectly) 10 percent or more of its issued and outstanding stock;

(B) a description of any previous experience that each person listed pursuant to subparagraph (A) has had with other gaming contracts with Indian tribes or with the gaming industry generally, including specifically the name and address of any licensing or regulatory agency with which such person has had a contract relating to gaming; and

(C) a complete financial statement of each person listed pursuant to subparagraph (A).

(2) Any person listed pursuant to paragraph (1)(A) shall be required to respond to such written or oral questions that the Chairman may propound in accordance with his responsibilities under this section.

(3) For purposes of this chapter, any reference to the management contract described in paragraph (1) shall be considered to include all collateral agreements to such contract that relate to the gaming activity.

(b) Approval

The Chairman may approve any management contract entered into pursuant to this section only if he determines that it provides at least—

(1) for adequate accounting procedures that are maintained, and for verifiable financial reports that are prepared, by or for the tribal governing body on a monthly basis;

(2) for access to the daily operations of the gaming to appropriate tribal officials who shall also have a right to verify the daily gross revenues and income made from any such tribal gaming activity;

(3) for a minimum guaranteed payment to the Indian tribe that has preference over the retirement of development and construction costs;

(4) for an agreed ceiling for the repayment of development and construction costs;

(5) for a contract term not to exceed five years, except that, upon the request of an Indian tribe, the Chairman may authorize a contract term that exceeds five years but does not exceed seven years if the Chairman is satisfied that the capital investment required, and the income projections, for the particular gaming activity require the additional time; and

(6) for grounds and mechanisms for terminating such contract, but actual contract termination shall not require the approval of the Commission.

(c) Fee based on percentage of net revenues

(1) The Chairman may approve a management contract providing for a fee based upon a percentage of the net revenues of a tribal gaming activity if the Chairman determines that such percentage fee is reasonable in light of surrounding circumstances. Except as otherwise provided in this subsection, such fee shall not exceed 30 percent of the net revenues.

(2) Upon the request of an Indian tribe, the Chairman may approve a management contract providing for a fee based upon a percentage of the net revenues of a tribal gaming activity that exceeds 30 percent but not 40 percent of the net revenues if the Chairman is satisfied that the capital investment required, and income projections, for such tribal gaming activity require the additional fee requested by the Indian tribe.

(d) Period for approval; extension

By no later than the date that is 180 days after the date on which a management contract is submitted to the Chairman for approval, the Chairman shall approve or disapprove such contract on its merits. The Chairman may extend the 180-day period by not more than 90 days if the Chairman notifies the Indian tribe in writing of the reason for the extension. The Indian tribe may bring an action in a United States district court to compel action by the Chairman if a contract has not been approved or disapproved within the period required by this subsection.

(e) Disapproval

The Chairman shall not approve any contract if the Chairman determines that—

    (1) any person listed pursuant to subsection (a)(1)(A) of this section—

        (A) is an elected member of the governing body of the Indian tribe which is the party to the management contract;

        (B) has been or subsequently is convicted of any felony or gaming offense;

        (C) has knowingly and willfully provided materially important false statements or information to the Commission or the Indian tribe pursuant to this chapter or has refused to respond to questions propounded pursuant to subsection (a)(2) of this section; or

        (D) has been determined to be a person whose prior activities, criminal record if any, or reputation, habits, and associations pose a threat to the public interest or to the effective regulation and control of gaming, or create or enhance the dangers of unsuitable, unfair, or illegal practices, methods, and activities in the conduct of gaming or the carrying on of the business and financial arrangements incidental thereto;

    (2) the management contractor has, or has attempted to, unduly interfere or influence for its gain or advantage any decision or process of tribal government relating to the gaming activity;

    (3) the management contractor has deliberately or substantially failed to comply with the terms of the management contract or the tribal gaming ordinance or resolution adopted and approved pursuant to this chapter; or

    (4) a trustee, exercising the skill and diligence that a trustee is commonly held to, would not approve the contract.

(f) Modification or voiding

The Chairman, after notice and hearing, shall have the authority to require appropriate contract modifications or may void any contract if he subsequently determines that any of the provisions of this section have been violated.

(g) Interest in land

No management contract for the operation and management of a gaming activity regulated by this chapter shall transfer or, in any other manner, convey any interest in land or other real property, unless specific statutory authority exists and unless clearly specified in writing in said contract.

(h) Authority

The authority of the Secretary under section 81 of this title, relating to management contracts regulated pursuant to this chapter, is hereby transferred to the Commission.

(i) Investigation fee

The Commission shall require a potential contractor to pay a fee to cover the cost of the investigation necessary to reach a determination required in subsection (e) of this section.

§ 2712. Review of existing ordinances and contracts

(a) Notification to submit

As soon as practicable after the organization of the Commission, the Chairman shall notify each Indian tribe or management contractor who, prior to October 17, 1988, adopted an ordinance or resolution authorizing class II gaming or class III gaming or entered into a management contract, that such ordinance, resolution, or contract, including all collateral agreements relating to the gaming activity, must be submitted for his review within 60 days of such notification. Any activity conducted under such ordinance, resolution, contract, or agreement shall be valid under this chapter, or any amendment made by this chapter, unless disapproved under this section.

(b) Approval or modification of ordinance or resolution

(1) By no later than the date that is 90 days after the date on which an ordinance or resolution authorizing class II gaming or class III gaming is submitted to the Chairman pursuant to subsection (a) of this section, the Chairman shall review such ordinance or resolution to determine if it conforms to the requirements of section 2710(b) of this title.

(2) If the Chairman determines that an ordinance or resolution submitted under subsection (a) of this section conforms to the requirements of section 2710(b) of this title, the Chairman shall approve it.

(3) If the Chairman determines that an ordinance or resolution submitted under subsection (a) of this section does not conform to the requirements of section 2710(b) of this title, the Chairman shall provide written notification of necessary modifications to the Indian tribe which shall have not more than 120 days to bring such ordinance or resolution into compliance.

(c) Approval or modification of management contract

(1) Within 180 days after the submission of a management contract, including all collateral agreements, pursuant to subsection (a) of this section, the Chairman shall subject such contract to the requirements and process of section 2711 of this title.

(2) If the Chairman determines that a management contract submitted under subsection (a) of this section, and the management contractor under such contract, meet the requirements of section 2711 of this title, the Chairman shall approve the management contract.

(3) If the Chairman determines that a contract submitted under subsection (a) of this section, or the management contractor under a contract submitted under subsection (a) of this section, does not meet the requirements of section 2711 of this title, the Chairman shall provide written notification to the parties to such contract of necessary modifications and the parties shall have not more than 120 days to come into compliance. If a management contract has been approved by the Secretary prior to October 17, 1988, the parties shall have not more than 180 days after notification of necessary modifications to come into compliance.

§ 2713. Civil penalties

(a) Authority; amount; appeal; written complaint

(1) Subject to such regulations as may be prescribed by the Commission, the Chairman shall have authority to levy and collect appropriate civil fines, not to exceed $25,000 per violation, against the tribal operator of an Indian game or a management contractor engaged in gaming for any violation of any provision of this chapter, any regulation prescribed by the Commission pursuant to this chapter, or tribal regulations, ordinances, or resolutions approved under section 2710 or 2712 of this title.

(2) The Commission shall, by regulation, provide an opportunity for an appeal and hearing before the Commission on fines levied and collected by the Chairman.

(3) Whenever the Commission has reason to believe that the tribal operator of an Indian game or a management contractor is engaged in activities regulated by this chapter, by regulations prescribed under this chapter, or by tribal regulations, ordinances, or resolutions, approved under section 2710 or 2712 of this title, that may result in the imposition of a fine under subsection (a)(1) of this section, the permanent closure of such game, or the modification or termination of any management contract,

the Commission shall provide such tribal operator or management contractor with a written complaint stating the acts or omissions which form the basis for such belief and the action or choice of action being considered by the Commission. The allegation shall be set forth in common and concise language and must specify the statutory or regulatory provisions alleged to have been violated, but may not consist merely of allegations stated in statutory or regulatory language.

(b) Temporary closure; hearing

(1) The Chairman shall have power to order temporary closure of an Indian game for substantial violation of the provisions of this chapter, of regulations prescribed by the Commission pursuant to this chapter, or of tribal regulations, ordinances, or resolutions approved under section 2710 or 2712 of this title.

(2) Not later than thirty days after the issuance by the Chairman of an order of temporary closure, the Indian tribe or management contractor involved shall have a right to a hearing before the Commission to determine whether such order should be made permanent or dissolved. Not later than sixty days following such hearing, the Commission shall, by a vote of not less than two of its members, decide whether to order a permanent closure of the gaming operation.

(c) Appeal from final decision

A decision of the Commission to give final approval of a fine levied by the Chairman or to order a permanent closure pursuant to this section shall be appealable to the appropriate Federal district court pursuant to chapter 7 of title 5.

(d) Regulatory authority under tribal law

Nothing in this chapter precludes an Indian tribe from exercising regulatory authority provided under tribal law over a gaming establishment within the Indian tribe's jurisdiction if such regulation is not inconsistent with this chapter or with any rules or regulations adopted by the Commission.

§ 2714. Judicial review

Decisions made by the Commission pursuant to sections 2710, 2711, 2712, and 2713 of this title shall be final agency decisions for purposes of appeal to the appropriate Federal district court pursuant to chapter 7 of title 5.

§ 2715. Subpoena and deposition authority

(a) Attendance, testimony, production of papers, etc.

By a vote of not less than two members, the Commission shall have the power to require by subpoena the attendance and testimony of witnesses and the production of all books, papers, and documents relating to any matter under consideration or investigation. Witnesses so summoned shall be paid the same fees and mileage that are paid witnesses in the courts of the United States.

(b) Geographical location

The attendance of witnesses and the production of books, papers, and documents, may be required from any place in the United States at any designated place of hearing. The Commission may request the Secretary to request the Attorney General to bring an action to enforce any subpoena under this section.

(c) Refusal of subpoena; court order; contempt

Any court of the United States within the jurisdiction of which an inquiry is carried on may, in case of contumacy or refusal to obey a subpoena for any reason, issue an order requiring such person to appear before the Commission (and produce books, papers, or documents as so ordered) and give evidence concerning the matter in question and any failure to obey such order of the court may be punished by such court as a contempt thereof.

(d) Depositions; notice

A Commissioner may order testimony to be taken by deposition in any proceeding or investigation pending before the Commission at any stage of such proceeding or investigation. Such depositions may be taken before any person designated by the Commission and having power to administer oaths. Reasonable notice must first be given to the Commission in writing by the party or his attorney proposing to take such deposition, and, in cases in which a Commissioner proposes to take a deposition, reasonable notice must be given. The notice shall state the name of the witness and the time and place of the taking of his deposition. Any person may be compelled to appear and depose, and to produce books, papers, or documents, in the same manner as witnesses may be compelled to appear and testify and produce like documentary evidence before the Commission, as hereinbefore provided.

(e) Oath or affirmation required

Every person deposing as herein provided shall be cautioned and shall be required to swear (or affirm, if he so requests) to testify to the whole truth, and shall be carefully examined. His testimony shall be reduced to writing by the person taking the deposition, or under his direction, and shall, after it has been reduced to writing, be subscribed by the deponent. All depositions shall be promptly filed with the Commission.

(f) Witness fees

Witnesses whose depositions are taken as authorized in this section, and the persons taking the same, shall severally be entitled to the same fees as are paid for like services in the courts of the United States.

§ 2716. Investigative powers

(a) Confidential information

Except as provided in subsection (b) of this section, the Commission shall preserve any and all information received pursuant to this chapter as confidential pursuant to the provisions of paragraphs (4) and (7) of section 552(b) of title 5.

(b) Provision to law enforcement officials

The Commission shall, when such information indicates a violation of Federal, State, or tribal statutes, ordinances, or resolutions, provide such information to the appropriate law enforcement officials.

(c) Attorney General

The Attorney General shall investigate activities associated with gaming authorized by this chapter which may be a violation of Federal law.

§ 2717. Commission funding

(a) (1) The Commission shall establish a schedule of fees to be paid to the Commission annually by each gaming operation that conducts a class II or class III gaming activity that is regulated by this chapter.

(2) (A) The rate of the fees imposed under the schedule established under paragraph (1) shall be—

(i) no more than 2.5 percent of the first $1,500,000, and

(ii) no more than 5 percent of amounts in excess of the first $1,500,000,

of the gross revenues from each activity regulated by this chapter.

(B) The total amount of all fees imposed during any fiscal year under the schedule established under paragraph (1) shall not exceed $8,000,000.

(3) The Commission, by a vote of not less than two of its members, shall annually adopt the rate of the fees authorized by this section which shall be payable to the Commission on a quarterly basis.

(4) Failure to pay the fees imposed under the schedule established under paragraph (1) shall, subject to the regulations of the Commission, be grounds for revocation of the approval of the Chairman of any license, ordinance, or resolution required under this chapter for the operation of gaming.

(5) To the extent that revenue derived from fees imposed under the schedule established under paragraph (1) are not expended or committed at the close of any fiscal year, such surplus funds shall be credited to each gaming activity on a pro rata basis against such fees imposed for the succeeding year.

(6) For purposes of this section, gross revenues shall constitute the annual total amount of money wagered, less any amounts paid out as prizes or paid for prizes awarded and less allowance for amortization of capital expenditures for structures.

(b) (1) The Commission, in coordination with the Secretary and in conjunction with the fiscal year of the United States, shall adopt an annual budget for the expenses and operation of the Commission.

(2) The budget of the Commission may include a request for appropriations, as authorized by section 2718 of this title, in an amount equal the amount of funds derived from assessments authorized by subsection (a) of this section for the fiscal year preceding the fiscal year for which the appropriation request is made.

(3) The request for appropriations pursuant to paragraph (2) shall be subject to the approval of the Secretary and shall be included as a part of the budget request of the Department of the Interior.

§ 2717a. Availability of class II gaming activity fees to carry out duties of the Commission

In fiscal year 1990 and thereafter, fees collected pursuant to and as limited by section 2717 of this title shall be available to carry out the duties of the Commission, to remain available until expended.

§ 2718. Authorization of appropriations

(a) Subject to section 2717 of this title, there are authorized to be appropriated, for fiscal year 1998, and for each fiscal year thereafter, an amount equal to the amount of funds derived from the assessments authorized by section 2717(a) of this title.

(b) Notwithstanding section 2717 of this title, there are authorized to be appropriated to fund the operation of the Commission, $2,000,000 for fiscal year 1998, and $2,000,000 for each fiscal year thereafter. The amounts authorized to be appropriated in the preceding sentence shall be in addition to the amounts authorized to be appropriated under subsection (a) of this section.

§ 2719. Gaming on lands acquired after October 17, 1988

(a) Prohibition on lands acquired in trust by Secretary

Except as provided in subsection (b) of this section, gaming regulated by this chapter shall not be conducted on lands acquired by the Secretary in trust for the benefit of an Indian tribe after October 17, 1988, unless—

> (1) such lands are located within or contiguous to the boundaries of the reservation of the Indian tribe on October 17, 1988; or
>
> (2) the Indian tribe has no reservation on October 17, 1988, and—
>
>> (A) such lands are located in Oklahoma and—
>>
>>> (i) are within the boundaries of the Indian tribe's former reservation, as defined by the Secretary, or
>>>
>>> (ii) are contiguous to other land held in trust or restricted status by the United States for the Indian tribe in Oklahoma; or
>>
>> (B) such lands are located in a State other than Oklahoma and are within the Indian tribe's last recognized reservation within the State or States within which such Indian tribe is presently located.

(b) Exceptions

> (1) Subsection (a) of this section will not apply when—
>
>> (A) the Secretary, after consultation with the Indian tribe and appropriate State and local officials, including officials of other nearby Indian tribes, determines that a gaming establishment on newly acquired lands would be in the best interest of the Indian tribe and its members, and would not be detrimental to the surrounding community, but only if the Governor of the State in which the gaming activity is to be conducted concurs in the Secretary's determination; or
>>
>> (B) lands are taken into trust as part of—
>>
>>> (i) a settlement of a land claim,
>>>
>>> (ii) the initial reservation of an Indian tribe acknowledged by the Secretary under the Federal acknowledgment process, or
>>>
>>> (iii) the restoration of lands for an Indian tribe that is restored to Federal recognition.
>
> (2) Subsection (a) of this section shall not apply to—
>
>> (A) any lands involved in the trust petition of the St. Croix Chippewa Indians of Wisconsin that is the subject of the action filed in the

United States District Court for the District of Columbia entitled St. Croix Chippewa Indians of Wisconsin v. United States, Civ. No. 86-2278, or

(B) the interests of the Miccosukee Tribe of Indians of Florida in approximately 25 contiguous acres of land, more or less, in Dade County, Florida, located within one mile of the intersection of State Road Numbered 27 (also known as Krome Avenue) and the Tamiami Trail.

(3) Upon request of the governing body of the Miccosukee Tribe of Indians of Florida, the Secretary shall, notwithstanding any other provision of law, accept the transfer by such Tribe to the Secretary of the interests of such Tribe in the lands described in paragraph (2)(B) and the Secretary shall declare that such interests are held in trust by the Secretary for the benefit of such Tribe and that such interests are part of the reservation of such Tribe under sections 465 and 467 of this title, subject to any encumbrances and rights that are held at the time of such transfer by any person or entity other than such Tribe. The Secretary shall publish in the Federal Register the legal description of any lands that are declared held in trust by the Secretary under this paragraph.

(c) Authority of Secretary not affected

Nothing in this section shall affect or diminish the authority and responsibility of the Secretary to take land into trust.

(d) Application of Internal Revenue Code of 1986

(1) The provisions of the Internal Revenue Code of 1986 (including sections 1441, 3402(q), 6041, and 6050I, and chapter 35 of such Code) concerning the reporting and withholding of taxes with respect to the winnings from gaming or wagering operations shall apply to Indian gaming operations conducted pursuant to this chapter, or under a Tribal-State compact entered into under section 2710(d)(3) of this title that is in effect, in the same manner as such provisions apply to State gaming and wagering operations.

(2) The provisions of this subsection shall apply notwithstanding any other provision of law enacted before, on, or after October 17, 1988, unless such other provision of law specifically cites this subsection.

§ 2720. Dissemination of information

Consistent with the requirements of this chapter, sections 1301, 1302, 1303 and 1304 of Title 18 shall not apply to any gaming conducted by an Indian tribe pursuant to this chapter.

§ 2721. Severability

In the event that any section or provision of this chapter, or amendment made by this chapter, is held invalid, it is the intent of Congress that the remaining sections or provisions of this chapter, and amendments made by this chapter, shall continue in full force and effect.

APPENDIX C

FEDERAL REGULATIONS RELATED TO INDIAN GAMING

The U.S. Secretary of the Interior is authorized to promulgate regulations and guidelines to implement the federal government's trust and other obligations to American Indian tribes, including applications to take land into trust. Congress also authorized the Interior Secretary to establish administrative procedures for federal acknowledgment or "recognition" of a tribe.

The Indian Gaming Regulatory Act of 1988 (IGRA) created and authorized the National Indian Gaming Commission to promulgate regulations and guidelines to implement much of IGRA's underlying policy goals. The Bureau of Indian Affairs in the Department of the Interior has issued regulations to implement several of IGRA's key provisions.

Secretary of the Interior/Bureau of Indian Affairs

25 C.F.R. pt. 83	Procedures for establishing that an American Indian group exists as an Indian tribe
25 C.F.R. pt. 151	Land acquisitions
25 C.F.R. pt. 290	Tribal revenue allocation plans
25 C.F.R. pt. 291	Class III gaming procedures
25 C.F.R. pt. 292	Gaming on trust lands acquired after October 17, 1988
25 C.F.R. pt. 293	Class III tribal state gaming compact process

National Indian Gaming Commission

General Provisions

25 C.F.R. pt. 501	Purpose and scope of this chapter
25 C.F.R. pt. 502	Definitions of this chapter
25 C.F.R. pt. 503	Commission information collection requirements under the Paperwork Reduction Act

233

25 C.F.R. pt. 513   Debt collection

25 C.F.R. pt. 514   Fees

25 C.F.R. pt. 515   Privacy Act procedures

25 C.F.R. pt. 516   Testimony of Commissioners and employees respecting official duties

25 C.F.R. pt. 517   Freedom of Information Act procedures

25 C.F.R. pt. 518   Self regulation of class II gaming

25 C.F.R. pt. 519   Service

Approval of Class II and Class III Ordinances and Resolutions

25 C.F.R. pt. 522   Submission of gaming ordinance or resolution

Management Contract Provisions

25 C.F.R. pt. 531   Content of management contracts

25 C.F.R. pt. 533   Approval of management contracts

25 C.F.R. pt. 535   Post-approval procedures

25 C.F.R. pt. 537   Background investigations for persons or entities with a financial interest in, or having management responsibility for, a management contract

Human Services

25 C.F.R. pt. 542   Minimum internal control standards

25 C.F.R. pt. 543   Minimum internal control standards for Class II gaming

25 C.F.R. pt. 547   Minimum technical standards for Class II gaming systems and equipment

Gaming Licenses and Background Investigations for Key Employees and Primary Management Officials

25 C.F.R. pt. 556   Background investigations for primary management officials and key employees

25 C.F.R. pt. 558   Gaming licenses for key employees and primary management officials

25 C.F.R. pt. 559   Facility license notifications and submissions

Compliance and Enforcement Provisions

25 C.F.R. pt. 571	Monitoring and investigations
25 C.F.R. pt. 573	Compliance and enforcement
25 C.F.R. pt. 575	Civil fines
25 C.F.R. pt. 580	Rules of general application in appeal proceedings before the Commission
25 C.F.R. pt. 581	Motions in appeal proceedings before the Commission
25 C.F.R. pt. 582	Appeals of disapprovals of gaming ordinances, resolutions, or amendments
25 C.F.R. pt. 583	Appeals from approvals or disapprovals of management contracts or amendments to management contracts
25 C.F.R. pt. 584	Appeals before a presiding official of notices of violation, proposed civil fine assessments, orders of temporary closure, the chair's decisions to void or modify management contracts, the Commission's proposals to remove a certificate of self-regulation, and notices of late fees and late fee assessments
25 C.F.R. pt. 585	Appeals to the Commission on written submissions of notices of violation, proposed civil fine assessments, orders of temporary closure, the chair's decisions to void or modify management contracts, the Commission's proposals to remove a certificate of self-regulation, and notices of late fees and late fee assessments

INDEX

Pages with tables are indicated by "T" in bold font. Names of cases, books and reports are in italic font.

non-reservation lands, 41
prohibited gambling devices on,
70–71
"reservation shopping," 44n29,
181–82
social problems, 22
tribal gaming success, disparity
between tribes, 156
unemployment on, 22, 32,
149n8, 150
Responsible Gaming Quarterly (web
site), 189, 196
restricted lands, 40
Return of the Buffalo (Lane), 193
revenue, Indian gaming, 65–68
audits, 56, 57
costs of regulatory activities, in
2012, 122
from early tribal gaming, in
1980s, 25
economic effects of, in 2010,
174–75
economic effects of, in 2012, 3,
146, 148, 149n10, 157
funding of NIGC, in 2012, 122
funding state economic development, 175
governance of, 121
industry estimates, 146
in Minnesota, from failed state-
tribe negotiations, 169n82
from Navajo casinos, 155n31
NIGC revised regulation, impact
of, 94–95
per capita payments, distribution
method, 66–67
restrictions on using, 65
tribal bingo, 33
tribal gaming facilities and total
revenue, 8T

tribal membership, based on, 67
tribal revenue paid to states, in
2012, 161
revenue, legalized gambling, 5
revenue-sharing agreements,
159–63, 183
California with all state tribes,
161
fixed compact payments and per-
centage payments, 160
Florida with Seminole Tribe,
108n118, 109n121
subject to litigation, 161–63
tribal-state negotiations, 9
Rhode Island
Carcieri v. Salazar (2009), 41–44
*Rhode Island v. Narragansett In-
dian Tribe* (1994), 41
RICO Act. *See* Racketeer Influenced
and Corrupt Organizations
(RICO) Act
The Rights of Indians and Tribes
(Pevar), 194
Rincon Band of Luiseno Mission
Indians, 161–63, 163n62
Roberts, Barbara, 45
Rocky Mountain Synod Evangelical
Lutheran Church, 142
*Roll the Bones: The History of Gam-
bling* (Schwartz), 194
Ross v. Flandreau Santee Sioux Tribe
(1992), 67
Rossum, Ralph A., 194
roulette, 58–59, 70n153, 76n11
*Rumsey Indian Rancheria of Wintun
Indians v. Wilson* (1994), 79,
113, 142

S

Salazar, Ken, 170